Savouring the East

by the same author
The Raj at Table

Savouring the East

Feasts and Stories from Istanbul to Bali

David Burton

faber and faber

For Andrea and Rea

First published in 1996
by Faber and Faber Limited
3 Queen Square London WC1N 3AU

Typeset by Faber and Faber Ltd
Printed in England by Clays Ltd, St Ives plc

Extract on page 159 taken from 'Mowgli's Songs Against
People', *The Second Jungle Book* by Rudyard Kipling.
By kind permission of A. P. Watt Ltd on behalf of The
National Trust for Places of Historic Interest or Natural Beauty.

A CIP record for this book
is available from the British Library

ISBN 0-571-17810-3

10 9 8 7 6 5 4 3 2 1

Contents

List of Illustrations

Introduction

What France, Italy and the Mediterranean were to Elizabeth David and her generation, the East has been to my own. Oriental food, once considered slightly 'alternative', has become mainstream: Asian recipes now fill women's magazines, spicy stir fry chicken pieces dominate butchers' window displays, and packets of Thai green curry mix cram supermarket shelves. Armies of restaurateurs – Chinese, Indian, Thai and Malaysian – march relentlessly on the outer reaches of suburbia everywhere.

Not since the discovery of the spice routes during the Middle Ages have the flavours of Asia so thoroughly infiltrated the Anglo-Celtic culinary idiom, not just in Great Britain, but throughout the entire English-speaking world – Canada, the United States (particularly California) and perhaps most dramatically of all in those two nations situated on Asia's doorstep – Australia and New Zealand.

This change is often said to have been inspired by Asian immigration, specifically that which in Britain followed the loss of empire, in America during the aftermath of the Vietnam War, in Australia after the abandonment of the White Australia policy, and in New Zealand with the Business Immigration Scheme initiated by the fourth Labour Government. An ethnic restaurant has always been the obvious business choice for those immigrants with little capital, a negligible grasp of the host language, and a large extended family to provide long hours of cheap labour. Typically, these restaurateurs began by serving fellow immigrants, but proudly welcomed European patronage when it began.

But while immigration undoubtedly facilitated the 'Asianization' of the Anglo-Saxon palate, a more fundamental cause was the upsurge in air travel and mass communications after the Second World War, which coincided with a massive international expansion of the middle class, determined to acquire not only the traditional trappings of paintings, music and books, but of culture in the wider sense of gardens, fine wine, cross-cultural cuisine and overseas travel.

It is hardly surprising, then, that after nearly twenty years of wandering, I find Asia greatly altered. Mass tourism exacts its price, and if certain regions and countries remain free of resort developers, it is only because revolutionaries have prevailed there instead.

The portents were obvious even when I first set out in 1977, as one of the last youthful pilgrims to tread in relative safety the well-worn trail overland from Istanbul to Bali. In Iran, a visible ferment of discontent was rising against the Shah, Afghanistan was busily destabilizing, while in Pakistan I found myself in the midst of political turmoil. Angry demonstrators roamed the streets of Rawalpindi in convoys of trucks, chanting and waving red flags, while phalanxes of helmeted riot police stood by, flaunting rifles and steel-tipped *lathis*. A few days later they opened fire, and the enlightenment of Prime Minister elect Zulfikar Ali Bhutto submitted to the tyranny of General Zia. Then Muslim fundamentalism spread to Iran, Afghanistan was invaded, and later still, internecine warfare closed off the Punjab and Kashmir. The hippie trail wilted with flower power itself.

Looking back on that era today, the self-righteous find the same succour for their reprobation as the excesses of late eighteenth-century England provided the Victorians. Yet for all our minutely catalogued faults, we of the Woodstock generation were probably the first Europeans ever to approach the East free of an attitude of racial superiority, and certainly the first to embrace its spirituality, culture and food without reservation.

True, we bought pakoras and puris from roadside vendors and ate nasi goreng at humble warungs primarily because we could not afford anything else. Yet much, much later, when we had all evolved into yuppies and finally got to sample the bland, denatured hotel fare of the Penang MegaContinental, we came to realize that the best food had been out on the street all along!

Until now, Westerners have generally been content to leave the preparation of Eastern food in the hands of the experts, enjoying it immensely when they go out to restaurants, but sticking to supposedly simpler Western fare when cooking at home. Yet, as anybody who reads the recipes in this book will realize, Asian food involves none of the complex patisserie and egg liaison sauces which so frustrate the amateur French chef. With the aid of a food processor and coffee/spice grinder, hours of laborious preparation can be reduced to minutes. Above all, now that Asian ingredients are beginning to cross over to supermarkets from the Oriental speciality stores, it is my hope that the recipes in this book will be seen for what they truly are – as nothing more than simple exercises in shopping, chopping and assembly.

Unless otherwise stated, the recipes serve four. Each has been tested in my kitchen at least once (some many times) during nearly fifteen years of writing a syndicated newspaper column for two New Zealand metropolitan dailies – the *Evening Post* and *The Press*. Together with some new material, they now comprise this book.

First Courses

Hong Kong

Yum char – literally 'drink tea meal' – is a delightful Cantonese custom of eating tiny titbits in tea houses from mid-morning to mid-afternoon, either as a substantial late breakfast or a heavy lunch. The custom has been around for a thousand years in China, where it began in the Imperial Court. The Emperor and his courtiers would be served dumplings filled with minced pheasant, or sweetened bean paste, and over the centuries less elaborate snacks found their way to the tea houses of the commoners, till by the turn of this century, yum char had evolved into a recognized speciality of the Cantonese. It is they who took the custom to the Chinatowns of the United States.

In the thriving commercial environment of Hong Kong, yum char restaurants are the ideal venue for business meetings, and with numbers swelled by office workers over lunch, there is generally such a babble that everybody must raise their voices to be heard. Above all this are the shouts of the waiting staff, bringing around offerings on trolleys or, at some of the more old-fashioned places, on tin trays with straps slung around their necks. As they often work on commission, the waiters tend to be pushy, but the beauty of yum char is, of course, that you only accept those dishes which take your fancy. In many restaurants, there is a list lying on the table, which is marked each time a dish is taken, but in other places, the waiting staff merely tot up the bill according to the number of empty dishes on the table, making sure that none have been stealthily removed to a neighbouring table.

An alternative name for yum char is dim sum, which means 'eating snacks for pleasure'.

Making the dough and shaping the dumplings which form so many of the dishes is so fiddly that a dim sum chef is a recognized specialist, and an increasing trend in Hong Kong is for yum char restaurants to order their wares wholesale from special factories that have been set up to manufacture them fresh each day.

Here then, are a couple of more accessible yum char recipes, neither of which involves making little dough dumplings likely to fall apart in the hands of a beginner.

Phoenix-tailed Prawns

In Chinese culture the mythical phoenix bird is an emblem of feminine beauty; special preparation prevents these prawns from curling up upon being deep-fried and the end result is supposed to resemble the graceful curve of the phoenix's tail.

500 g (1 lb) raw giant prawns or scampi
salt and pepper
150 g (6 oz) plain flour
5 tbsp cornflour
1½ tsp baking powder
½ tsp salt
2 tbsp peanut oil, plus enough for deep frying
1 large green pepper, cut into rectangles

Defrost the prawns or scampi and remove the heads. Peel the shells from the bodies, but leave the tails intact. If necessary, remove the black vein down the back by making a shallow slit down the back and pulling it out.

Turn the prawns over and make three shallow slits in the abdomen of each; this prevents the tail from curling up. Pat each prawn dry with a kitchen towel. Lightly sprinkle with salt and pepper.

Sift the flour, cornflour and baking powder into a bowl. Gradually work in 225 ml (8 fl oz) cold water and beat until smooth. Allow this batter to rest for 45 minutes, then beat in the salt and 2 tbsp peanut oil. Beat till the batter takes on a shiny consistency.

Heat the remaining peanut oil in a wok until bubbles form around a chop-stick plunged down into it. Holding the prawns by their tails, dip them and the pieces of green pepper into the batter, allow the excess to drip off, then deep fry the prawns and the pieces of green pepper for several minutes, until the batter turns golden. Remove and drain on kitchen towel.

Serve immediately.

Black Bean Steamed Spare Ribs

750 g (1½ lb) pork spare ribs
salt
2 tbsp salted black beans, chopped
2 large cloves garlic, crushed
100 ml (4 fl oz) chicken stock
1 tbsp dark soy sauce
1 cm (½ in) piece of fresh root ginger, chopped
1 tsp sugar
1 tbsp Chinese rice wine or dry sherry

Cut spare ribs into individual lengths, then with a sharp knife or cleaver, chop across the bone into 5 cm (2 in) segments (or have your butcher do this for you).

Rub the spare ribs with salt, allow to stand for 30 minutes, then blanch in boiling water for 5 minutes.

Mix together the remaining ingredients and coat the spare ribs with this mixture. Place on a heatproof plate and arrange either on a rack in a pot, or in a Chinese steamer in a wok. Have about 5 cm (2 in) of water boiling in the vessel. Cover and steam for an hour till the spare ribs are tender, topping up the level of boiling water when necessary.

India

If you thought you had to spend hours making stock in order to produce a really tasty soup, then consider the rasam of south India. This consommé can be made in minutes from a wealth of more-or-less instant ingredients – tamarind, garlic and a mass of spices and fresh herbs – which do not in the least resemble soup powder, stock cubes, monosodium glutamate or other contemporary chemical horrors.

A rasam is perhaps better described as a rice-mixer than a soup, as the concept of drinking soup as a first course is foreign to Indian cuisine. The Indian way is to bring on the entire meal at once, without separate courses. The rasam is intended to be spooned over plain white rice, in order to moisten the grains sufficiently to allow them to be bunched together and picked up with the fingers of the right hand. The rice also has the effect of absorbing some of the very strong fiery flavour of the rasam.

Rasam is derived from the Tamil word *ras*, meaning 'essence'. On the west coast of India rasam is known as saar, which also means essence when used metaphorically. And so they are. To add to the confusion, a virtually identical mixture of spices, tamarind and water is also known in Tamil as 'pepper water'. Served both with rice or after a heavy meal as a digestive, this 'moloo tunny' is the direct ancestor of that most famous Anglo-Indian soup, mulligatawny.

At their most basic, these rasams, pepper waters and saars, are made by boiling a little dal in plenty of water then adding fried mustard seeds, chilli and curry leaves. Sometimes the Indian cook obtains a ready-made base for a rasam simply by scooping some of the water off the top of a pot of bubbling dal. For special occasions, garlic, ginger, turmeric, coriander, cumin and mustard seeds are added.

Perhaps the most delicious rasam I ever tasted was made from a base of tomato rather than dal, in the massive kitchen of Sathya Sai Baba's ashram in the state of Andhra Pradesh:

South Indian Tomato Rasam

4 large or 8 small tomatoes
2 tbsp dried tamarind
1 tbsp oil
1/2 tsp black mustard seeds
1 medium onion, finely diced
10 cloves garlic

1 small red chilli
1 tsp ground cumin
½ tsp ground black pepper
3 tbsp fresh coriander, chopped

Place the tomatoes in a large pot with 1 litre water and boil until the tomatoes burst. Pick out the skins and discard, then mash the tomatoes into the water.

Meanwhile break the dried tamarind into small pieces and soak in 250 ml (scant ½ pt) of boiling water for five minutes. Massage the pieces to release the tamarind juice, then strain the liquid into the pot containing the tomato and water.

Heat the oil in a pan, add the mustard seeds, cover, and cook over a high heat until the mustard seeds pop. Add the onion and sauté until cooked. Add to the rasam.

Pulverize the cloves of garlic and the chilli. Add to the soup along with the cumin and black pepper.

Boil for a few minutes longer. Sprinkle with the freshly chopped coriander just before serving. Use to spoon over portions of snowy white rice.

More than any other city in India, Bombay is a kaleidoscope of practically every race, caste and community which exists in the sub-continent. In addition to the core population of native Maharashtrians wearing their homespun white Gandhi caps, you are likely to see on any street, traders from Gujarat in traditional dhotis, wealthy Parsi industrialists in Western business suits, Sikhs with their turbans, Baghdadi Jews in the advertising business, and Catholic priests from Goa in flowing white habits.

Since each community has clung steadfastly to their food traditions, the variety of ingredients available in Bombay is bewildering. At Crawford Market, fresh produce pours in each morning from every corner of India: oranges and grapefruit from Nagpur, tea from Darjeeling, perfumed Alphonso mangoes from Goa.

The building itself is a tourist attraction. Built by the British in 1869 with the object of better controlling the business activities of their subjects by containing them all under the one roof, a police station is still conveniently situated opposite. Architecturally, Crawford Market is typical of many Bombay buildings erected during the Raj: a weird mix of Victorian Gothic, Flemish and Swiss chalet, with Moorish arches and thick flagstones from Caithness. An indoor fountain may have long ago run dry, but mythological beasts still hold up the spouts, and generations of pigeons' droppings have failed to corrode completely the dragon-shaped lamp brackets on the walls.

You are scarcely allowed the luxury to contemplate such details, however, as basket boys jostle past, shouting at you to make way. Spirited bargaining echoes from within the main hall, between customers and the greengrocers who perch, magisterially, high above ground level on wooden tiers, surrounded by meticulously arranged pyramids of fruit and vegetables.

Having already bought a huge bag of dates, a young man clad in white is haggling over a huge bundle of fresh coriander, together with potatoes, cucumbers and tomatoes. Come nightfall, you will find him down at Bombay's Chowpatty Beach, behind the brightly striped awning of a fast-food stall. For he is a seller of bhel puri, Bombay's most famous snack, and has spent the day chopping up vegetables and making two fresh chutneys – one sweet-sour (tamarind and date) and one hot and spicy (coriander).

To maintain the crispness of the dried ingredients, each order has to be assembled on the spot. Taking a little from each of a row of bowls, and pouring in the two chutneys, the bhel puri man puts them in one big bowl together with some crumbled crispy-fried wheat bread known as puris, and gently tosses everything up into the air to mix it through.

Bhel puri can be made at home fairly easily, as it is more a shopping and assembly job than a difficult cooking task. The only fiddly part is making the puris, though even these can be dispensed with. Some variations on the recipe call for potato splinters instead, a convenient substitute for which would be crumbled potato crisps.

Nowadays, many supermarkets stock one or two of the vast family of Indian snack foods based on spicy chickpea flour paste extruded into various shapes then deep-fried until golden and crisp. They are known variously as ghajia, sev, bhujia, chiura or chivda (which is a mixture of them all, plus peanuts and fried dal). Any will suffice here. Crispy rice cereals are essentially the same product as Indian puffed rice (kurmura or mumra).

Bhel Puri

100 g (4 oz) puffed rice
1 cup chivda
1 cup sev
1 potato, boiled and finely diced
1 small cucumber
2 shallots or 1 small onion
1 medium tomato, finely diced
2 tbsp desiccated coconut

TIKHI CHUTNEY
1 cm (½ in) piece of cinnamon stick
8 peppercorns
seeds of 2 cardamom pods
2 cloves garlic
walnut-sized piece of fresh root ginger
2 or more fresh green chillies
1 bunch fresh coriander
handful of fresh mint leaves
¼ tsp salt

MITHI CHUTNEY
piece of dried tamarind the size of a small egg
15 dates, stoned
pinch of salt

PURIS
100 g (4 oz) self-raising flour
pinch of salt
1 tsp oil
oil for deep frying

First, make the chutneys. For the tikhi chutney, finely chop in a food processor the cinnamon, peppercorns, cardamom seeds, garlic, ginger and chillies (minus stalks and seeds). Reserve a few of the best looking leaves of
coriander and finely chop the rest also – leaves, stalks, roots and all – along
with the mint and salt. Add a dash of water – just enough to turn the mixture
into a thick paste.

To make the mithi chutney, break the tamarind into small pieces and soak
in a cup of boiling water for 5 minutes. Massage the tamarind to release the
pulp, then press the mixture through a sieve, to eliminate tough stones and
pith. Mince or finely chop in a food processor along with the dates and salt.

Next, make the puris. To the flour, add the salt and oil and just enough
water to form a stiff dough. Knead for a few minutes, then leave aside for a
further 15 minutes. On a floured surface, roll out and cut into tiny rounds,
the size of a 2p piece. Deep fry in a wok, a few at a time and on both sides,
until puffy, crisp and golden. Drain and set aside. Crumble most, leaving a
few for garnishing.

To assemble the final dish, mix together the dry ingredients and the
crumbled puris with the chopped vegetables and some of each of the chutneys. Pour more of both chutneys over the top. Sprinkle each serving with 1
tsp desiccated coconut and top with a whole puri and a few of the reserved
coriander leaves.

SERVES 6 AS A SNACK.

Indonesia

In an Indonesian village all the chickens you eat will have ranged freely in the most literal sense – around the family compound, through the neighbours' gardens, and more than likely out on to the road, where they dart back and forth in front of passing traffic and get flattened with great regularity.

The one great drawback to such an athletic lifestyle is that, in comparison to battery-produced hens, the Indonesian chicken is fairly tough, in addition to being a small size. Indeed, the domesticated Indonesian chicken resembles what we would call a bantam, the reason being that it is not far removed from the wild jungle fowl, the ancestor of all chickens.

The red jungle fowl is native to a wide crescent stretching from Bangladesh through Burma, Malaysia and down into Indonesia. They are still to be seen in the jungle today, especially in clearings and in lowland shrub. Despite being a prized bag for hunters, they survive through being extremely fast and agile flyers. The closely related green jungle fowl is native to Java, Bali and the chain of islands which lead down to Timor. It is found around rice paddies and on rocky parts of the coasts. I have seen them for sale at village markets in Bali, distinguished from their domestic counterparts by their feathered legs, their lowered tails and their overall scragginess.

The toughness of Indonesian chickens no doubt accounts for the popularity of this delicious and substantial soup-stew, which originated in the Madura region of Java but is eaten throughout the republic.

I was shown how to make Soto Ayam by my cooking teacher in Bali, and here is the recipe as I recorded it:

Soto Ayam (Indonesian chicken soup)

2 chicken breasts
salt

GARNISHES
1 medium potato
6 shallots or 1 medium onion, sliced
oil, preferably coconut oil
6–8 kerupuk (prawn crackers)
2 eggs, hard-boiled and quartered
60 g (2 oz) beansprouts
4–5 spring onions, sliced
2 small sprigs seledri or curly-leaved parsley

BUMBU SOTO
2 cloves garlic, minced
walnut-sized piece of fresh root ginger
1 cm (½ in) fresh turmeric root or ½ tsp ground dried turmeric
2 candle nuts or macadamia nuts (optional)
1–2 tbsp oil, preferably coconut oil
8 cm (3 in) piece of fresh lemon grass, or 4–5 leaves dried
2 daun salam leaves or 8 curry leaves
salt
1 tbsp kecap manis or molasses

Place the chicken breasts in a tightly covered pot with a generous litre (2 pt) of water and salt to taste, and simmer until well done.

Meanwhile, prepare the garnishes. Cut the potato into thin slices, then cut the slices into quarters. Fry the sliced shallots in 3–4 tbsp oil in a wok, on a high heat initially, which can then be turned down. When browned and crisp, remove with a slotted spoon and allow to drain. Add the sliced potato to the oil remaining in the wok, and fry, stirring constantly, until golden brown. Remove and set aside.

Add some more oil to the wok and fry the kerupuk one at a time, spreading them with two fish slices as they expand. Drain on absorbent paper.

Place the shallots, potato and kerupuk in separate bowls and set to one side, along with the remaining garnishes.

When the chicken breasts are ready, remove them from the cooking liquor and shred them finely with a fork.

Now prepare the 'bumbu soto' (soup condiments). Heat 1–2 tbsp oil and briefly fry the garlic, ginger, turmeric and nuts. Add 375 ml (⅔ pt) of the chicken cooking liquor along with the lemon grass, daun salam or bay leaves and salt to taste. Stir and cover well, and cook on a very high heat for 5–8 minutes. Add soy sauce and kecap manis or molasses, the shredded chicken, and the remaining chicken cooking liquor.

Dilute the soup with extra water if necessary, and heat through.

Take four bowls, and in each place equal amounts of the beansprouts, seledri or parsley and hard-boiled eggs. Pour the cooked soup over. The bowls of shallots, potato and kerupuk are served separately.

There is a great deal of flexibility with this recipe. Very often it includes chilli and fine noodles and I have even had it with small kidney beans.

Iran

Central to Persian cuisine is a stew-like soup known as ash, which typically consists of pulses, meat, grains, herbs and spices slowly simmered in water. In fact, ash is so important that the Farsi word for a cook is *ashe-paz*, or ash-maker and the kitchen too is known as *ash-paz-khanah*, the place where the ash is prepared.

So thick and hearty are these soup-stews that in Iranian roadside cafés I have seen heavily built truck drivers make a whole meal of them, accompanied by a flat, wholewheat bread with a pebbled surface.

To an Iranian, as to most Middle Easterners, sharing a bowl of soup has special meaning as a gesture of reconciliation, in much the same way as sharing a peace pipe had for Native Americans. One of the greatest acts of intimacy for two lovers or close friends is to drink soup from the same spoon, and in neighbouring Turkey, there is a special wedding soup, made from mutton and marrow bones and thickened with beaten egg and lemon juice.

When unexpected guests arrive, they can always be offered soup, even if it means stretching it further by adding more stock. In Iran, as everywhere, however, this hospitality is open to abuse. There is a delightful story of the Kurdish folk hero Nasrudin Hodja, who had a relative come from the country bearing the gift of a duck. This was duly cooked and shared, but after this, friends of the relative kept appearing on the doorstep, expecting hospitality. The final straw was one visitor who announced himself as 'a friend of the friend of the friend of the man who brought you the duck'. Nasrudin welcomed him in, sat him down, and some soup was brought in and placed before him. On tasting it, the visitor found it was little more than warm water, and he asked Nasrudin what sort of soup it was. 'This,' Nasrudin replied, 'is the soup of the soup of the soup of the duck!'

Ashe Miveh (Persian sweet-sour soup)

This soup reflects the Iranian penchant for mixing dried fruit into savoury dishes, and works in very well with the sweet-sour idea, which may possibly have been borrowed from the Chinese.

80 ml (3 fl oz) oil (preferably olive oil)
2 onions, chopped
2.5 litres (4 pt) water
400 g (14 oz) yellow split peas
1/2 tsp ground turmeric

1/4 tsp ground allspice
1 1/2 tsp salt
1/4 tsp pepper
75 g (3 oz) brown rice
100 g (4 oz) prunes, stoned but left whole
100 g (4 oz) dried apricots, stoned but left whole
2 tbsp chopped fresh mint leaves
250 ml (9 fl oz) wine vinegar
50 g (2 oz) sugar
large handful of finely chopped parsley
5 spring onions (include some of the green top), finely sliced
30 g (1 oz) chopped walnuts

GARNISH
4 cloves garlic, chopped
1 tsp dried mint

Measure 4 tablespoons of the oil into a large saucepan. Heat, then add the chopped onions. Fry, stirring frequently, until the onions are lightly browned, then add the water, yellow split peas, turmeric, ground allspice, salt and pepper. Bring to the boil, skim off the scum, cover, lower the heat and simmer for 30 minutes.

Add the rice and simmer for 30 minutes, stirring occasionally, then add the prunes and simmer for a further 15 minutes.

Add the apricots and mint and simmer for a further 45 minutes. Keeping the fruit whole will prevent them from completely disintegrating with the long cooking. Stir from time to time to prevent the split peas from sticking and burning (and hence tainting the flavour).

Stir in the wine vinegar, sugar, parsley, spring onions and walnuts. Simmer for 5 minutes longer.

Just before serving, prepare the garnish:

In a small frying pan, heat the remaining oil until very hot, then sauté the garlic until brown and crispy. Add the dried mint. Serve the soup and pour a little of this garnish over the surface of each bowl.

Serve with heated pitta bread, cut into quarters. Sometimes a handful of cinnamon-flavoured lamb meatballs is added to this soup. Traditionally, the parsley and walnuts are added early on in the cooking, but frankly this is bad culinary practice as lengthy stewing turns parsley bitter and softens walnuts.

SERVES 4–6.

Singapore

When you are eating scorpions, it helps to remember they look like little crayfish, and that crisply fried black ants bear a vague resemblance to caviar. Even better is the thought that, having successfully downed such a repast at the Imperial Herbal Restaurant in Singapore, you are going to walk out feeling very virtuous and healthy. For the restaurant, which boasts its own resident Chinese physician to give you a checkup and then prescribe appropriate dishes, emphasizes the inseparable link between food and medicine in Chinese cuisine.

The Chinese consider all material things as an organic cosmos in which all parts belong and interact, with the same fundamental principles governing the weather, plants, animals and people. As all foods are considered to have curative value, they are to be used to maintain harmony between the body and its nutritional needs. This is achieved by striking a balance between the two main categories of foods, those classified as 'cold' and those classified as 'hot'. In between are those foods which are considered 'cooling', 'warming' or merely neutral.

Hot and warming foods generate heat in the body, stimulating appetite, blood circulation, nerves and perspiration. Obvious examples of hot foods are chilli and ginger, though it seems any dense food, such as red meat, carrots or chestnuts, is likely to be classified as warming. Hot and warming foods are prescribed for conditions such as colds and flu, but on the downside, they are likely to cause inflammation, such as skin eruptions or ulcers, and to exacerbate infection.

Cold and cooling foods, on the other hand, cleanse toxic heat, and are prescribed for fever or for losing weight. The negative side of cooling foods is said to be that they may cause weakness, diarrhoea and running noses. Foods with 'cold' energy include seafood such as fish, crabs, shrimps, oysters and clams and most bitter foods. Most leafy vegetables are considered cooling, as is the sourness of citrus fruits, and indeed fruits in general (though lychees and mangoes, oddly, are considered hot). Honey and white sugar are cooling, whereas brown sugar is warming. Red vinegar, because of its colour, is considered warmer than white.

It is fairly obvious, then, that such classifications have no scientific basis, though from the cook's point of view, the Chinese requirement to balance heating and cooling foods has led to some very felicitous partnerships: the cooling tendencies of fish or cabbage, for example, benefit from a clove of garlic or some slices of spring onion and ginger for 'warmth'.

The following dish demonstrates the harmony of opposites even more strongly. The 'cold' shrimps and squid are balanced by the chilli, which is one of the few foods which are considered not merely warming but downright 'hot'. Chinese from Hunan and Sichuan may consider chilli an essential stimulant, but the Cantonese tend to be very wary of it, particularly where a person is suffering from any sort of inflammation.

Be that as it may, this recipe was given to me by a Cantonese chef living in Singapore, after I had been particularly impressed with the dish at a Cantonese restaurant which forms part of the Shangri-la's plush Rasa Sentosa Resort on the western tip of Sentosa Island. Sitting on the veranda, fanned by the sea breeze, it is hard to believe you are only 15 minutes from Singapore's central business district, and even more astounding to reflect that the setting – an immaculate white sandy beach fringed with coconut trees and complete with blue lagoon – was imported en masse from Indonesia!

Deep-fried Squid with Minced Shrimp in Spicy Sauce

150 g (6 oz) squid (body pouches, not tentacles)
1 red chilli, sliced
200 g (7 oz) shrimps, minced
beaten egg
breadcrumbs
oil for deep frying
salt
dash of chilli sauce

Cut the squid flesh into rectangles. Mix the minced shrimp with a little beaten egg, place a heaped teaspoon on each rectangle of squid, and fold the squid over. Roll the parcels in beaten egg, then in breadcrumbs and deep fry until golden brown. Briefly stir fry them with the red chilli and add salt and a dash of chilli sauce.
   SERVES 2–3.

In addition to the heating and cooling classifications, there are foods which exert 'wet' or 'dry' influences on the body's intrinsic balance. Dampness in the body shows itself in fluid retention and a tendency towards oozing sores and fungal infections, whereas 'dryness' manifests itself through thirst, coughs, dry skin and constipation. The water balance of the body is said to be affected not only by the types of vegetables we eat, but also by the way in which they are cooked.

Traditionally, Chinese believed that a doctor, having correctly diagnosed his patient, must order the patient to eat certain foods. Only when the food failed should the doctor prescribe medicine. Even here, however, there are overlaps. The Chinese word for wine, for example, shares the same linguistic root as that for medicine, while certain everyday foods, such as dates, crystal sugar, vinegar and cinnamon, are considered to be so beneficial that they can be bought both from regular food stores and from the traditional herbalists found throughout China, Hong Kong and Singapore.

Looking at all the displays which fill the windows and cabinets of these shops – dried deer penises, sea horses, deer antlers and wild ginseng roots in the shape of human torsos – a Westerner is tempted to dismiss it all as so much hocus pocus. But then, we once held similar contempt for acupuncture. I remember as a child some missionaries visiting our Sunday School fresh from China and recounting in a mocking tone the 'crude' Chinese belief that by sticking needles into a patient, 'the evil spirits could be released'.

As long ago as the second century BC, a Chinese book titled *The Inner Classic of the Yellow Emperor* was making the link between diet and health, a connection health authorities in the West are only too eager to emphasize today. And who can argue against the Chinese attitude that meat should be consumed in moderation, and that *fan* foods (grains) and *cai* (vegetables) are the foundations of longevity and good health?

Thailand

Like many Oriental cuisines, Thai food does not involve frustratingly difficult techniques or tricky sauces, but is more a straightforward process of assemblage. A food processor to take care of all that monotonous pulverizing makes the job easier still.

The only real secret is getting hold of the ingredients in the first place, for Thai cuisine hinges upon a small number of absolutely vital flavourings, without which you may as well not bother. Many of these are already familiar to contemporary cooks: chillies, garlic, coconut cream, fresh coriander, fresh basil. Others, such as fish sauce (nam pla), lemon grass, galangal and kaffir lime leaves, may only be found in Asian food stores, but are becoming increasingly widely available (*see* Glossary of Ingredients, pp. 251–63).

One dish which incorporates nearly all the above ingredients is the famous tom yum soup. Most Thai restaurants make a good deal of fuss about these soups, and with good reason. My favourite is a variation known as tom kar kai – chicken with coconut cream and galangal.

Having hung out on a few verandas and watched home cooks at work in Thailand, I know how difficult it is to prise recipes out of them. The fact is, they don't use them! A pinch of this, a handful of that, and then an adjustment of the seasonings just before the dish is served – no wonder the written recipes vary so widely.

Thus, while none of the three recipes I have referred to for this soup specifies chicken stock, I know for a fact the nicest tom kar kai I have been served, both at home and in Thailand, has contained it. So here is my approximation.

Tom Kar Kai Soup

1 chicken
2 sticks celery, plus any tops
2 onions
2 roots coriander, bruised
handful of dried lemon grass
6 kaffir lime leaves (can be frozen or dried)
3 pieces of dried galangal
2 tbsp lemon juice
4 tbsp fish sauce
1 tsp sugar
1 tsp finely chopped fresh chilli
100 g (4 oz) button mushrooms

400 ml (¾ pt) coconut cream
handful of coriander leaves

Skin the chicken and place in a large pot. Cover with water and add the celery, onions and coriander roots. Bring to the boil and simmer for about an hour. During the last 15 minutes of simmering, throw in the lemon grass, kaffir lime leaves and galangal.

Strain the stock. There should be about 1.5 litres (2½ pt). Break about a quarter of the chicken into small pieces and reserve the rest for some other use. Pick out the galangal and slice thinly into sticks.

Add the chicken pieces and the galangal to the strained stock, along with the lemon juice, fish sauce, sugar, chilli and button mushrooms.

Bring to the boil, then lower the heat and simmer for 5 minutes. Now add the coconut cream. Reheat, and just before serving sprinkle over freshly chopped coriander leaves.

Turkey

It is ironic that the Greeks and the Turks, whose relations could not be described as exactly cordial, share so much of a common culinary heritage. Each nation borrows extensively from the other's repertoire of recipes, and the list of ingredients favoured by both Greek and Turkish cooks is virtually identical. For this reason the boom in popularity of Greek food in recent years is good news also for fans of Turkish cooking. Now we can buy and enjoy good quality olive oil, many types of olives, feta cheese, preserved vine leaves, pine nuts – and filo pastries.

In Turkey, filo is known as yufka. As most people know by now, this pastry comes in sheets rolled so thin you could literally read this book through one.

Because filo consists simply of flour, salt, and a little oil and water, it is possible to make it at home. However, the technique of rolling it out paper thin is difficult to master. Most people are likely to take the easy way out and buy a packet of filo from the local delicatessen. Even the Turks usually buy theirs ready-made from a pastry shop.

I saw dozens of these pastry shops throughout Turkey, the windows of all of them piled high with superb examples of the confectioner's art. In one of them I counted half a dozen varieties of Turkish delight and seven of halva. These shops also sell biscuits and pastries, including baklava, the famous Greek speciality. There is a Turkish version too, which comes as individual pastries shaped like sultans' turbans.

Individual filo pastries filled with a savoury mixture are known as borekler. They are very typical of the Turkish habit of rolling their food into small bundles, a survival perhaps, from the days when most Turks were nomads and needed foods which could be easily carried around and quickly reheated over a fire.

The borek pastries are usually served as mezze, or appetizers, either at the beginning of a meal or as a snack at other times during the day. Other simpler mezze include olives, cheeses, caviar and roasted almonds or pistachios. They might accompany a mid-morning coffee break, or a heavier drinking session lasting until the early hours of the morning.

A whole spread of assorted snacks and morsels is known as a raki table, taking its name from the strong aniseed-flavoured liquor drunk with them. Tasting very much like ouzo, raki also turns milky when water is added, leading to the wry comment that this fools Allah into thinking his abstemious followers are drinking milk.

The following borekler are all variations on a theme; suggestions for fillings are given below.

Sigara Boregi (cigarette pastries)

The Turks are a nation of chronic smokers. On the streets of Istanbul I saw boys of no more than seven or eight not only hawking black-market American cigarettes, but lighting them up quite nonchalantly, without a bat of an eyelid from adult passers-by. Small wonder, then, that they have a pastry so named.

20 sheets filo pastry
1 egg, beaten with a little milk
oil for deep frying

Cut the sheets of filo pastry into rectangles about 9 x 6 cm (3½ x 2½ in) and put a teaspoon of filling (see below) across one end. Fold the end over the filling, then fold the sides of the pastry inwards. Roll up the pastry like a cigarette and seal the edges with water, or dip the whole pastry in beaten egg mixed with a little milk. Deep fry in oil for several minutes, turning them until all sides are golden brown. Drain on absorbent paper and serve hot with drinks.

Burma Borek (baked pastry rolls)

These are rolled up in exactly the same way as the pastry cigarettes, only the pastry is brushed with melted butter first. The rectangles of pastry are also larger, and a tablespoon or more of filling is used. They are baked in a hot oven for 20 minutes or until lightly browned. Being more substantial, they can be served as either a main course or an appetizer.

Kol Boregi (pastry coils)

Brush whole filo sheets (about 10–12) with melted butter, place a line of filling (see below) down one edge, then roll up into a tube. The pastry should stick together; brush with butter again if it does not. Now coil each tube into a snail-shell shape. Brush them with beaten egg, and bake in the oven at 200°C/400°F/Gas Mark 6 for 20 minutes or until browned. These may also be served as a main course.

MEAT FILLING
2 tbsp butter
1 large onion, diced
500 g (1 lb) minced beef or lamb
salt and pepper
handful of chopped parsley

Melt the butter, fry the onion until transparent but not browned, then add the mince and fry until cooked. Season to taste with salt and pepper, take off the heat and add the parsley.

That is the traditional recipe, but rather plain I think. Some toasted pine nuts and sultanas liven up the flavour considerably.

WHITE CHEESE FILLING

Feta cheese is the nearest equivalent we have to beyaz peynir which would be used in Turkey.

500 g (1 lb) feta cheese
1 egg
handful of parsley
pepper

Crumble the cheese and beat in the egg and parsley. Add pepper to taste.

SPINACH FILLING
500 g (1 lb) spinach
2 tbsp olive oil
1 medium onion, diced
75 g (3 oz) feta cheese, crumbled
1 egg, beaten
pepper

Wash the spinach thoroughly to remove all grit, but do not dry. Place in a covered saucepan with no extra water and steam for five minutes or so until limp.

Meanwhile, fry the onion in olive oil until transparent. Mix together the spinach, onion, feta cheese and egg, and season to taste with pepper.

Stuffed Mussels with Currants and Pine Nuts

I hesitate to call this recipe by its Turkish name, Midya Domasi, since I have changed the method of cooking completely, and added wine to the list of traditional ingredients.

18 fresh mussels
125 ml (4 fl oz) red or white wine
2–3 tbsp olive oil
1 medium onion, diced
75 g (3 oz) brown rice
$\frac{1}{2}$ tsp ground allspice
$\frac{1}{2}$ tsp chilli powder or $\frac{1}{2}$ tsp ground cinnamon
30 g (1 oz) dried currants
40 g (1$\frac{1}{2}$ oz) pine nuts
1 tbsp chopped parsley

Rinse the mussels well in running water and scrub the shells clean. Leave in a sink of warm water until the shells barely open (in order to dissipate the saltiness). Place in a large, tightly lidded pan with the wine. Bring to the boil and steam until the mussels have opened. Set them aside and reserve the cooking liquor, of which there should be about 250 ml (just under ½ pt). Taste to check it is not too salty (you will have to dilute it with water if it is).

Heat the olive oil and fry the onion until transparent. Add the brown rice and stir until the grains are well coated with oil, stir in the spices and pour over the mussel liquor. Bring to the boil, reduce heat to low, cover the pan tightly, and allow to simmer until the rice has cooked and absorbed most of the liquid. This should take anywhere between 45 minutes and an hour, depending on the age and the type of the rice. You may have to add extra water if it dries out before the rice is cooked. Ten minutes before the end of cooking, add the currants.

Meanwhile, remove the beards from the cooked mussels, take them carefully from their shells and slice each into three pieces.

Place the pine nuts in a small heavy frying pan without any oil and toast them to a golden brown on all sides over a medium heat, shaking the pan often. Mix with the cooked rice, along with the mussels and the parsley. Spoon a little of this mixture back into each of the mussel shells.

This quantity serves three as a main meal (say, with French bread and a salad) or between four and six as a starter.

My method, as outlined here, is far less trouble than the traditional Turkish way, which is to prise open the raw mussels, fill them with the partially cooked mixture, bind each mussel up with string, then boil them again in water. To my mind, the drawbacks of this method are that the mussels get overcooked, the pine nuts turn soft and, most importantly, much of the flavour disappears into the water which is then thrown out.

Meat

Afghanistan

In a quest for ever more exotic food, it would be difficult to go much further than Afghanistan. It is, after all, one of the more remote ends of the earth. And desolate. How could anybody produce crops in this country, let alone a cuisine worth anything, I asked myself, as I chugged through barren brown hills and deserts towards the western city of Herat, aboard an ancient wooden bus that resembled a gypsy caravan with its all-over floral decoration.

The fact is, however, that farmers do coerce vegetables from the meagre soil, and run flocks of the comical fat-tailed sheep. Moreover, Afghanistan's strategic position on the ancient spice and silk trade routes meant that its cuisine evolved long ago into a mosaic of influences from all over the East. Anybody familiar with the food of Turkey, Iran, Pakistan or India would be equally at home with the pilaus, kebabs, stuffed peppers, korma curries and flat breads which form the backbone of Afghan cuisine.

Ensconced in a Herat guest house for a week, I watched with fascination as the cook turned out these sophisticated delicacies with nothing more than pots and pans over a wood fire, using water drawn from a deep clay well in the yard with a black rubber bucket constructed from the inner tube of a truck tyre.

'Hey, Spaghetti!' shouted the cook one day to a disconsolate young Italian named Franco, the guest house's only other occupant. 'Why are you so sad? Homesick? Tonight, I cook you some spaghetti – Afghan spaghetti.'

At first I though he was joking, but no, he insisted the spicy variation on spaghetti and meatballs he turned out as an appetizer that evening, was a famous Afghan national dish, a speciality of Mazar-i-Sharif in the north.

Aush

2 small onions, grated
500 g (1 lb) lamb or beef, minced
1 tsp ground cumin
1 tsp salt
½ tsp ground black pepper
small handful of chopped fresh coriander
   or 1½ tsp ground coriander seeds
3 tbsp oil

2 medium onions, sliced
3 tomatoes, peeled
3 cloves garlic, crushed
1 tbsp chopped fresh root ginger
1–2 fresh green chillies, finely chopped
225 g (8 oz) spaghetti
75 g (3 oz) cooked chickpeas
500 ml (18 fl oz) plain yoghurt
dried mint

Mix the grated onions into the minced meat, along with the cumin, salt, black pepper and coriander. Set aside the mixture.

To make the sauce, heat the oil in a large pot and fry the sliced onions until lightly browned. Pour in 750 ml (1½ pt) water and add the tomatoes. Bring to a slow boil.

Now form the meat mixture into meatballs and drop into the pot. Cook, uncovered, over a medium heat for about 20 minutes, until the meatballs are cooked through. Turn over the top layer of meatballs to ensure even cooking. Five minutes before the end of cooking, add the garlic, ginger and chillies.

Cook the spaghetti for 10 minutes until *al dente*. Have ready the cooked chickpeas and yoghurt at room temperature.

To serve, place equal amounts of spaghetti in six small bowls. Pour over the meatballs and sauce, then top with a generous spoonful of yoghurt. Sprinkle with the cooked chickpeas and a little dried mint.

SERVES 6 AS AN APPETIZER, 2–3 AS A MAIN COURSE.

Hong Kong

Although we do not normally associate taro with Chinese cooking, the great hairy tuber has been cultivated in China for over 2000 years. It was first mentioned in Chinese writings about 100BC. However, though it may be beloved by the Polynesians, the Chinese until very recently tended to treat taro with suspicion. This is not entirely without justification, for it is true many of the 200-odd varieties of taro contain nasty microscopic calcium oxalate crystals, which when raw can cause allergic reactions in some people.

This I once discovered for myself, when a friend began to clutch her throat and cough alarmingly after a rather disastrous experiment of mine: I had decided to try delicately steaming taro nouvelle cuisine-style, rather than subjecting it to prolonged boiling – as indeed you must do. Either that, or it can be braised long and slow, Chinese-style, with chicken and coconut milk, or cut into small pieces and thoroughly deep-fried.

The Cantonese associate taro with oil, or with oily birds such as ducks, because they believe the tuber affects the stomach. A little may aid digestion, but too much will hinder it. For this reason, the Cantonese cook taro with oil, in order to lubricate its path through the digestive passages, and to discourage the diner from eating too much of it. In Hong Kong, however, the taro began to enjoy a definite vogue in the 1980s, served in the form of elegant shredded and deep-fried 'bird's nests', and filled with seafood, vegetables or beef.

If you can't get hold of taro, use yams or even potato instead. In Hong Kong, special moulds are available to shape the nests, but they can be made equally well with two sieves, one of which will fit inside the other. Choose a taro which seems light for its weight, which will be nice and starchy. A heavy taro indicates a high water content, which is not good for making bird's nests.

Fried Beef in Taro Nest

150 g (5 oz) beef fillet
4–5 tbsp oil
1 tbsp dark soy sauce
1 tsp cornflour
½ tsp sugar
¼ tsp sesame oil
white pepper

1 tsp bicarbonate of soda (optional, *see* over)
50 g (2 oz) celery, cut into matchstick lengths
50 g (2 oz) carrot, cut into matchstick lengths
50 g (2 oz) green pepper, cut into matchstick lengths
4 tinned water chestnuts, sliced
1 clove garlic, finely chopped
small piece of fresh red chilli
30 g (1 oz) preserved cabbage (optional)

SAUCE
$\frac{1}{2}$ tsp cornflour
3 tbsp water
2 tsp light soy sauce
$\frac{1}{4}$ tsp sesame oil

BIRD'S NESTS
1 taro
3 tbsp flour
1 tsp mirin (Chinese wine)
$\frac{1}{2}$ tsp baking powder
$\frac{1}{2}$ tsp salt
white pepper

Wash and wipe the beef fillet, slice thinly across the grain, then shred. Mix with 1 tablespoon of the oil, dark soy sauce, cornflour, sugar, sesame oil and a few shakes of white pepper. (If you suspect the beef is tough, add a teaspoon of bicarbonate of soda mixed with a tablespoon of water.) Leave to marinate for half an hour.

Mix together the celery, carrot, green pepper, water chestnuts, garlic and red chilli, adding, if possible, preserved cabbage (which may need to be soaked in water if it is too salty).

Mix together the sauce ingredients and set aside.

Peel the taro and shred 180 g of it. Ideally, this should be done on a mandoline, which provides nice long strands. Pat the strands dry with a paper towel, then place in a bowl with the flour, wine, baking powder, salt and a few shakes of white pepper.

Half-fill a wok with oil for deep frying, and heat. Test by plunging a chopstick down into it. A steady stream of bubbles coming up the sides of the chopstick shows the oil is getting warm, but it is not properly hot until it is bubbling strongly.

Dip the nest mould or sieves in the hot oil to heat them, then arrange the shredded taro evenly across the bottom sieve. Press the top sieve down over the taro and dip the assembly in the oil. Deep fry the nest in oil until golden and crispy, continually ladling hot oil around the rim to ensure even cooking. Remove and drain on absorbent paper.

Heat the remaining 3–4 tablespoons of oil in a wok, sauté the beef for one minute, then remove. In the same oil, stir fry the vegetable mixture. At the last moment, return the beef to the wok along with the sauce.

Place the taro nest on a platter garnished with shredded lettuce, then fill it with the beef and vegetable mixture.

SERVES 3.

India

India is a sub-continent so full of religious and geographical diversity that it is difficult to come up with a single list of dishes which could collectively constitute a national cuisine. This is clearly seen in the case of meat cookery, where it is impossible to make generalizations for the whole country. It is not true, for instance, that all Indians abstain from beef, since a Christian minority on the south-west Malabar coast eat it, as their ancestors always did both before and after their conversion to Christianity by the apostle Thomas ('doubting Thomas') in AD 52.

It is true, however, that the slaughter of cattle in India is the subject of angry debates in Parliament, petitions and letters to newspaper editors.

'The cow is your mother,' a wizened old café proprietor in Benares told me in response to an innocent question. 'Would you eat your mother? Cow is very holy, very sacred,' he continued querulously, wagging his finger under my nose for extra effect. A few feet away one of the venerable beasts in question paused in the street (they are allowed to roam freely through that holiest of Hindu cities) and began to munch its way ponderously through a discarded cardboard carton.

The diet of Indian pigs in the state of Goa is even more unmentionable and it is not only for religious reasons that Muslims and Hindus alike have an abhorrence for what they consider is unclean meat. The heat in India is said to be conducive to bacteria and pigs breeding in the same conditions. Nevertheless, the Goan Christians still enjoy roast suckling pig on Christmas Day, and have exotic dishes combining pork with radishes, or pig's heads stuffed with brains, or pork sausages made partly with liver.

Hindus practise vegetarianism with varying degrees of devoutness. Members of the Brahman caste, for instance, are usually held up as being particularly strict, yet those in the remote vale of Kashmir, impervious to the Hindu move to vegetarianism elsewhere in the fifth century BC, have always eaten lamb and game (although, strangely enough, not chicken). A number of Brahmans in Bengal eat seafood, while the more lax Hindus of other castes today eat all kinds of meats, sometimes even buffalo meat or beef.

In the north of India, where most of the country's 60 million Muslims live, is found the richest and most lavish of all Indian meat cookery. This is a legacy of the Moghuls, the Muslim invaders who began sweeping down through the Khyber Pass in the eighth century, eventually establishing the Delhi Sultanate in the twelfth century in what is now Pakistan. By the fourteenth century they had taken control of northern India.

In their noble courts a grand luxurious cuisine was established, not one born of necessity but a style of cooking that was rich in spices, herbs and sauces. The Moghul rulers were not by tradition great eaters of seafood, and geography did not encourage them to begin. Finding themselves in a predominantly Hindu country, the eating of beef was not looked upon kindly by their subjects. And pork, of course, was ruled out by their religion. This left chicken, which became popular but not nearly to the extent of lamb, on which the reputation of Moghul cooking ultimately rests. It is said that a good north Indian cook can create a different lamb dish for every day of the year.

Among the more famous Moghul dishes are spicy kebabs made with cubed or minced lamb (there are dozens of variations), biryani (a lamb and rice dish) or pulau (similar to a biryani except that the rice predominates).

Badam Gosht (lamb with yoghurt, coconut cream and almonds)

A truly noble dish worthy of the most lavish Indian feast.

1 kg (2¼ lb) boned lamb (shoulder or leg)
1 tsp salt
1½ tsp caraway seeds
500 ml (18 fl oz) plain yoghurt
1 tsp saffron threads (optional)
5 tbsp ghee or oil
1 tsp cardamom seeds, ground
8 cm (3 in) cinnamon stick
6 whole cloves
2 medium onions, finely chopped
2 cloves garlic, crushed
½ tsp chilli powder
75 g (3 oz) ground almonds
375 ml (⅔ pt) coconut cream

Cut the lamb into 2–3 cm (1 in) cubes, sprinkle with salt and caraway seeds, pour over yoghurt, then mix until each cube is coated. (If you have saffron, soak it in 2 tablespoons of boiling water and add this mixture to the yoghurt.) Leave to marinate for half an hour.

Meanwhile, fry the ground cardamom seeds, cloves and cinnamon stick in ghee or oil for about a minute, then add onion and garlic and fry another seven or eight minutes until lightly browned.

Remove lamb from yoghurt with a slotted spoon and fry until browned.

Add yoghurt, chilli powder and ground almonds mixed to a paste with 4 tablespoons of water. Bring to the boil and simmer about ten minutes, then add coconut cream and simmer for a further 20 minutes or until the lamb is tender. Remove cinnamon stick and cloves and serve with rice or chapattis.
   SERVES 6.

Over forty years after the British quit India, the ghost of the Raj lingers at the Darjeeling Planters Club. Like the whole of the Darjeeling hill station, this club was built at the height of Britain's involvement in the Darjeeling tea industry, which still survives to this day, albeit in a reduced form.

The last British tea planter departed in 1972, but the club continues, with an Indian membership, as if they had never left. A huge armoured Maxim gun, the very symbol of British imperial might, guards the entrance to the club, a large rambling wooden building with verandas running along the entire length of its two floors. From a cane armchair one can contemplate the majesty of the Himalayan skyline across the valley, culminating in Kanchenjunga, the third-highest peak in the world.

Would it be possible, I asked the club secretary, for us to have a meal, a quiet browse in the library, and perhaps a game or two of billiards?

'Yes, yes,' he replied impatiently. 'But first,' he added with an air of self-importance, 'it is obligatory to furnish application for temporary membership.'

He handed me a yellowed and much mildewed form, fifty years old at the very least, which enquired, besides the usual questions, whether civilian or military membership was required, and to which recognized London clubs the applicant belonged.

Then he led us down a corridor lined with tiger skins, English fox-hunting prints and mounted bear's heads, into a vast room filled with overstuffed armchairs, and sofas, with blazing fireplaces at either end. Around the walls was a series of faded framed watercolours, depicting Englishmen in khaki pith helmets with long spears, in the various stages of a tiger hunt. I paused at one showing a hunter being tossed from his horse, backside-first into a stream.

'That one's a ripper, eh?' commented a tall Indian with a perfect Oxford accent, standing warming himself in front of the fire. He was fortyish, urbane, handsome, with wavy hair greying about the temples and the beginnings of jowls and bags under this eyes. He was clutching a tumbler filled almost to the brim with brandy.

Would we care to join him for a drink, he asked and, pressing a button on the wall, rang for the butler. An ancient Nepali appeared, resplendent in a white tunic with brass buttons, with a tray of 'brandy-panis' – tumblers of brandy mixed with boiling water and a chit for the man to sign.

We chatted for a good half hour about the walks we had been on around the district, the horse races at Calcutta, the absence of decent Scotch whisky in India, and his frightfully jolly way of playing golf, which involved having a drink after every hole. Then, realizing we had not been introduced, I asked him his name.

At this point the club secretary, whose head all this time had been darting silently and very nervously back and forth from one speaker to the other as our conversation had progressed, spluttered into his drink. His eyes widened and a look of abject horror spread over his face.

'But . . . but,' he hissed at me sideways through his buck teeth, 'dammit, man, don't you know? This is the Maharajah of Cooch Bihar!'

Later, we adjourned to the dining room for dinner. Though there must have been seating for a hundred in that room, we were the only guests. Around the walls were framed photographs of various Himalayan mountains and group portraits of past club officials, solemn Englishmen with handlebar moustaches and knee-high boots. The table was impeccably laid with silver cutlery on a starched white tablecloth, with a menu neatly typed out and placed in a silver scallop-shaped holder in the centre of the table.

We began with some excellent fried fish, freshly caught from a nearby mountain lake. For the main course, there was a dish of beef, an old Anglo-Indian favourite.

Beef Vinthaleaux

1 kg (2¼ lb) cheap cut of beef, such as shin or braising steak
2 tsp ground chillies
1 tsp ground coriander
½ tsp ground cumin
2 cloves
a few whole peppercorns
pinch of ground cardamom
1 cinnamon stick
2 tbsp crushed garlic
4 tsp chopped fresh root ginger
½ tsp salt
80 ml (3 fl oz) vinegar
4–5 tbsp ghee or butter

Cut the beef into large squares.

In a dry frying pan, toast the ground chilli, coriander, cumin, cloves, peppercorns, cardamom and cinnamon for a minute or two to allow the flavours to mellow. Ideally, the spices should have been ground freshly, either in a coffee mill, a blender, or with a mortar and pestle. Add to the beef, along with the garlic, ginger, salt and vinegar. Mix well and leave the beef to marinate for 24 hours. Stir occasionally.

Heat the ghee or butter and add the meat mixture. Cover and simmer over a very low heat for two hours, stirring occasionally, until the meat is tender.

Who has not had fantasies about Oriental marble palaces, lolling on fine carpets dressed in rich brocades, running fingers through trunks overflowing with rubies, diamonds and emeralds? Dream we may, as dream nowadays we all must, even those descendants of the princes who once ruled a third of India.

Deprived of their independent princely states when India became one nation in 1948, taxed heavily and stripped even of their titles by Mrs Gandhi in 1971, the ex-maharajahs of contemporary India are a bruised and sorry lot. The Nizam of Hyderabad, whose notoriously miserly grandfather was once the richest man in the world, today wears jeans and farms sheep in the Australian outback, while the Rajah of Katodia was reduced to riding a bicycle each day to his clerk's job in Gujarat, responding to official invitations only when a return fare was provided.

There is, however, one great consolation for all who are born several centuries too late to rule the Moghul Empire: in this democratic age each of us can afford to dine like a maharajah. Indeed, in some instances Westerners are able to eat very much better.

Take lamb, for example. It is generally accepted that the supreme culinary achievement of the Moghuls was their treatment of lamb, yet the raw product would sorely disappoint us today. The sheep of sixteenth-century India was a small and lean animal, yielding tough, microscopic joints about half the size of ours. True, the lamb of the Patna breed from the north-west was good, as was some of that from the green pastures of the Deccan plateau, while the gram-fed mutton of Bengal was famous. But on the whole, Indian stock breeding only came of age with the arrival of the British, who established 'mutton clubs' in areas where goat meat was often all that was available. The mutton club was a cooperative of English residents who kept their own flock of sheep, organizing its feeding and supervision. By the 1890s the clubs were no longer needed, as good gram-fed lamb and mutton was now sold in village bazaars.

The following recipe translates roughly as 'royal lamb curry'. Originally it came from the royal court of the Shah of Isfahan in Persia, where the grand cuisine, the glittering fabrics, the fine carpets, poetry and miniature painting formed the basis for all that flourished in India under the Moghul emperors.

However, India has a habit of changing all that touches it, and soon the Shahi Korma was being cooked with more spices than had been the case in Persia. Rich and spicy though it may be, this curry is very mild. Indeed for many, the total absence of chilli forms its main attraction. It is excellent as the centrepiece for a dinner party.

Shahi Korma

1 kg (2¼ lb) lamb, cut into large cubes
300 ml (½ pt) meat stock or water
1 cinnamon stick
8 cm (3 in) strip lemon peel
3 bay leaves
3 large onions, minced or finely diced
100 g (4 oz) clarified butter
250 g (9 oz) ground almonds
3 tbsp grated fresh root ginger
10 cloves garlic, crushed
3 tbsp ground coriander seed
8 cardamom pods
1 tsp ground cloves
3 tbsp chopped mint leaves
1 tsp paprika
½ tsp ground black pepper
¾ tsp salt
185 ml (6 fl oz) plain yoghurt
185 ml (6 fl oz) cream
pinch of saffron strands or ¼ tsp ground turmeric

Place the cubes of lamb in a saucepan with the stock or water, cinnamon, lemon peel and bay leaves. Bring to the boil and simmer very, very gently for 20 minutes.

Meanwhile, fry the onion gently in the clarified butter in a large pot (preferably a cast-iron casserole dish). Stir from time to time, until they have turned light golden and shrunk to half their original volume.

Preheat the oven to 180°C/350°F/Gas Mark 4.

Strain the stock from the lamb and put the meat to one side (picking out and discarding the cinnamon, bay leaf and lemon peel). Boil the stock vigorously until it is reduced by half.

To the onions in the pot, mix in the ground almonds, ginger, garlic, coriander seed, the crushed seeds from the cardamom pods, cloves, mint, paprika, black pepper and salt. Stir in the yoghurt and cream, then the reduced stock and lamb.

Cook in the preheated oven for 15 minutes, until the meat is heated through. The volume of ground almonds and onions will prevent the yoghurt from curdling, but the texture will still not be completely smooth.

Before serving, grind a pinch of saffron strands with a little boiling water, and add. Failing saffron, use turmeric.

SERVES 6.

Indonesia

Hidden away in the hills of Bali are scattered villages inhabited by a people who are, quite literally, a race apart. These are the Bali Aga, descendants of the original inhabitants of the island, who were there even before immigrants began to flow in from Java more than a thousand years ago. So intensely isolationist and conservative are the Bali Aga that to this day they retain their own religion, art forms, festivals – and food.

While many of these villages remain cool or even openly hostile toward outsiders, there is one, Tenganan, which is not. Even Tenganan once employed a person to sweep away the footprints of any visitor and had a village wall with only one gate opening to the outside world, which was so narrow that a fat person would have had difficulty squeezing through. Today this gate has been widened, and although visitors are now admitted without previous permission, one must first sign a visitors' book and make a compulsory donation. Once inside, the rows of long-houses with mist-shrouded jungle impinging from the surrounding hills evoke more of the atmosphere of Borneo than Bali.

The Bali Aga villages are ruled by a council of elders who also serve as the priests of their religion. They worship nature spirits and those of their ancestors, believing that from time to time their ancestral spirits can be called to earth to visit them. Unlike the mainstream Balinese, who have a relaxed attitude toward sexuality, the Bali Aga strictly segregate their adolescents into clubs of virgins (*seka daha*) and adolescent boys (*seka truna*), believing that only virgins are sufficiently pure to be able to perform certain rites and to be the guardians of the village's magical implements.

Each year there is a ceremonial meeting of the club of virgins. Dressed in gold head-dresses and rich cloth, the girls arrange themselves into two lines, from the oldest down to the youngest, and perform the redjang, a dance so simple that it consists only of turning one's head to each side and holding out a coloured scarf, while a primitive gamelan orchestra plays in a nearby pavilion.

In former times, each of the girls would later step forward and dance solo, whereupon a would-be suitor from the boys' club would gingerly attempt to join her, risking public ridicule and humiliation should she refuse him. I did not see any of this happening in 1989, however.

Accompanying the ceremony was the inevitable feast. As with most other villages in Bali, it is the men rather than the women who are responsible for preparing it, and three of them were busy dishing it out on to neat green squares of palm leaf, using coconut shell ladles. There were three dishes: ground coconut, a somewhat unappetizing gelatinous grey substance, and another I identified as a variation on lawar babi – shredded spicy pork, a famous Balinese festival dish.

'But how do you get that pretty red colour?' I asked innocently of one of the cooks, a toothless old man.

'Pig's blood,' he replied, beaming proudly, 'fresh today!'

Lawar Babi (shredded spicy pork)

Lawar, which means 'sliced thinly', is a style of cooking meat, fruit or vegetables practised throughout Indonesia. Only in Bali is pork used, however, and non-Transylvanians should note that outside Bali Aga villages the blood is an optional ingredient.

3 shallots or 1 small onion
3 cloves garlic
500 g (1 lb) lean, boneless pork, cut into thin strips
1 tsp ground cumin
1 tbsp ground coriander seed
1 tsp ground galangal (optional)
1 tsp salt
2 tbsp peanut oil
1 fresh red chilli, finely chopped
1 daun salam leaf or 4 curry leaves
250 ml (9 fl oz) coconut cream
1 tbsp dried tamarind

Pulverize the shallots or onion and the garlic in a food processor or with a pestle and mortar. Rub this mixture into the meat, along with the cumin, coriander, galangal (if using) and salt.

Heat the peanut oil in a pan and sauté the pork mixture for several minutes. Add the chopped chilli, daun salam or curry leaves and coconut cream. Simmer, uncovered, until the meat is tender and the liquid has reduced.

Meanwhile, break the tamarind into small pieces, place in a small bowl and cover with boiling water. Leave for 5 minutes, then squeeze to extract all the juice. Rub through a sieve to remove any pith and stones, and stir the strained juice into the pork.

It sometimes seems as if the first rule of South-East Asian cooking is coconut with everything: grated, toasted, made into cream, moulded into sweets. It has always been this way, since the palm is older than South-East Asian civilization itself. Indeed, the Malay archipelago is thought to be the coconut's first home, whence the individual nuts bobbed and floated around the world on ocean currents, taking root on tropical islands everywhere.

For one third of the population of this planet, the coconut tree yields food and drink, vessels and clothing, habitations for themselves and a heritage for their children. Little wonder that the mystical Javanese revere the coconut palm as the symbol of knowledge, or that in neighbouring Bali, women were formerly not even allowed to touch the tree, for fear they would drain off its fertility.

The eighteen varieties under cultivation in Indonesia have different uses. In Bali, for example, the small nyuh bulau or moon coconut is used for religious ceremonies, since its skin is the holy colour, saffron yellow. The nuts are also graded according to age: young coconuts are used for their water, with the jelly-like flesh eaten as a snack and middle-aged coconuts are grated for cooking. Most Indonesians would recoil in horror at the brown hairy coconuts sold at greengrocers in the West. In Indonesia, such elderly specimens are used either for boiling down in vats of water to extract the oil which is scooped off the surface, or for drying out into copra. When coconuts are plentiful, these old coconuts might even be fed to animals.

Unfortunately, most imported coconuts tend to be elderly, if not downright infirm. But they can still be used for home-made coconut cream.

Why bother making your own coconut cream when you can buy the stuff in tins? Well, it's like the difference between tinned evaporated cream, and the fresh product. Tinned coconut cream is a perfectly acceptable substitute, but a connoisseur, cooking for friends who will appreciate the extra effort, will demand that extra edge of freshness and fragrance which can only be obtained by making coconut cream on the spot. Here's how you do it.

Coconut cream

First, before buying, shake your coconut, and if you can't hear the water sloshing around inside, reject it; once the water has dried up, the coconut is almost certainly going bad.

Back home, extract the water and flesh. Perhaps you have read the standard instructions about how to do this: 'Put it in a vice, drill two holes through the brown eyes, and shake out the water. Now take a hammer, a set square, a circular saw and . . .'

Forget it. Here's how an old farmer showed me in Bali: with a heavy machete (or a meat cleaver), give the coconut good smack in the midriff, to crack the shell. Now work the blade further into the crack, prise the coconut open a little, and drain the coconut water into a bowl. Outside, on concrete, bash the coconut on all sides, to loosen the white flesh. Break the shell into large pieces. Using a table knife with a flexible blade (a beat-up old bone-handled knife is perfect), prise out the flesh. For the purposes of making fresh coconut cream, it is not necessary to peel off the thin brown outer skin. Indeed, it is better that you don't, since the brown skin will make for a thicker, oilier cream, which is precisely what we are after.

Cut the pieces into smallish chunks and in a food processor, reduce to a paste. Failing a food processor, use an ordinary grater. In Indonesia, the traditional utensil is a board spiked with hundreds of little teeth, known as a *parut* in Java and in Bali as a *kikian* (a rapidly vanishing sight in modern Bali; in most villages the hand grater has been replaced with a simple machine).

Having grated your coconut, cover it with boiling water. 500 ml or 1 pint will give you coconut cream of an average thickness; add less or more water according to how thick you want your cream.

Allow it to cool a little, then wash your hands and squeeze the grated coconut until the water turns white and thick. Strain off the liquid through a sieve, giving the fibres a final squeeze.

Discard the by-now tasteless coconut fibres (or, better still, feed them to your chickens, as the Indonesians do).

Lombok Beef Curry

4 shallots or 1 small onion
4 cloves garlic
2–4 fresh red chillies (according to taste)
walnut-sized piece of fresh root ginger
walnut-sized piece of galangal root (optional)
4 tbsp oil
500 g (1 lb) beef, cubed
400 ml (¾ pt) coconut cream (*see above*)
1 tsp salt
1½ tsp ground coriander
½ tsp ground turmeric
½ tsp ground cumin

¹⁄₂ tsp ground black pepper
¹⁄₄ tsp ground cloves
¹⁄₄ tsp ground cinnamon
¹⁄₄ tsp ground nutmeg

In a food processor or with a mortar and pestle, grind together the shallots or onion, garlic, chillies, ginger and galangal if using.

Heat the oil, and brown the meat, then add the ground flavourings and sauté for a further 30 seconds. Now add the coconut cream and simmer until the meat is tender. How long this takes will depend on the quality of the beef you bought in the first place. It is vital the mixture be stirred from time to time and be left to simmer uncovered, otherwise the coconut cream may curdle. The sauce will reduce and thicken with cooking.

About 5 minutes before the end of cooking, add the salt and remaining spices. Serve with plain boiled white rice.

SERVES 3.

Despite all the twentieth-century advances in kitchen technology, it seems there is still nothing to surpass the flavour of meat cooked over a charcoal grill.

To see such a grill amid all the gleaming hi-tech gadgetry of a modern hotel kitchen strikes me as somewhat ironic, considering it is surely the most primitive form of cookery known to humanity, varying from culture to culture only in the details of how it is done.

The Arawak Indians of Haiti, for instance, grilled their meat on a frame of thin green sticks set upon posts. Known as a *barbacoa*, it is from this that our most popular form of outdoor cooking is named. The Maori barbecuing technique was to skewer birds or fish on sticks and lean them over the glowing embers of a fire. Birds were also roasted on a spit and the fat collected in a trough below, later to be poured over the birds to preserve them. I sometimes fear we are beginning to lose sight of the barbecue's origins. A few years ago, I attended a poolside barbecue on a concrete patio without a leaf or twig in sight.

However, gas-fired barbecues do the job pretty well. While the meat loses the faint smoky tinge it does retain most of the true barbecue flavour, which results from juices dripping down from the meat and then being vapourized by the heat rising below. The steam impregnates and flavours the meat. This explains why a true barbecue effect cannot be achieved by putting meat under the grill of a household stove. Because the heat is coming from above rather than below, the juices simply drip down and are lost. An ordinary grill is also not hot enough to turn the surface of a steak brown while retaining a moist and pink centre. By the time a steak has browned under a griller the centre will probably be too dry.

How long you should leave a steak on the barbecue depends on a number of factors, such as the heat of the charcoal and the thickness of the steak, but a good rule of thumb is to wait until the juices just begin to rise to the top surface of the steak before you turn it. A steak should be turned once and only once. For a rare-to-medium steak, wait until the juices just begin to appear again. For a well-done steak, allow the juices to collect for a few minutes before removing. For an average steak of say, 2 cm thickness, allow about 4 minutes per side for rare, up to 6 for medium and 8 or more minutes for well done. You can always test for doneness at the end of cooking by stabbing a knife into the middle and parting the edges.

Those who want a little more out of a barbecue than a charred sausage with a gooey pink centre should consider going to the effort of marinating the meat and making kebabs, such as satay.

There are many versions of this famous South-East Asian speciality, but there is one I consider the most delicious. The magic ingredient is dried tamarind, which replaces the more usual lemon juice and soy sauce.

Satay

1 kg (2¼ lb) lamb or beef
1½ tbsp dried tamarind
1 large onion
2–3 cloves garlic
walnut-sized piece of fresh root ginger
1 tbsp ground coriander
1 tsp ground fennel seeds
1 tsp ground turmeric
1 tsp lemon peel
2 tsp brown sugar
1 tsp salt

The best cut of lamb for kebabs is the wide end of a leg of lamb, since there is little wastage with bone.

Bone the meat, then cut across the grain into fairly thin slices, about 7–8 mm (⅓ in) thick. Cut these slices into smaller pieces, aiming for squares where possible. The idea of thin, flat squares is to allow the marinade to penetrate over a wider area, and to ensure quick cooking later.

Break the tamarind into small pieces, pour over 4 tablespoons of boiling water, and allow to stand five minutes.

Meanwhile, peel the onion, garlic and ginger and pulverize in a food processor (or pound or chop very finely by hand).

Squeeze the tamarind in the water to extract the pulp from the pith and seed, then strain it into the onion mixture and add the remaining ingredients. Mix well, stir in the meat and leave, covered, to marinate for at least 6 hours, preferably overnight.

Soak bamboo skewers in cold water for an hour. Thread three or four pieces on to each skewer and cook over glowing charcoal, turning when the meat begins to show brown patches. They should only need a few minutes per side.

Serve with the following sauce:

Peanut Sauce

75 g (3 oz) roasted peanuts
6 dried small hot chillies, soaked
1 medium onion
1 clove garlic
5 candle nuts or macadamias
¾ tsp finely grated lemon peel
2 tbsp oil
375 ml (⅔ pt) coconut cream
2 tsp dried tamarind
1 tsp brown sugar
salt to taste

Pulverize the peanuts in a food processor with a little oil (or substitute 5 tablespoons of peanut butter). Set aside.

Pulverize the chillies, onion, garlic and nuts in a food processor (or pound or chop very finely by hand). Fry in oil over a low heat for 4–5 minutes, stirring frequently. Add the lemon peel and coconut cream and bring almost to the boil, then add peanuts, tamarind (soaked in a 4 tablespoons of boiling water and strained), brown sugar and salt to taste. Serve at room temperature.

Macau

When Western chefs begin talking about the spicing of European dishes with Oriental flavourings as something revolutionary, Macanese cooks such as Julie de Senna Fernandes might justifiably reply that their families have been at it for centuries.

Fernandes belongs to a tiny Eurasian community known as the Macanese, descendants of Portuguese traders who married the Chinese women of Macau, after the Portuguese government, in the middle of the sixteenth century, had wrested control of this tiny trading post at the southern tip of China.

As might be expected, the Macanese combine the cuisines, cultural traditions and languages of Portugal and China. More interesting from the cook's point of view, however, is the way their cuisine has assimilated flavourings and recipes from all over Portugal's former empire.

'Rice is our staple,' Fernandes explains, 'because we are of China, but our dishes come from our travellers and traders from Africa, India and the Moluccas as well. Furthermore, Macau has always provided a place of refuge – we have opened our door in past centuries, for example, to persecuted Japanese Christians, who introduced miso into our cuisine. We use and we compromise. From Portugal we have preserved meats – our hams, chouriços, and blood sausages – our pork stews. From our Chinese heritage we have preserved ducks and pork.'

All these ingredients and more – including chicken, fried pork skin, Chinese white cabbage, turnip, cabbage and carrot – go into a stew known as tacho, served to herald the beginning of winter and particularly enjoyed by the devoutly Catholic Macanese on Christmas Day. 'Tacho originated from the Portuguese cozido,' says Fernandes, 'but it is not nearly as bland.'

Luckily, I was able to verify this for myself, for while in the territory I chanced upon the Macau Gourmet Festival, a contest to decide who could cook best the best tacho in Macau. The participants were mostly elderly Macanese women, and all proudly urged me to sample their finished dishes.

The contest had been organized by Fernandes and a group known as the International Ladies Club of Macau, as part of a concerted effort to keep alive Macanese cuisine, which is in dire danger of extinction. Already many dishes have been forgotten or lost. One example of this was readily obvious at the contest, where most entrants had been forced to make do with a concoction of belachan (Malaysian shrimp paste), wine, lemon and bay leaves, as a substitute for an important old

Macanese condiment known as balichao, traditionally eaten with tacho and other dishes.

At one time the manufacture of balichao formed a thriving industry in Macau; today, only a handful of private families still make it, and of these, just one, the Eusebios, provide the public with a chance to sample it, at their restaurant called, appropriately, Balichao. The reason for this state of affairs is simple: of the estimated total population of 60,000 Macanese, 40,000 have left Macau, and are dispersed all over the world, in the United States, Canada, Brazil, Australia and Portugal. With the handing of Portuguese administration of Macau back to China in 1999, sadly, many Macanese feel they can no longer regard Macau as their home.

There have been several waves of Macanese emigration, the first of which was to neighbouring Hong Kong in 1840, when the establishment of the British colony led to a huge demand for Macanese multi-lingual skills. It was about this time that one of the most famous of all Macanese dishes was perfected – minchi.

Almost certainly an adaptation of the English term 'minced meat', it is still a staple of many Macanese households. Like all Macanese dishes, it is descended from a tradition of home cooking, and as such is subject to a multitude of family variations. I was given four or five recipes in Macau, all of them different. Here then is my own amalgamation.

Minchi

1 large potato, cut into cubes
oil for frying
1 medium onion, finely diced
2 cloves garlic, crushed
500 g (1 lb) minced beef or pork (or a mix of both meats, half and half)
4 tbsp soy sauce (preferably a mixture of dark and light soy sauces, plus the sweet Indonesian kecap manis)
2 tsp sugar

Parboil or microwave the potato cubes and set aside.

Into a wok, pour a little oil and stir fry the onion until transparent. Add the garlic and minced meat and stir fry until cooked.

When the mince is almost ready, fry the potato cubes until golden brown. Drain on a kitchen towel.

To finish the minchi, add the soy sauce and sugar. Serve on plain steamed rice, sprinkled with the potato cubes.

SERVES 2.

Malaysia

When Tamil Indians and Hokkien-speaking Chinese were imported to Malaysia to work the rubber plantations and tin mines in the nineteenth century, they brought their ancient cooking traditions with them. Living in such close proximity to each other, it was inevitable that the three communities should exchange techniques and ingredients. Thus, today we have Malays adopting Indian curry leaves and spices, Indians routinely adding Malay lemon grass and Chinese soy sauce to their curries, and Chinese eating their Hokkien-style noodles with fiery Malay sambals of shrimp paste and chilli.

The following dish, which was demonstrated to me by a Malaysian chef, illustrates this concept very well. Although the dish is thought to have come originally from Muslim West Sumatra, it brings an Indian interpretation with its use of coriander, cumin, turmeric and curry leaves. And that star anise is so unmistakably Chinese.

Daging Rendang

1.5 kg (3–3½ lb) topside steak
4 cloves garlic
2 tsp fresh root ginger
2–4 small red fresh chillies, or 2 tsp chilli sauce or sambal ulek (*see* p. 227)
2 stalks lemon grass
100 g (4 oz) desiccated coconut
2–3 tablespoons oil
2 cinnamon sticks
2 star anise seeds
2 medium onions, finely sliced
2 tsp ground coriander
2 tsp ground cumin
2 tsp ground turmeric
1 tsp salt
½ tsp ground black pepper
5 daun salam leaves or 20 curry leaves
750 ml (scant 1½ pt) coconut cream

Cut the steak into cubes.

Mince the garlic, ginger, chillies and lemon grass or, better still, place these ingredients in a food processor and grind to a paste.

Place the desiccated coconut in a shallow dish and roast in a hot oven for about 20 minutes, stirring from time to time, until the coconut turns dark tan.

Meanwhile, heat the oil in a wok, add the cinnamon sticks, star anise and the onions. Sauté until the onion is transparent but not browned. Add the garlic, ginger, chillies and lemon grass, along with the coriander, cumin, turmeric, salt, black pepper and daun salam or curry leaves.

Sauté for another 3–4 minutes, then add the beef and sauté on all sides until browned. Add the coconut cream, bring slowly to the boil, then reduce the heat. Gently simmer for about an hour or more, until the coconut cream has nearly all evaporated away. The meat by this stage should be almost falling apart. Lastly, stir in the roasted desiccated coconut, which will soak up the remaining moisture and coat the cubes of meat with the sauce. Serve with rice.

SERVES 6–8.

Morocco

In the middle of a dry, scrubby, tan-coloured plain in northern Morocco lies the ancient city of Fez, the oldest of the kingdom's four imperial towns and arguably the most fascinating of them all.

Walking through the old part of the town, you might well believe you are in a time warp back to the ninth century, when it was built, for there have been few concessions to the twentieth century here. The inhabitants still fetch their water from communal, patterned-tile fountains, the shops carry no advertising, and no motor vehicle could possibly penetrate this maze of narrow, winding sloping alleyways closed in on both sides by tall crumbling walls. The sole means of transport here is still convoys of donkeys, laden down on both sides by huge sacking side-saddles, their drivers precariously on top, shouting down to the pedestrians to make way.

The streets are choked with swarthy Moroccans, a good half of whom still wear the traditional dress, especially the older people. Sitting at a table in an outdoor café over a Moroccan tea (a bunch of fresh mint stuffed down into a glass and hot, sweet China tea poured over), you can watch the costume parade pass by – the men in yellow or grey pointed slippers and long striped gowns with attached hoods like Wee Willie Winkie, or perhaps a patterned skull cap, a turban or a crimson fez with the characteristic black tassel. The women wear full-length gowns and head-dresses rather like a Catholic nun's, only they also have a white, lace-fringed handkerchief over their mouths.

Now and again a pair of Berber tribeswomen might wander by, well hidden beneath layer upon layer of striped dresses, capes and aprons. and a huge straw sombrero with lengths of plaited wool leading down from the crown to the brim, like the spokes of a wheel.

For the gourmet, Fez holds the added attraction of being Morocco's gastronomic capital. It is here, in the many restaurants and higher class cafés, that one can taste the country's best pastillas, (pigeon, chicken, almond and egg pie set in a sort of flaky pastry, and sprinkled with cinnamon and sugar) and there are a large number of local elaborations of national dishes which carry the designation 'Fassic' – that is, cooked in the style of Fez. Thus we have couscous d'agneau à la fassic – a piece of lamb on the bone served with peas and a sauce atop a pile of couscous (the semolina-wheat grain which is Morocco's most celebrated contribution to international cuisine) – or tagine d'agneau à la fassic – lamb casserole with a thin, spicy, tasty sauce.

The 'tagine' in the title of this recipe refers to a peculiarly Moroccan

48

casserole dish with a tall conical lid. Made of dark brown ovenproof pottery, they come in many sizes and are usually decorated with diamond-shaped Berber tattoo motifs. (These tattoos, seen on the chins of Berber women, serve them not only as a form of permanent make-up but also as a means of identifying the woman's home region, essential in the Berber culture which has four main languages and many more dialects.)

The tagine is either placed over direct heat or into an oven. In Fez, or at least in the old part, the houses do not have ovens, so the dishes must be taken along to the local bakery to be cooked. I must have passed five or six of these neighbourhood bakeries in the space of a morning, each of them a scene from medieval Europe – a large dingy room lit only by a carved, glowing orange hole in the wall. To one side is a pile of firewood, and beside the oven a baker at the ready with a long-handled wooden paddle used to take out the bread. The local Moroccans mix their own dough and bring it along to be cooked, for a small fee, into loaves.

Tagine Fassia

Traditionally, the ingredients of this recipe are placed in a tagine and left to cook overnight in the glowing embers of the baker's oven. Obviously this is not a practical proposition for the European cook, but I have found very passable results can be obtained with a pressure cooker.

$\frac{1}{2}$ tsp saffron
1.5 kg (3–3$\frac{1}{2}$ lb) knuckle of veal, including bone
1 tbsp paprika
1 tbsp coriander, ground
1 tbsp ginger
$\frac{3}{4}$ tsp salt
3 large onions, sliced
4 medium tomatoes, skinned and halved
6 cloves garlic, peeled but left whole
80 ml (3 fl oz) olive oil

Grind the saffron with a mortar and pestle and pour over a tablespoon of hot water to dissolve. (If you don't have saffron, use turmeric to colour the dish.)

Place meat, onions, tomato and garlic in a pressure cooker or heatproof casserole and pour over the oil and 375 ml ($\frac{2}{3}$ pt) water. Sprinkle over the spices and salt and put on the lid. It will take 20 minutes in a pressure cooker or 1$\frac{1}{4}$ hours over a low heat.

Serve with rice.

Singapore

Searching for the British colonial legacy in Singapore, you need do no more than sip a gin and tonic in the Cricket Club and peer through the Elizabethan-style mullioned windows at the comings and goings of wing-collared lawyers over at the Supreme Court. Who, however, would expect to find a lasting Anglo-Saxon influence on the food of a people possessed with such healthy esteem for their own Chinese, Malay and Indian culinary heritage? Nevertheless, it is there, not only in the roast beef and grilled lamb chops which the Eurasian community liven up with chilli sauce and sambal belachan, but also in the cooking of the Hainanese Chinese, favoured by the British as house servants.

Indeed, the island of Hainan has so little indigenous cuisine that its emigrant sons were forced to invent their own dishes in the Singaporean kitchens of their British masters. The most famous of these is Hainanese pork chops – breaded, fried and served with trimmings of mashed potato, quartered tomatoes, onions and peas, and a gravy of starch-thickened soy sauce.

It was also a Hainanese Chinese, Ngiam Tong Boon, who invented Singapore's most famous drink, the Singapore Sling. This was some time before 1910 at the Long Bar of Raffles Hotel which, even then, set the standard for European fine dining in Singapore.

Today at the hotel's museum, visitors may view the safe in which Mr Ngiam locked away his precious recipe books, as well as his cocktail shaker and the Sling recipe hastily jotted down on a bar-chit in 1936 by a customer who asked the waiter for it:

SINGAPORE SLING
Combine one half-measure gin, one quarter cherry brandy, one quarter mixed fruit juices (orange, lime or lemon, pineapple), a few drops of cointreau and Benedictine and a dash of Angostura bitters. Top with a cherry and a slice of pineapple.

Ngiam Tong Boon also invented the Million Dollar cocktail, once as popular as the Singapore Sling and immortalized in one of Somerset Maugham's most famous barside tales, 'The Letter'. Maugham made the first of his visits to Raffles Hotel in 1921; he returned again in 1926 and then in 1959. Legend has it that he worked every morning under a frangipani tree in the Palm Court, turning the bits of gossip and scandal overheard at dinner parties into his famous stories.

Today Raffles boasts of its former guests like a public school would list its famous sons. They include singers (Michael Jackson, Diana Ross), actors (Marlon Brando, Richard Burton, Elizabeth Taylor, Orson Welles, Grace Kelly, Jean Harlow, Mary Pickford and Charlie Chaplin) and heads of state (Haile Selassie, Pierre Trudeau, Malcolm Fraser, Valery Giscard d'Estaing, Chou En-Lai). Indira Gandhi also slept here – though not as President of India. George Bush wanted to, but his advisers decreed the security was not up to scratch.

But it is the literati, not the glitterati, that have become the hotel's greatest trump card: James Michener, Günter Grass and Maxine Hong Kingston are merely the latest in a list which began with Joseph Conrad, a year after the main building of the hotel opened in 1889. Not everybody was impressed. Herman Hesse wrote in his diary in 1911: 'We are staying expensively but well in Raffle's Hotel. The food is bad here too.' For Kipling it was the other way round: 'The food is as excellent as the rooms are bad. Let the traveller take note. Feed at Raffles and sleep at the Hôtel de l'Europe.'

Raffles was almost alone in Singapore at this time in having a French chef, and French cuisine is a tradition which continues to this day at the Raffles Grill. From the Raffles Grill, here is:

Tian of Roasted Lamb Loin, Ratatouille and Tapenade

2 kg (4½ lb) chopped lamb bones
600 g (1¼ lb) onions
225 g (8 oz) celery
225 g (8 oz) carrots
2 bay leaves
2 sprigs of fresh thyme
20 whole white peppercorns
600 g (1¼ lb) lamb loin fillet
salt and ground pepper
2 tbsp vegetable oil

TIAN OF RATATOUILLE
1½ tsp chopped garlic
125 ml (4 fl oz) olive oil
500 g (1 lb) aubergine, diced
500 g (1 lb) courgettes, diced
500 g (1 lb) tomatoes
1 tsp fresh thyme
salt and ground white pepper

TAPENADE SAUCE
50 g (2 oz) sun-dried olives (stones removed)
4 cloves garlic
3 anchovy fillets
30 g (1 oz) capers

To make the stock, brown the lamb bones (without any oil) in a heavy frying pan over a high heat, then add the onions, celery, carrots, bay leaves, thyme and peppercorns. Place the lamb bones and vegetables in a stock-pot, add water and bring to the boil. Reduce to a simmer for 2 hours, skimming occasionally to remove fat and sediment. Strain through a very fine sieve into a smaller cooking pot. Reduce the stock to one third by slow cooking. Set aside until needed.

For the tian, lightly brown the garlic in olive oil in a medium-sized sauté pan. Add the aubergine and courgette and cook for 2–3 minutes, then add the tomatoes and fresh thyme. Season with salt and ground white pepper. Set aside until needed.

Make the tapenade by puréeing the olives with the garlic, anchovy fillets and capers in a blender, slowly adding olive oil to form a paste. Remove from the blender. Bring the reduced lamb stock to the boil and add the olive paste. Reduce to a simmer, add the remaining thyme and adjust the seasoning. Set aside.

Preheat the oven to 180°C/350°F/Gas Mark 4. Remove the silver skin from the lamb if not already done, and season with salt and pepper. Grease a heavy frying pan with vegetable oil and brown the fillet well over a high heat. Transfer to the preheated oven and roast for 3–4 minutes or until medium rare. Remove from the oven and rest for 5–10 minutes before slicing.

Bring the tapenade sauce to the boil, reduce the heat and simmer over low heat. Reheat the ratatouille.

To serve, spoon a portion of the ratatouille on to the centre of each warmed dinner plate. Slice the lamb fillet thinly and lay over the ratatouille. (A small stainless steel ring about 10 cm (4 in) in diameter, such as one for making crumpets or poaching eggs, can help with the presentation: place the ring on the plate, fill with ratatouille, place the meat on top of the ratatouille inside the ring and then remove the ring.) Pour the hot tapenade sauce around.

Serve immediately.

Thailand

Considering their official religion is Buddhism, the Thais are a fairly carnivorous people. In many areas fish and seafoods are eaten almost daily, while chicken, pork and beef also feature in traditional Thai cookery. But then the Thais are also a sensual people who have never let religious strictures interfere with simple pleasures. A sight which never failed to amuse me in Thailand was Buddhist monks, shaven-headed and saintly in their saffron robes, seriously dragging away on tailor-made cigarettes.

Besides, Thai fishermen have a marvellous rationalization: the fish are stupid to swim into their nets. And they don't kill the fish, they merely take them from the water. If the fish should happen to die as a result, then what does it matter if their carcases are eaten afterwards?

It has been estimated that more than 60 per cent of rural-dwelling Thais still depend on catching fish for their regular home supplies. I have watched them by rivers, ponds and even paddy fields, using a variety of rods, nets and baskets. Carp and eel are common freshwater species, while on the southern coasts there are sea bass, mackerel, tuna, shark, cat-fish, squid, lobster, oysters, crab, shrimp and prawns.

The Thais themselves are rather more squeamish about slaughtering the other animals they eat. The pork and poultry butchers in Thailand are mostly Chinese, while the slaughtering of the buffalos used for beef (which is surprisingly tender) is left mainly to the Muslim descendants of Pathan immigrants from north-western Pakistan.

Chicken is common enough to be sold from the carts of street vendors, but pork and beef tend to be reserved for more special occasions.

Kaeng Masaman (Thai Muslim curry)

CURRY PASTE
6 dried red chillies, seeded
3/4 tsp ground black pepper
1 tbsp coriander seeds
1/2 tbsp cumin seeds
4 cm (1 1/2 in) cinnamon stick
4 whole cloves
4 cardamom pods
1/4 tsp nutmeg
4–5 cloves garlic, crushed
5 shallots or 1 small onion, finely chopped
1 tbsp grated root ginger

¼ tsp salt
½ tsp belachan or kapee (preserved shrimp paste) (optional)
bunch of dried lemon grass
1 tbsp brown sugar
1 tbsp tamarind pulp
juice of 2 limes or 1 lemon

CURRY
750 g (1½ lb) chuck steak, cubed
2 tsp butter
625 ml (1¼ pt) coconut cream
2 tbsp Thai fish sauce
5 cardamom seeds
5 cm (2 in) cinnamon stick
4 bay leaves
100 g (4 oz) peanuts, skinned

To prepare the curry paste, lightly smear a frying pan with oil, place in first eight ingredients, and toast over a medium heat until they just begin to darken and give off a spicy aroma. Remove and place in a blender (or electric spice grinder) and grind. Finish off with a mortar and pestle, grinding the spices as finely as possible.

In the same frying pan, gently fry garlic, shallots (or onion) and ginger for two minutes. Add this to the ground spices along with the salt and shrimp paste (if using) and grind to a smooth paste.

Take a small bunch of dried lemon grass about the thickness of your little finger, barely cover it with 4–5 tablespoons of water in a pan, bring to the boil and simmer for 5 minutes. Discard the lemon grass, and in the hot liquid dissolve the brown sugar and the tamarind pulp. Stand for several minutes, then drain off the liquid, squeezing all the moisture from the tamarind. Add this liquid to the ground spices along with the lemon or lime juice.

Sauté the cubes of beef in butter until browned on all sides. Add the coconut cream, fish sauce, cardamon seeds (seeds, note, not whole pods), cinnamon stick and bay leaves. Bring to the boil and simmer for 15–20 minutes until the beef is tender.

With a slotted spoon, remove the beef and keep warm and covered in a medium-low oven. Bring the coconut cream mixture in the pan to a rapid boil and reduce its volume by half, stirring to prevent it sticking. Pick out the cinnamon stick and bay leaves and discard.

Stir in the curry paste and the peanuts, then put the meat back in the pan and heat through for several minutes.

SERVES 4–6, depending on how many other rice and vegetable dishes you serve with it.

Neua Pad Prik (chilli beef)

Were it not for the chillies in this dish, it might well be mistaken for a Chinese recipe and indeed would fit in well with a Chinese meal.

500 g (1 lb) chuck steak
2 tbsp soy sauce
1 tbsp brown sugar
2 cloves garlic, crushed
1 tbsp grated fresh root ginger
1 medium onion
2 green peppers
8 Chinese dried mushrooms (or use fresh)
4 tbsp cooking oil
4 red chillies, fresh or dried
1 small tin baby corn cobs
125 ml (4 fl oz) beef stock
1 tbsp cornflour
3 tbsp oyster sauce
1 tbsp Thai fish sauce

Trim all fat and gristle from the beef and slice as thinly as possible, aiming for wafer-thin pieces about 2–3 cm (1 in) square. Add soy sauce, sugar, garlic and ginger and mix well. Leave to marinate for a minimum of half an hour.

Cut the peeled onion in half and then slice very thinly lengthways. Cut the green peppers in half, remove seeds and pith, and slice into 3 cm (1 in) squares. Soak the dried mushrooms in hot water and slice, or slice fresh mushrooms.

Heat the oil in a wok (or large frying pan), add chillies, beef, mushrooms and onions and stir fry over a high heat for one minute. Add the green peppers and baby corn and stir fry for another minute. Pour in the beef stock, reduce the heat and simmer for three minutes, continuing to stir.

Mix the cornflour with 2 tablespoons of cold water and stir into the mixture to thicken. Stir in oyster sauce and fish sauce.

SERVES 4–6, depending on what else you serve with it.

Turkey

Café society abounds everywhere in Istanbul, but its focal point is a solid bunch in sixty-odd cafés, doner kebab stalls and restaurants lining an alleyway known as Gigek Pasaji, or Flowery Passage.

You have to know how to find this bohemian enclave, because around nightfall you could walk down the adjacent, deserted boulevard and easily miss the tiny inconspicuous entrance. Once inside, however, we are confronted with a seething mass of citizenry, virtually all male, squeezing past each other and milling about the open-air cafés. At the tables, men sit smoking hookahs and drinking ouzo (only, please, in Turkey we call it raki).

After the raki-drinking is over for the night, maybe somebody will get socked in the jaw, but in the meantime, a kid with a *dabruka* (a drum with a horn attached) is pounding out a happy rhythm, grinning with a mouth that begins and ends a little beneath both ears, thrusting his head back and singing for all he's worth. At each of the tables he deigns to stop at on his way down the alley, the song ends with a shower of coins and notes sent fluttering down the mouth of his *dabruka*.

Around dinner time, a sprinkling of women and their escorts can be seen picking their way through the unruly crowd towards the stairs that lead to the respectable restaurants on the first floor.

There is music here, too, from an orchestra no less, seated on a stage at the end of the dining room. Besides the *dabruka* player there is a tall, skinny man on the *gumbus* (a banjo-like instrument), a piano accordion player, and a violinist in white shirt and tie, the jacket of his powder-blue suit unbuttoned to release his bulging folds of flesh.

During one of their breaks, a startling Frenchwoman of about sixty appears. A proud crumbling statue, round-shouldered, shambling around the tables on twisted heels, she is dressed all in funereal black: black sequined dress, black bouffant hair, black eyeliner and bright red lipstick, her pot tummy conveniently jutting out from her abdomen like a shelf. Conveniently, because upon it she rests an enormous black piano accordion, which accompanies the songs of Edith Piaf, sung in her throaty, masculine voice. Her tips come in the form of drinks and cigarettes as well as the coins and notes she drops into the pocket of a tiny apron.

Ah, our food is arriving now, borne aloft on a tray: stuffed mussels, beetroot in vinegar with sugar and garlic, cold steamed shrimps, a plate of crumbly white beyaz peynir (the Turkish version of feta), an intact steamed sheep's brain and the pièce de résistance, Ali Nazik: aubergine purée with yoghurt sauce, topped with minced lamb enriched with tomato and chilli.

Ali Nazik

Although this is a common Turkish restaurant dish, you don't need the skill of a chef to make it; indeed, it is little more than an assembly job. Strictly speaking, the meat should be lamb, but standard minced beef works just as well.

1 large or 2 small aubergines
2 large cloves garlic, crushed
½ tsp salt
500 ml (18 fl oz) plain yoghurt
2 tbsp olive oil
1 small onion, finely chopped
250 g (9 oz) lamb or beef, minced
1 small red pepper, finely chopped
2 tbsp tomato paste
½ tsp dried thyme
½ tsp paprika
½ tsp or more chilli powder (or fresh paste or sauce)
250 g (9 oz) rice

Stab the aubergine in the side with a knife, then place under the grill and cook on all sides until the skin is blackened and the aubergine has collapsed into a wrinkled heap. The flesh will now be infused with a delicious, mildly smoky flavour.

Lift the aubergine, shaking off any oil (which may be bitter) and transfer to a chopping board. Peel off the charred skin and discard, then finely chop the aubergine until it is reduced to a rough purée.

Stir the garlic and salt into the yoghurt. Set half of this to one side, and mix the other half with the aubergine purée. Set aside.

Put the rice on to boil or steam while the meat is being cooked.

Heat the oil in a frying pan, add the onion and sauté several minutes. Add the meat and the pepper, and fry for 7–8 minutes, mashing the mince with a spoon to separate the lumps. Towards the end of cooking, add the tomato paste, dried thyme, paprika, and chilli.

Spread a layer of rice over a platter, and over this spread the aubergine purée. Spoon over the yoghurt sauce, and then the reddened mince mixture, which will look most appetizing set against the background of snowy white.

SERVES 3.

Like most countries of Asia Minor, Turkey is rich in vegetables and fruit of exceptional quality, a result of mineral-rich soils and long hours of sunshine. The variety and abundance which confronts one at Turkish markets can be quite bewildering. On market day in the town of Bodrum on the Aegean Coast, for instance, I was amazed to find the stalls lined not just one street but the entire eight or so blocks of the town centre.

Huge stacks of spinach, some waist-high, competed for space with piles of blood-red carrots, and aubergines of every conceivable shape and colour – long and thin, short and squat, white, mauve or purple. The tomatoes, deeply ribbed and strongly flavoured, were two or three times the size of what one would call a medium-sized specimen. Green peppers, that other mainstay of Turkish cooking, were everywhere and there was an astonishing array of string beans – not only green but red, pink and white.

In Turkish cooking the distinction between a meat and a vegetable dish is often blurred, as the two are commonly cooked together. This is especially so with dolmas, or stuffed vegetables, in which meat is often combined with rice or cracked wheat, nuts, dried fruit and spices, to provide a filling for any of a number of squat, round vegetables, such as peppers, aubergines, courgettes, tomatoes, onions or artichokes.

Like koftas or the individual pastries known as borekler, dolmas reflect a Turkish passion for serving their food in little bundles. This may reflect their nomadic past, but it is more likely that dolmas were introduced to Turkey from elsewhere in the Middle East. Vegetable-coring implements dating back between 5000 and 6000 years have been found in archaeological sites as far apart as Knossos in Crete and Medzamor in the southern USSR. The savage Turkish tribes from Central Asia, who founded the Ottoman Empire in the fourteenth century, had only a very primitive cuisine of their own, but following the capture of Constantinople (modern Istanbul) in 1453, a luxurious style was created for the rich and mighty sultans, drawing on the cuisine of all the other Middle Eastern cultures. It was during this period that dolmas, as we know them today, were perfected. Later the recipe spread to all corners of the Ottoman Empire – to North Africa, Iran, Saudi Arabia, Greece and the Balkans.

When a grape vine leaf, silver beet or cabbage leaf is wrapped around the filling, the dish is known in Turkish as sarma. The following recipe is very popular in Turkey today, although the cracked wheat and the yoghurt sauce belie an Armenian origin.

Gaghampi Patoug (meat-filled cabbage leaves)

100 g (4 oz) coarse cracked wheat (burghul)
1.5 kg (3–3½ lb) cabbage
vinegar
500 g (1 lb) minced lamb or beef
oil for frying
1 large onion, finely chopped
2 cloves garlic, crushed
100 g (4 oz) walnuts, chopped
1 tsp ground allspice
1 tbsp chopped fresh basil
1 tbsp chopped parsley
salt and pepper
100 g (4 oz) prunes, stoned and halved
100 g (4 oz) dried apricots, roughly chopped
1 small onion, cut into thin rings
750 ml–1 litre (1½ pt) stock or water
3–4 tbsp tomato paste

YOGHURT SAUCE
500 ml (18 fl oz) plain yoghurt
1 tsp dried mint
2–3 cloves garlic, crushed

Cover the cracked wheat with water and leave to soak for 30–45 minutes.

Break the leaves off the cabbage and steam until they are just pliable. Drain the leaves, sprinkle with vinegar, then cut away the protruding part of the central rib (to enable the leaf to lie flat).

Stir fry the mince in a little oil until the pinkness disappears, then add the chopped onion, garlic, walnuts, allspice, basil, parsley, and salt and pepper to taste.

Place a good tablespoon of this mixture on each cabbage leaf, fold both sides over, and roll up the leaf like a cigar.

Line the bottom of a pot with the outside leaves of the cabbage (to prevent the dolmas sticking to the bottom) and pack in your cabbage parcels. Sprinkle over the prunes, apricots and onion rings and pour over the stock or water mixed with the tomato paste. Boil for 10–15 minutes.

Mix together the sauce ingredients and heat but do not allow to boil.

Serve with the yoghurt sauce handed round separately.

Poultry and Eggs

China

Five eggs

I was five years old
when I buried under the tree
five eggs as white as snow.

I was ten years old
when I had the urge to see
what had become of them.

I was fifteen years old
and had completely forgotten about the eggs
as I journeyed far from home.

I was twenty years old
and on my wedding day
the memory of those five eggs came back,
buried there under the tree.

I did as I was advised,
went and sprinkled the spot with lime
and poured some water over it.

I was twenty-five years old,
my eldest son was five,
his brother two years younger
when their little sister was born.

Then I dug up those five eggs
transformed by the years
into a rare delicacy
and I meditated
on the transformation those eggs
and on the transformation of my life.

Chinese poem

Twenty years would be a respectable age indeed for one of Chinese cooking's celebrated 'ancient eggs', for while they are often called 'Hundred-Year-Old Eggs', in the curing process one year is usually taken to mean one day, and sometimes they are left for as little as fifty days.

While I am not seriously suggesting they be made at home, the recipe sounds easy enough, being fresh ducks eggs coated with a combination of six parts pine wood ash to one of lime, mixed to a paste with strong black tea, allowing a pinch of salt per egg. The coated eggs are then buried in an earthenware container, separated from each other by several centimetres of packed earth, and left in a cool place for a hundred days.

An ancient Chinese text warns: 'While making ancient eggs, avoid strangers, ignore too many people, especially friends and acquaintances, and do not gossip or talk more than is absolutely necessary.'

For my own initiation into this culinary curiosity I have a Chinese host in Thailand to thank. I must admit that seeing some mud-coated specimens in the market had not exactly fired my ambition to try them, but having two of these olive-green coloured eggs now placed before me as the principal dish of an otherwise simple meal, I had no choice.

Each had been neatly sliced in half to reveal the yellowish circles which emanated outwards from the centre of the yolk, and on the outside the white had turned to a dark amber-coloured jelly. The flavour however was a pleasant surprise – salty, pungent and a little reminiscent of a well-matured cheese.

A considerably more practical proposition for Western kitchens are these delicately flavoured eggs boiled in tea and soy sauce.

Ch'a Tan (tea eggs)

6 eggs
2 tbsp Indian tea
2 tbsp soy sauce
1 tbsp salt
1 tsp aniseed
1 cinnamon stick (optional)

Hard boil the eggs (allowing no more than 10 minutes) then tap each egg lightly all over, or roll them across a bench. The shells should be finely cracked all over. Do not peel.

Place in 600 ml (1 pint) water and add all other ingredients. Bring to boil and simmer, covered, for 1½–2 hours. The eggs can now be peeled and eaten, but will improve with a further 8–10 hours seeping in the cooled liquid (with the shells still on). Surprisingly enough, the yolks still stay yellow. The whites take on a subtle tea-flavour and the visual effect is startling, like that of delicate cracked porcelain.

These eggs make an effective table decoration and are a pleasant variation on plain old hard-boiled eggs for packed lunches. They are also an idea to keep in mind for Easter.

Another unique Chinese technique with eggs is to trail a fine thread into soups:

Chi Tan T'ang (egg drop soup)

1.2 litres (2 pt) chicken stock
2 tsp freshly grated fresh root ginger
1/2 tsp sugar
1 1/2 tbsp cornflour
2 eggs
1 tsp sesame oil
1–2 spring onions, finely sliced
salt and pepper

Bring chicken stock to the boil, add ginger and sugar and boil together for one minute. Mix the cornflour with 4 tablespoons of water, stir into the soup, and boil a further minute. Meanwhile beat the eggs with 2 teaspoons of cold water until frothy. Now take a chopstick and, stirring the soup vigorously, trail a fine thread of the egg mixture into it as slowly as you can. Top with sesame oil and spring onions, and season with salt and pepper to taste.

The Taoist philosophers of China have considered the egg a perfect embodiment of the principle of yin and yang, or the union of opposites. Like the outer circle of the famous yin-yang symbol, the egg shell signifies the origin of creation, which is divided into two constituent parts, the white and yolk, or yin and yang. These respectively symbolize female and male, darkness and light, moon and sun, earth and heaven, quietude and force, absorption and penetration. So ponder upon that next time you fry your breakfast egg, only remember the case of Sir Isaac Newton, who was so absentminded that, having his pocket-watch in one hand and an egg in the other one morning, he fried the pocket-watch and held the egg.

India

Indian chickens, like their kin throughout the East, are scrawny but tasty. They are by far the most common bird to be eaten, although ducks and small birds are sometimes seen in markets. Since Moghul days, the nobility had enjoyed shooting smaller quarry as well as tigers and in maharajahs' palaces game birds were often on the menu. Evidently too often. At a Mayfair restaurant, one visiting prince of the Raj ordered becasse au fumet – woodcock – watched as it was brought to the table on a silver platter and flamed in brandy, then, with a languid wave of his hand, ordered the waiter to take it away uneaten. 'I'm not hungry,' he explained to a bevy of young Englishwomen at his table, 'but I loved the show.'

In the south of India, a creamy sauce for chicken might be based on coconut milk, but in the north it would be more likely to be yoghurt or curds. A korma, basically meat braised in yoghurt, is spiced without being fiery and makes a good introduction to Indian food for a newcomer wary of throat-scalding chillies. It is more traditional to use lamb, but chicken is a delicious and acceptable alternative.

Chicken Korma

750 g (1½ lb) chicken meat, boned
3 medium onions, sliced thinly
2 tbsp ghee or oil
1 tsp ground coriander
½ tsp ground turmeric
2 tsp grated fresh root ginger
¼ tsp cardamom seeds, ground
½ tsp fenugreek
1½ tbsp desiccated or shredded coconut
375 ml (13 fl oz) plain yoghurt
salt

Place chicken bones in a little water and boil for 15–20 minutes.

Cut the chicken meat into 2–3cm (1 in) pieces. Fry the onions in ghee or oil, then add all the spices except cardamom. Stir in the coconut and fry the mixture until the spices darken in colour. Now add the cardamom along with the chicken, a quarter of the yoghurt and some of the chicken stock. Cook until the chicken is tender (about 30 minutes) adding more stock as necessary, and salt to taste. Stir in the remaining yoghurt at the end of cooking and heat through.

Serve on rice.

Of the many religious and ethnic minorities in India, few have such a distinctive style of cooking as the Parsis of Bombay.

The largest remaining enclave of the ancient Zoroastrian fire-worshipping religion of Iran, the modern Parsis are descendants of a group which fled Iran more than 1200 years ago to avoid conversion to Islam by Arab invaders. They settled in the state of Gujarat, where most of them still live, particularly in the main city of Bombay, although I have also spotted them in the streets in the far north of India.

Their dress is quite distinctive – the women wear a sari over a Western style dress, the men Western style suit tops but with tight-fitting white trousers which give their legs a spidery appearance, and sometimes on their heads a black rimless hat of stiffened black shiny cloth.

As a class the Parsis are essentially upper-middle and professional, and are among India's top businessmen and industrialists. They are also well-known as public benefactors, although they tend to show a certain reserve when dealing with outsiders.

They show no desire to convert others to their faith, and indeed no non-Parsi, however trusted, is allowed into their temples to observe the purification rites before the holy fire, symbol of their supreme god, Ahura Mazda. Since fire is sacred to them, they do not desecrate it by cremating their dead, preferring instead to leave the corpse to resident vultures perched atop their eerie towers of silence.

During the era of British rule in India, the Parsis contributed greatly to the relative harmony of Indo-British relations in Bombay as compared to Calcutta, and frequently entertained the British with afternoon tea parties. In his *British Social Life in India* (1938), Dennis Kincaid has an account of one such occasion:

> Nestling modestly in the shadow of the teapot [was] a plate of Indian potato-cakes. 'One of our little native preparations. My wife insisted on making them for you. Oh yes, like sampling foreign dishes.' The ungloved hand advanced, selected one of the soft, luke-warm yellowish blobs. A moment of panic; had the cook remembered not to put any chillies in? The Englishwoman's face was inscrutable in the shadow of that huge hat with its pyramid of vertical flowers nodding on green wire stems. A whalebone-stiffened collar enclosing the throat almost concealed the faint swallowing motions. There was an encouraging nod. 'Yes, very nice. An unfamiliar taste, of course. And now I would like a cucumber sandwich, please.'

Fortunately the Parsis persisted with their 'native preparations' which in fact amount to a highly individual cuisine, particularly in its treatment of eggs.

Parsi Poro (Parsi omelette)

200 g (7 oz) potatoes
1 tbsp oil
1 medium onion, finely chopped
4 eggs
$\frac{1}{2}$ tsp salt
black pepper
$\frac{1}{2}$ tsp ground cumin
$\frac{1}{2}$ tsp ground turmeric
$\frac{1}{2}$ tsp chilli powder or 2 fresh chillies, chopped
2 tbsp chopped fresh coriander leaves
1 tbsp ghee or butter
1 tomato, chopped (optional)
1 green pepper, chopped (optional)
175 g (6 oz) green peas (optional)

Peel the potatoes and parboil in water for five minutes. Remove and cut into small cubes. Heat the oil in a pan, fry the potatoes, and when nearly cooked, add the onions and fry until both are cooked.

Meanwhile, separate the eggs, beat the whites until very frothy but not quite stiff, then stir in the egg yolks, salt, a few grinds of black pepper, the cumin, turmeric, chilli, and coriander or parsley.

Heat the ghee or butter in a frying pan, pour in the omelette mixture and cook over a medium heat until most of the egg has set. About a minute before the end of cooking, sprinkle over the potatoes and onion and, if using, the vegetables. Fold over and serve.

SERVES ONE HEARTY EATER, TWO MODERATE EATERS.

Keema per Eenda (spiced mince with eggs)

2 tbsp ghee or oil
2 medium onions, finely diced
4 cloves garlic, crushed
walnut-sized piece of fresh root ginger, grated
2 fresh chillies, chopped or 2 tsp chilli powder
2 tsp ground coriander
$1\frac{1}{2}$ tsp ground cumin
1 tsp ground turmeric
pinch of ground cloves
pinch of ground cinnamon
750 g ($1\frac{1}{2}$ lb) lamb or beef, minced
1 tsp salt
$\frac{1}{4}$ tsp brown sugar

2 medium tomatoes, peeled and chopped
3 tbsp fresh coriander leaves, chopped
4 eggs
salt and pepper

Heat the ghee or oil in a pan and fry onions, garlic, ginger, chilies or chilli powder, coriander, cumin, turmeric, cloves and cinnamon for 2 minutes. Add the mince, salt and sugar and cook for several minutes longer, mashing with a wooden spoon until it is browned on all sides. Add the tomato, 2 tablespoons of the coriander leaves and 250 ml (9 fl oz) of water and cook, covered, until the water is almost all absorbed.

Preheat the oven to 190°C/375°F/Gas Mark 5.

Spread the mixture over a lightly buttered ovenproof dish. Separate the eggs. Beat the whites until fairly stiff, fold in the egg yolks, add a little salt and pepper, and pour over the meat in the dish.

Bake in a the oven for about 20 minutes until the egg rises like a soufflé. Sprinkle the remaining coriander leaves over the top.

Variation: instead of beating the eggs, make four dents in the top of the meat with a large spoon and break in the eggs whole. The dish will then only need 10–15 minutes in the oven.

Indonesia

If the small man's complex can be extended to the animal kingdom, then a prime example must be the Balinese rooster, a wiry little beast who makes up with ferocity what he lacks in size. Just to be placed in front of another male is enough to flare his ruff and reduce his beady pupils to angry pinpricks.

This goes a long way to explaining the popularity of cockfighting in Bali, and indeed Indonesia in general. Every Balinese man, it seems, keeps a pet fighting cock. Each day these are placed in bell-shaped cages by the side of the road, so that they might amuse themselves by watching the passing traffic.

At dusk, groups of men can be seen in the villages, squatting in circles clutching their prized birds, massaging them and comparing them. Occasionally they let them loose at each other, brushing their heads against each other to goad them into a sparring session. The performance of the birds at these practice bouts is carefully noted, as it will influence the betting on the day of the real fight, when razor-sharp spurs are attached to their right legs and the battle is to the death.

Such occasions are tightly regulated by the Indonesian government: since 1974 it has been necessary to obtain a permit for every cockfight. In Bali these are generally issued only when a rooster's blood is needed for religious ceremonies. At the festival of Nyepi, for example, the spilling of a rooster's blood is said to purify the earth, infected by the devils lately cast out by the Lord of Hell, Yama.

A cockfighting permit would also be issued to a private individual who wished to appease the evil spirits during a ceremony to open a new house. The blood would be used in opening the ceremony and again in closing the ceremony three days later.

A common ploy, however, is to obtain permits for two or three cockfights, and then carry on and hold fifteen or twenty. The police might come to break them up, but conveniently not arrive until after the last fight. But not always. Approaching a hamlet near Ubud one day, I was confronted by a huge commotion. The police, most discourteously, had appeared amid an illegal cockfight, and men were scattering in all directions. One enterprising youth roared off on his trailbike down a narrow track between the paddy fields, where the police jeep would not be able to follow. I have also heard of Balinese wives who, in a matter of seconds, are able to usher fleeing men into their homes and make out they are holding a tea party by the time the police arrive on their doorstep.

Cockfights are not for the faint-hearted. At one fight, having watched an American tourist rudely push and shove her way to the front, I could not help but smile at the poetic justice as she returned moments later a pale shade of green.

The Balinese are genuinely puzzled by the attitude of many Westerners, who eat chicken yet decry the sport as cruel. To the Balinese there is no difference whether the rooster on the kitchen table has met its fate in a cockfight or the slaughterhouse.

Being a somewhat stringy specimen, a deceased fighting cock is often used for this recipe, where the idea is to shred the meat. A good substitute would be a retired laying fowl, bought cheaply. The beauty of the recipe is that it uses meat which is often discarded by wasteful Western stock-makers.

Abon Ayam

4 chicken breasts
1 tbsp dried tamarind
1 clove garlic, crushed
$\frac{1}{2}$ tsp ground coriander
2 tsp brown sugar
2–3 tbsp oil

Boil the chicken breasts in water for about an hour. Remove from the stock (which can be reserved for other uses) and cool, then shred the meat finely, either by hand or with a fork. This is the most laborious part, the aim being to get as fine and fibrous a texture as possible.

Break the tamarind into small pieces and pour over 3 tablespoons of boiling water. Leave for 5 minutes, then squeeze the pieces of tamarind to extract the juice. Strain off the tamarind stones and pith, and sprinkle the juice over the chicken. Add the garlic, coriander and sugar, and mix well.

Heat the oil in a wok, and add the chicken a handful at a time, stir frying until golden brown. Drain on absorbent paper. Repeat until all the chicken is done.

Once cooked, abon ayam should dry sufficiently to keep in an airtight jar in the fridge for two weeks. It is usually served a little at a time, as a side dish to accompany a rice-based meal.

Bebek tutu, stuffed roast duck, is Bali's most celebrated dish, if only because of the immense effort needed to produce it correctly. The duck is rubbed and stuffed with innumerable flavourings and spices, then for three long days cooked in a pit of smouldering rice husks.

Nowadays, every other restaurant in the island's resort centres offers the dish on their menu, usually stipulating that it be ordered 24 hours in advance. However, most tourists who try bebek tutu in such places are likely to wonder what the fuss is all about: a steamed, slightly smoky-flavoured duck, not over spicy, certainly very pleasant, but nothing to rave about.

This is hardly surprising, given that they are very likely the latest victims of a minor swindle. Three days' preparation time, even at meagre Balinese rates of pay, means huge labour costs for Balinese restaurateurs. But since the average tourist has not the slightest idea of how the dish ought to taste, the restaurateurs surmise, they may as well take a short cut. And so they do. The standard practice is to steam the duck or roast it in the oven, then finish it off for an hour or so by burying it in ashes, to give it a slightly smoky tinge. All of which is an excellent illustration of the havoc wreaked by mass tourism upon indigenous cultures.

This piece of inside information came to me courtesy of my cooking teacher in Bali, who also introduced me to a group of cooks in the village of Peliatan, near Ubud, where the dish is still prepared according to tradition.

Many villages in Bali are famous for a particular art form, and Peliatan, besides having a famous dance troupe, prides itself on producing some of Bali's best bebek tutu. I was not surprised to find the cooks were all men; as with much Balinese food, the everyday dishes are cooked by the women, but the preparation of the special, festival-style dishes is the domain of the men.

Here is how it was done. First the duck was cleaned, and a hole cut to remove the innards. Some terasi (preserved shrimp paste), salt and a little tamarind and coconut oil were mixed together and massaged into the duck, the idea being to impregnate the flavour through the duck and at the same time tenderize the flesh. Then the gut cavity was filled with nutmegs, cloves and a mixture the Balinese call 'base gede'. The same mixture is known in Indonesian as 'bumbu serebu' and is widely available from village markets. Since the name translates roughly as 'mixture of a thousand roots', I did not feel up to the task of analysing it too thoroughly! I did, however, detect a presence of ginger and galangal. The opening in the duck carcass was sewn up with a length of thin bamboo, more of which was used to bind betel leaves around the body of the duck. The use of betel leaves here is unique in Balinese cooking.

Then I was led out to the back of the compound where a number of holes, each about 80 cm (2½ ft) deep and the same wide, contained slowly smouldering fires of rice husks. Each of these holes contained a pot carved from limestone, enclosed by a lid, and inside each lay a duck similarly prepared. A Balinese boy wandered about desultorily tending the fires, checking they were still alight, so slowly did they burn.

The cooking continues like this for three days, at the end of which the duck is withdrawn, a parcel of deeply browned, though not greatly charred leaves.

Having haggled over the price of one of these ducks, as custom demands, we took it back to my teacher's house. Unwrapped, it revealed an ambrosial-smelling (if not looking) mass of duck meat, falling off the bone yet still moist. The flavour had a slight smoky tinge reminiscent of hangi food, the earth-oven dishes of the Pacific Islands, and in the background the scent of the thousand mysterious roots and spices. It was as different from the restaurant versions I had tasted as real chicken soup is from the stuff out of a packet. Let anybody dare tell me the cuisine of Bali is that of a 'primitive' culture!

The Indonesian civilization, it is sometimes said, is founded on four plants: rice, banana, bamboo and coconut. Apart from being eaten, the coconut serves all sorts of useful purposes: the half-shells form drinking vessels and cooking ladles, and in Bali are considered the best fuel for spit-roasting pigs and satay; the coarse outer fibres of the coconut are woven into mats and ropes, and the wood of the tree is used for the beams and rafters of the houses. Occasionally in Bali, you also see the stump of a coconut tree carved into a giant throne-like chair.

Everywhere throughout Indonesia young coconuts are sold from the side of the road as a refreshing drink. With the fresh water supply being as dodgy as it is for Western travellers with delicate stomachs, this certainly makes a welcome change from bottled mineral water and sticky soft drinks.

Having been bargained down to something approximating a non-extortionate price, the seller will whack the coconut skilfully with a machete until a little hole appears in the top of the outer fibrous coating. You then siphon out the slightly sweetish water with a straw provided and hand the empty coconut back to the seller. He now lops off a small round piece of shell. This becomes a scraper, used to remove the thin, jelly-like meat from the interior of the shell. When this young meat is shredded and mixed with ice and the coconut water, it becomes a popular Indonesian drink, es kelapa muda.

Only young, green coconuts will yield this treat, but even the brown hairy ones available in greengrocers and supermarkets in the West can be used to make fresh coconut cream which exceeds the tinned variety (see pp. 39–40).

Opor Ayam (Indonesian coconut chicken)

This famous Indonesian chicken dish is an excellent way of using coconut cream, as the condiments are forced into a background role and not allowed to drown the delicate coconut flavour.

1 large chicken, cut into 8 pieces
salt
5 macadamia or candle nuts
2 medium onions
3 cloves garlic
walnut-sized piece of fresh root ginger
1 tbsp ground coriander
1 tsp ground cumin
$\frac{1}{4}$ tsp ground turmeric
$\frac{1}{4}$ tsp terasi (preserved shrimp paste)
oil for frying
8 curry leaves (or, ideally, 2 daun salam leaves)
1 tsp salt
1 tsp brown sugar
400 ml ($\frac{3}{4}$ pt) coconut cream

Rub the chicken pieces with salt and grill for 4–5 minutes on each side.

Meanwhile, in a food processor, grind the nuts, onions, garlic and ginger. Add the coriander, cumin, turmeric and terasi.

Heat a little oil in a wok, add the onion/spice mixture and fry for 3 minutes. Add curry or daun salam leaves, salt and brown sugar. Now add the coconut cream and the chicken pieces, and simmer for another 15 minutes until cooked.

Since China is reckoned to possess one of the world's greatest cuisines, it is hardly surprising that its influence has trickled down into the kitchens of the rest of South-East Asia.

While Indonesian cuisine also shows influences of the Arabs, the Indians and, to a lesser extent, the Dutch, it was the Chinese who arrived there first. Many centuries before the Arab traders and the advent of Islam, migrants from the fabled kingdom of Cathay were settling in Indonesia. The first records of their settlement are wall paintings and porcelain from about 200–100BC.

The wok, known in Indonesia as the wajan, was probably introduced by the Chinese, as also were carp, lychees, bamboo shoots, beansprouts, mange tout and Chinese cabbage (*Brassica chinensis*). Today these are turned into such Sino-Indonesian classics as pu yung hai – Chinese mixed vegetable omelettes – and the stir-fried meat and vegetables known as cap cai ca.

Indonesia, with the exception of Hindu Bali, is Muslim, but the Chinese have always ensured a ready supply of pork throughout the islands. Consequently, nearly all Indonesian pork dishes show a Chinese influence: pork in hot and sour sauce, pork and noodles, pork in soy sauce, pork and mushroom buns.

Chinese food products such as tofu (known in Indonesia as tahu), and so-un (rice flour noodles, called laksa by the Indonesians) have been thoroughly integrated into the local cuisine, and Indonesian noodle dishes are mostly variations on a Chinese theme. The famous bami goreng, for example, owes more than a little to Chinese lo mein. Most Indonesian soups are Chinese, and the restaurateurs who serve them invariably so. Soy sauce, too, is hugely popular, and in Indonesia it has given birth to the wonderful sweet-salt kecap manis.

Sino-Indonesian Soy Flavoured Chicken

This dish needs an adaptation to make it suitable for Western produce, and I prefer not to call it by its original name – ayam goreng kecap. As the *goreng* in this title suggests, the chicken is traditionally deep-fried. This is fine in Indonesia, where the chickens need a little oil to counteract their dryness as they are free-range and rather scrawny. The average battery-fed chicken, by contrast, is these days so fatty that from both a health and a gastronomic point of view, I consider the only acceptable cooking method is to grill or roast it in order to extract some of this fat.

In Bali, shallots are more commonly used for the dish than onions. In a curious reversal, shallots in Bali are very cheap, while onions are expensive, comparatively rare, and regarded as a luxury, something to be fried separately and used as a garnish.

1 large chicken, cut into 8 (or 8 ready-cut pieces)
oil
1 large onion, diced
125 ml (4 fl oz) kecap manis or soy sauce and 1 tbsp honey
3 cloves garlic, crushed
walnut-sized piece of fresh root ginger, finely grated
3 tbsp lemon juice
terasi (preserved shrimp paste) (optional)

Brush the chicken pieces with oil, and place under a hot grill, but not too close, or the skin will burn before the chicken is cooked. Turn from time to time until the skin is golden brown and crisp all over. Test by piercing the thickest piece with a knife – if the juice comes out clear, the meat is done, but if the juice is pink, it needs more cooking.

Meanwhile, make the sauce. Fry the onion in 2 tablespoons of oil. When it has begun to turn brown, add the kecap manis or soy sauce/honey mixture, the garlic, and ginger. Cook for 2–3 minutes, then stir in the lime or lemon juice. (Traditionally the wondrously aromatic little Indonesian lime known as jeruk limau is used to flavour this dish.) Use a little of this sauce to baste the chicken toward the end of cooking, then pour the rest over the cooked chicken. Serve on a bed of rice to soak up the excess sauce.

A little terasi may be added to this dish if desired.

Perhaps the most audacious Chinese claim is to have invented satay. The name, the story argument goes, derives from the Chinese habit of placing only three pieces of meat on the skewer. 'Satay', it is claimed, derives from the Cantonese words, *sah* (three) and *tay* (piece). However, the principle of sticking small pieces of meat on a skewer is so universal – kebabs are found in one form or another from Morocco eastwards – that such a claim seems unreasonable. What is beyond argument is that the dish reaches its apotheosis in Indonesia.

In the kitchen of a family compound in Bali, I watched the grandfather of the house spend two laborious hours pounding raw chicken meat to a paste. It was a perfect illustration of how differently we Westerners and the Balinese view time; first the old man took a tomahawk and used the blunt end to bash the meat, handful after handful, for an hour, by which time you might have thought every fibre and tendon had been obliterated. But no, he transferred it to an oversized wooden mortar, took a pole which served as the pestle, and pummelled it for another full hour.

After mixing in various spices and condiments, he then twirled the paste around large bamboo skewers and got his nephew to grill it, the result being a delicious Balinese variation on satay known as satay pentul.

Once back in my own kitchen, I reproduced the dish using my food processor. As I suspected, this noisy but obliging servant will do the same job as the blunt end of a tomahawk and a rice pounder – one hour and fifty-four minutes faster.

Satay Pentul

1 large chicken or 500 g (1 lb) boned pork
1 tbsp dried tamarind pulp or 2 tbsp lemon juice
3 cloves garlic
1 small fresh red chilli (or 1 tsp chilli sauce)
2 tsp chopped fresh root ginger
1 tsp coriander seeds
½ tsp ground turmeric
1 tsp brown sugar (this is a substitute for Balinese palm sugar)
1 tbsp soy sauce
1 egg
3 tbsp fresh grated or desiccated coconut

Skin the chicken, trim off and discard the fat. Cut the meat off the bones (these make excellent stock, and the discarded skin can be grilled). Chop the meat into small pieces. Mince in the processor, in two batches, for 3–4 minutes or until it is a fine paste.

Break the dried tamarind into tiny pieces, picking out any stones, and steep in 3 tablespooons of boiling water for 5 minutes. Strain.

Crush the garlic with the chilli or chilli sauce, ginger and coriander seed. Add to the meat in the processor, along with the strained tamarind juice, ground turmeric, brown sugar, soy sauce, egg and coconut. Process for a further 1–2 minutes until these ingredients have been well mixed in.

The processing will have heated the mixture slightly, making it sticky and difficult to work with, so it is preferable to let it cool in the refrigerator before attempting to apply it to the skewers.

The bamboo skewers used by the Balinese for this type of satay are not the usual thin variety, but are about the thickness of a pencil. Work the paste around these sticks, so they look like miniature hot dogs. Grill for 5–6 minutes under a hot grill, turning often, until they have spots of brown all over.

They can be eaten either by themselves, with a standard peanut satay sauce (see p. 43) or with a dipping sauce such as the following:

SAMBAL KECAP
2 tbsp soy sauce
juice of 1 lemon or 2 limes
1 clove garlic, crushed
1 small red chilli, crushed

Mix ingredients together with a dash of water.

Different versions of satay pentul are found on Java and Lombok, the islands that flank Bali on either side. In Lombok it is made with beef and terasi (preserved shrimp paste) and called satay pusut. In Java it is also made with beef, and the spicing is more complicated: in addition to the Balinese list of ingredients, you would use $\frac{1}{4}$ tsp cumin and a pinch each of nutmeg and ground cloves. Prior to grilling, the sticks are precooked in coconut cream, to which has been added 4–5 leaves dried lemon grass, a small piece of cinnamon stick, a teaspoon each of sugar and the spice/garlic/ginger mixture which went into the meat. This sauce is also used to baste the satay during grilling.

A distant cousin of satay pentul also exists in northern India. In Kashmir, a dish known as goshtaba, commonly served at weddings, consists of lamb which may be beaten all day to get the correct smooth consistency, and then combined with a heady mixture of cardamom, cumin, cloves, black pepper, badiani (a type of dried flower) and curds. It is then formed into large balls and deep-fried.

Macau

Among the delightful jumble of dishes from China, Portugal and its former empire which constitute the cuisine of Macau, none is more likely to confuse the traveller than African Chicken.

The dish is probably Macau's most famous and is found on restaurant menus all over the Portuguese enclave.

At roadside cafés, African Chicken might simply comprise a chicken which has been splayed out, rubbed with fiery Mozambique piri-piri chillies and an assortment of spices such as Chinese five spice powder, cumin, coriander, turmeric, paprika, bay leaves and curry powder, then grilled and served without further adornment. Some chefs add white wine or dry sherry to the marinade, which is later boiled down to make a rudimentary sauce. At its highest level, African Chicken is marinated, baked, jointed, and then served with a rich, spicy coconut sauce.

The dish was brought to Macau with a contingent of Angolan soldiers in the 1960s, yet curiously no two chefs seem to agree on the recipe. 'The sauce should include peanut butter,' says one chef. 'What? He told you to put peanut butter in the sauce?' asks the next. 'But you don't serve a separate sauce at all,' insists a third who, as instructor in Macanese cuisine at Macau's Hotel and Tourism Training School, must be taken seriously. Done correctly, he says, the sauce mixture is brushed on to the chicken in a thin layer and left to dry. While the chicken is being grilled over charcoal, the sauce is brushed over again and again.

The nicest African Chicken I ate in Macau was at Henri's Galley, a restaurant established in 1976. Its mainland China-born owner, is one of those people who were made for the restaurant trade: jovial, personable, able to sustain a conversation with absolutely anybody and not averse to the cup that cheers (and does inebriate). He presides over a restaurant which reflects his nautical beginnings as a trainee cook aboard ships of the Dutch-South African line. Around the wall are paintings of sailing ships and series of flags whose signals seem to plot my progression through a bottle of Portas Dos Cavelleiros 1989. 'I require a pilot', reads the first. After a few glasses, I read: 'Keep clear of me, I am manoeuvring with difficulty', while at the end of the bottle: 'I require assistance'.

Here is the version of the famous dish I ate there.

African Chicken

1 tsp minced dried hot chilli
1 tsp minced garlic
2 tbsp minced shallot
1 tsp sweet paprika
2 tsp five spice powder
2 tsp crumbled fried rosemary
1 chicken, weighing about 1.5 kg (3–3½ lb), halved

SAUCE
1 onion or 4 shallots, minced
6 cloves garlic, minced
2 medium red peppers, minced
4 tbsp corn oil
1 tbsp sweet paprika
185 ml (6 fl oz) coconut cream
4 tbsp peanut butter
375 ml (⅔ pt) chicken stock
½ bay leaf
3 tbsp vegetable oil
1 boiling potato, cubed

In a bowl stir together the spices and flavourings for the chicken and rub the mixture into the chicken. Place in a shallow bowl, cover and leave to marinate, chilled, for at least 6 hours or overnight.

Next, make the sauce. Cook the shallots or onion, garlic and red pepper in the corn oil over a moderately low heat, stirring until the vegetables are softened. Stir in the paprika, coconut cream, peanut butter, stock and bay leaf. Bring the liquid to the boil and simmer, stirring, for 10 minutes. Discard the bay leaf.

Preheat the oven to 200°C/400°F/Gas Mark 6.

In a large frying pan, heat the vegetable oil over a moderately high heat until it is hot but not smoking, then add the chicken and the potato cubes. Brown well, then transfer to a baking dish. Spoon 500 ml (scant 1 pt) of the sauce over the potato and chicken and bake in the middle of the oven for 25–30 minutes or until the chicken is cooked through. Serve the chicken with the potato and the remaining sauce, heated through.

SERVES 2.

This is a domestic adaptation of the Angolan soldiers' method, which was to pick the leaves of a particular tree, wrap the chicken, and then pit-roast it in charcoal.

Malaysia

Nestled in a leafy side street of the comfortable Kuala Lumpur suburb known as Petaling Jaya, is the Zainon family bungalow. Behind curly wrought iron gates a Mercedes-Benz is parked on the courtyard, next to a lush tropical garden overflowing with umbrellas of perfumed screwpine leaves.

We have been invited to join the family for lunch, Malaysian style, and the patriarch, Encik Mohd Zainon, is there to greet us at the door. He nods approvingly as I remove my shoes without having to be asked, and we enter a spacious living room, the marble flagstones underfoot cooled by fans whirring overhead. It is high summer in a country where there are really only two seasons – hot and hotter.

Mr Zainon motions me to a sofa. Unlike traditional Malay houses still found in parts of the countryside, there are no raised seating platforms and, indeed, little to distinguish this home from its Western counterparts, apart from details such as the wall plaque inscribed with a passage from the Koran.

Today being Friday, Mr Zainon has cancelled his regular trip to the mosque in our honour. Between heavy drags on his cigarette, he tells me he has recently retired after thirty-three years with the Malaysian Tobacco Company, beginning as an accounts clerk in 1958 and working his way up to employee relations manager. His wife, Puan Rosekilah Baba, runs a small company which prints business cards. Like many modern Malaysian wives with school-age children (she has five), she comes home to cook lunch for the children who then go to school for the afternoon (Malaysian schools being run in two shifts a day).

Giving me a pair of house slippers to wear, Rosekilah ushers me out to her white-tiled kitchen, where the makings of a feast are laid out. There is sayur lodeh, a vegetable dish of long green beans, chilli and tempeh, cooked in coconut cream with bean thread noodles and prawns. On a platter lies a whole bawal puteh, or white pomfret, the most expensive and highly esteemed fish in the Malaysian markets. The fish has been coloured yellow with turmeric and fried whole, ready to be finished in a sauce of tomato ketchup and sweetened soy sauce, and garnished with fried onions and green and red chillies. A side dish of prawns, sambal tumis udang, is fried with plenty of chilli, sweetened with sugar and then given a sour edge with tamarind.

The pièce de résistance, however, is the Malaysian national dish, rendang. Most commonly it is made with beef (*see* p. 46), but today Rosekilah is making it with chicken. Rendang has many regional variations but, broadly, there is a division between north and south. In northern Malaysia, and especially in Penang, everything is simply thrown into the pot and boiled all at once, resulting in a softer, wetter rendang, whereas Rosekilah's recipe here is more typical of the drier southern version, where the chicken is fried first.

In order not to compromise the authenticity of this recipe, it appears here as Rosekilah gave it to me. Not all ingredients may be obtainable, but see the Glossary of Ingredients (pp. 251–63) for acceptable substitutes.

Chicken Rendang

6 stalks lemon grass
walnut-sized piece of fresh root ginger
walnut-sized piece of galangal
1 tsp cumin
1 tsp fennel
10 shallots
1 medium onion
3 cloves garlic
20 chilli padi
25 pieces of dried red chilli, soaked for 15 minutes in water
2 turmeric leaves (optional)
2 coconuts
1 large chicken, cut into 8 pieces
salt
2 tsp ground turmeric
10 tbsp oil for deep frying
10 whole cloves
5 cm (2 in) cinnamon stick
walnut-sized piece of belachan (preserved shrimp paste)
4 tsp sugar
3 pieces of gelugur or 2 tsp dried tamarind pulp, soaked in 4 tbsp hot water

In a food processor or blender, or with a mortar and pestle, grind the lemon grass, ginger, galangal, cumin, fennel, shallots, onion, garlic, chilli padi and pieces of soaked and drained chilli. Set aside this ground mixture (or rempah as a Malay cook would term it). Finely slice the turmeric leaves, if using – they do not have lot of flavour and are not crucial to this recipe.

Break open the coconuts and make coconut cream (see pp. 39–40). For this recipe, also take off the tough brown layer adhering to the white flesh. Process in two batches, using 500 ml (scant 1 pt) water with each. Set aside.

Rub the chicken with 1 teaspoon salt and the ground turmeric and leave to marinate for 5–10 minutes.

Heat the oil in a wok and deep-fry the chicken until half cooked. Set aside. Drain off all but several tablespoons of this oil. Put in the ground flavouring mixture and continue frying the mixture for half an hour, by which time the chilli flavour will have mellowed considerably.

Add the coconut cream, along with the cloves, cinnamon stick and belachan. Leave to simmer for another 45 minutes, then add the sugar, gel-ugur and salt to taste. If using tamarind, use the strained liquid and discard the pith. Only now add the pieces of half-cooked chicken. Cook another 30 minutes if you want gravy, or 45 minutes if the dish is wanted dry.

Dry, indeed, is how a rendang is often cooked, for the sake of extending its shelf-life. If cooked dry, a chicken rendang will last two or three days, and a dry beef rendang will last a week.

This explains why rendang is such a popular dish over festival time, when nobody has time to cook. In particular, it is served at hari raya, the Muslim new year festival, when Malaysian homes are thrown open to all comers – including Indians and Chinese. A huge pot of rendang is often on hand, ready to serve to visitors. Rendang is also known as the traveller's dish, and sealed jars are sometimes sent to homesick relatives overseas.

Steeped in history, Malacca is Malaysia's oldest city, and from the gourmet's point of view one of the most important. The marriage of a Chinese princess and the Malay Sultan Mansor Shah in 1403 set the tone, many centuries later, for the delicious Nyonya style of cooking that has come from the intermarriage of these two cultures. Successive occupations of Malacca by the Portuguese, the Dutch and the English have also left their mark.

The former Dutch Governor's residence, known as the Staathuus, marks the centre of the old city, a tiny chunk of Europe transported curiously to the tropics. The illusion is nicely rounded out by Christ Church (built in 1753) next door, which borders a square dominated by a Gothic clock tower and a fountain marking Queen Victoria's coronation.

The architectural legacy of the Portuguese in Malacca may be less impressive, yet of the three colonial conquerors, its influence on the local culture has been by far the most profound. This is for the simple reason that, unlike the stand-offish Dutch and British, the first Portuguese traders and soldiers married the local Malay women. Amazingly, this Portuguese community has clung together for nearly 500 years, in a small fishing village on the coastal side of Malacca. The

Malaysian government formally recognizes these Portuguese as bumi putra, or people of the land.

The Malaysian Portuguese claim that what is today Malaysia's national dance was derived from their own Christi dance, still performed on Catholic feast days and on Saturday nights for the benefit of tourists, at the restaurants which today line Portuguese Square.

The way they cook is different from how a Malay cooks. Obviously, being a fishing settlement, there is big emphasis on fish and, unlike the Muslim Malays, their Catholic faith permits the consumption of pork and alcohol. While they don't drink hard liquor, the average wedding party would polish off thirty barrels of beer without any trouble! Their Portuguese curries are distinguished from their Malay counterparts by being heavily thickened and seasoned with chilli. One of their core dishes is Curry Debal, better known as:

Curry Devil

30 dried red chillies
walnut-sized piece of fresh root ginger
24 shallots (or 7 small onions)
7 cloves garlic
1 tbsp coriander seeds
1 tsp ground turmeric
1 stalk lemon grass (optional)
1 large chicken, cut into pieces
salt
4 fresh red chillies
8 tbsp oil for stir frying
1 tbsp mustard seeds, lightly bruised
2 tbsp vinegar
2 tsp dark soy sauce
1 tsp sugar

Soak the dried chillies in warm water for 15 minutes to soften them, then drain. Using a food processor, blender or mortar and pestle, grind these chillies to a paste with the fresh ginger, 16 of the shallots (or 4 small onions) 4 cloves of the garlic, the coriander seeds, ground turmeric, and lemon grass (if using). Add a small amount of water if necessary, to facilitate the grinding process. Set this ground spice mixture aside.

Sprinkle the chicken pieces with salt and set aside. Slice the remaining shallots (or onions) and garlic and the fresh chillies.

Heat the oil in a wok and stir fry the sliced onions, garlic and chillies until lightly browned. Add the ground spice mixture along with mustard seeds, and continue to stir fry for 3–4 minutes. Add the chicken pieces, fry for 5 minutes, then add 375 ml (⅔ pt) water. Bring to the boil, reduce the heat, cover the wok and simmer for 15–20 minutes, until the chicken is tender.

Just before serving, add the vinegar, soy sauce and sugar.

Morocco

Around the world there are various species of pine whose cones yield a delicious edible seed. The most famous of these is the stone pine (*Pinus pinea*), a native of the Mediterranean region which thrives on coastal areas from Portugal across to the Black Sea, and down to North Africa. It is a beautiful umbrella-shaped tree, often featured in romantic Italian landscape paintings.

The huge glossy brown cones are gathered during the winter and stored until the summer, when they are spread out under the heat of the sun until the scales split open. The seeds are then shaken out, the hard shells cracked open, and the tear drop-shaped nuts extracted. In the past this had to be done by hand, a laborious process, but despite the recent invention of machinery to do the job the nuts remain expensive.

Eaten raw, the ivory-coloured nuts have a faint pine fragrance, which dissipates on heating and develops into a delicious deep nutty flavour. Care should be taken when toasting pine nuts (they are best done in a pan without any oil) as they can turn from white to charcoal in a matter of seconds.

The Italians have enjoyed pine nuts since Roman times. Husks have been found on rubbish tips left by the Roman legions in Britain, and Ovid listed them as part of his diet for lovers:

> Eat the white shallots sent from Megara
> Or garden herbs that aphrodisiac are,
> Or eggs, or honey on Hymettus flowing,
> Or nuts upon the sharp-leaved pine trees growing.

The Roman gourmet Apicius suggested pine nuts and raisins as an accompaniment for broccoli, a combination which still survives in Italian cookery (with the addition of tomatoes, garlic, olive oil and lemon juice) as a sauce for pasta. Other Italian uses for pine nuts include marinated aubergine, as a stuffing for green peppers (along with olive oil, breadcrumbs, anchovies, olives, currants and parsley) or pounded with basil leaves, garlic, parmesan cheese and olive oil to make pesto, Genoa's celebrated sauce for pasta.

Pine nuts are used only to a very limited extent in French cookery, but in Spain, Greece and the Middle East they are enormously popular. They are often included in minced meat dishes such as koftas or kibbeh, the Lebanese and Syrian dish of baked mince, cracked wheat and onion. The following chicken dish is found in various forms throughout most of the Arab states.

Dajaj Mahshi (chicken stuffed with rice and pine nuts)

200 g (7 oz) long-grain rice
100 g (4 oz) butter
1 medium onion, finely chopped
1 chicken, weighing about 1.5 kg (3–3½ lb), plus its giblets
2 tbsp pine nuts
3 tsp salt
1½ tbsp currants
¾ tsp cinnamon (optional)
2½ tbsp plain yoghurt

Place the rice in a sieve and rinse under hot running water until the water runs clear. Set aside.

Melt half the butter in a medium heavy-bottomed saucepan, add onion and sauté for several minutes, then add giblets and pine nuts and continue frying until the onion is transparent and the pine nuts have turned a light brown. Add 2 tsp of the salt, the currants, cinnamon and rice, and stir until the rice begins to glisten.

Add 450 ml (¾ pt) water, bring to the boil, cover, reduce heat to low and cook for about 25 minutes until the water is absorbed and the rice is cooked. Stir in the other half of the butter until it is melted and well blended.

Preheat the oven to 200°C/400°F/Gas Mark 6.

Stuff as much of the rice mixture into the cavity of the chicken as it will comfortably take (do not cram it in or it will ooze out during cooking), tie up with string or secure with skewers. Place the rest of the rice mixture aside to reheat and serve separately with the chicken when it is cooked.

Mix the remaining salt with the yoghurt and spread half this mixture over the chicken. Place in a roasting dish on a rack or with a little water in the bottom of the pan.

Roast the chicken for 15 minutes, then spread over the other half of the yoghurt and salt, reduce the oven heat to 180°C/350°F/Gas Mark 4 and roast for about an hour. Test for doneness by pressing a skewer into the thigh. If pink liquid comes out, put it back for another 5 minutes or so; if the liquid comes out yellowish or clear the chicken is cooked.

Very closely related to the stone pine is the alpine Swiss stone pine (*Pinus cembra*) whose seeds have been crushed and used for lamp oil, and there is also a variety from the Siberian mountains.

In North America seeds from the Mexican or American nut pine (*Pinus cembroides*) and several related species are still gathered and baked by the Indians. There are two Himalayan species (one of which is also found in Afghanistan) whose nuts are used in north Indian pilau dishes. The Koreans float the nuts of their native species (*Pinus koraiensis*) in cups of ginseng tea.

Chile and Brazil both have distant relatives of the pine which produce edible kernels, and stands of the bunya-bunya pine, an Australian member of the same genus (*Araucaria*) provide the venue for picnics among the Aborigines, who gather for up to a fortnight to feast on the nuts roasted among hot embers.

Now that all our supermarket eggs come with a convenient 'use by' stamp, it is as well to understand why they should indeed be used by the date shown.

As an egg moves from youth through to old age, the most dramatic change which takes place is a rise in the alkaline level, a result of the egg expiring carbon dioxide through its shell (which has to be porous in order to allow air to enter and develop the chick).

This might only be of academic interest, were it not associated with another change which is most unfortunate for the cook – the thinning out of the egg white. Furthermore, with time, water begins to seep from the egg white, through into the yolk, stretching the yolk membrane and thus weakening it. This means the cook has to deal with an egg which is more likely to break its yolk, as well as having a white which runs all over the pan. The white of an old egg is also less likely to foam up, when beaten, not only because it is so thin but also because it contains fat which has leaked out from the yolk over time.

The effect of both moisture and carbon dioxide loss on an old egg is that it shrinks within the shell, enlarging the empty space at the wide end of the shell. It is this phenomenon which accounts for the reliability of the age-old test for the freshness of an egg: putting it in a basin of water. If it is less than fresh, the wide end will rise up from the bottom, and if the egg is stale or downright rotten, it will begin to float under water.

Even this test is not foolproof, however. I remember my Sunday School teacher, who used to be a missionary in East Africa, telling us how he successfully carried out this test for years and then all of a sudden could not work out why even the most rotten of eggs were sitting firmly on the bottom of the basin. It turned out the egg sellers had devised a cunning way to get around the test by boiling the eggs ever so slightly before they sold them!

In its raw state, an egg white comprises water in which are suspended protein molecules, each consisting of a chain of amino acids which is coiled up into itself in a ball. When the egg is heated, these protein balls begin to unravel and bump into each other. Parts of the chains become interconnected with their neighbours, trapping water in the interstices of the meshwork. Now that the proteins are woven together, they begin to deflect rays of light, and thus the colour of the white turning from clear to white.

So far so good, but this is assuming that we have been applying gentle heat to the egg, and not for too long. When excessive heat is applied, the protein chains, already close, begin to squeeze together ever more tightly and the water, which is held within and around the coiled proteins by relatively weak hydrogen bonds, is literally wrung out. The net result is either a rubbery egg or, in the case of a sauce in which liquid has been added, a series of tiny lumps of egg floating in the water; in other words, the dreaded curdles.

When poaching an egg, there are three tricks to keep the white nice and compact, and prevent it spreading all over the pot like a piece of drunken lacework. The first is to add a good dash of vinegar (or lemon juice) which speeds up coagulation, and adds a not unpleasant flavour. Second, the water should only just be boiling and no more, as too much turbulence will spread the white. Third, the most important, you must create a whirlpool before you drop the egg in. Do this by stirring a chopstick around and around the inside edge of the pot so a whirlpool is formed in the centre. Drop the egg neatly into the centre of the whirlpool, and the circular motion will wrap the egg white neatly around itself.

Having just said all that, here is a poached egg recipe to which none of the above rules need apply, since the egg is solidly trapped in a bed of sauce.

Moroccan Poached Eggs

The idea of dropping whole eggs into a sauce or stew as a garnish goes right back to a cooking manual written in Baghdad by one al-Baghdadi in 1226 and, as I discovered, is still very much alive in Morocco today.

4–5 large ripe tomatoes
4 tbsp olive oil
6–8 cloves of garlic, chopped
2 tbsp paprika
1 tsp whole caraway seeds
2 tsp ground cumin
1/2 tsp cayenne pepper
large handful of finely chopped parsley
handful of finely chopped fresh coriander leaves
8 large eggs

Pour boiling water over the tomatoes, leave for about 30 seconds, then peel off the skins. Chop the tomatoes.

Heat the olive oil in a large saucepan, add the garlic, sauté for 30 seconds, then add the tomatoes, along with 125 ml (4 fl oz) water, the paprika, caraway, cumin and cayenne pepper. Allow the sauce to cook for about 20 minutes on a low heat, stirring from time to time. Five minutes before the end of cooking, add the parsley and coriander leaves. (Although not traditional, fresh basil leaves make a good substitute for the coriander.)

Make little indentations into the thickened sauce, and place in the eggs, cover the pot, and cook until the whites are firm. Serve directly from the pot, and accompany with French or pitta bread for an informal but tasty lunch or dinner.

Singapore

'Here, take a whiff of this,' invites Peter Wee, lifting the lid off a large earthenware jar to reveal bun-shaped cakes of dark brown belachan, or preserved shrimp paste. A fishy odour immediately fills his Singapore antique shop. 'We call this Peranakan cheese – the smellier the better!' he chuckles.

Emptying a glass jar of dried flowers on to a plate, he shows how the dried violet stems of the wild blue pea flower (*Clitorea ternatea*) are removed, before boiling with vinegar and lime to produce a natural blue dye, traditionally used to colour cakes and confectionery. 'I feel a duty to continue stocking these Peranakan foodstuffs, for like the antiques I also sell in this store, they are now virtually extinct.'

Peter Wee personifies the identity crisis faced by the dying Straits Chinese community in modern Singapore. Officially known as Peranakan (meaning 'local born'), and colloquially called *baba* (men) and *nonya* (women), they are the descendants of fifteenth-century Hokkien Chinese traders who are said to have taken Malay wives. Originating in Malacca, numbers of Peranakan migrated first to Penang, then flocked in droves to Singapore in the early nineteenth century, on hearing news of Stamford Raffles' new trading post.

Exactly how much intermarriage with Malay women took place, if any at all, is now a topic of debate among anthropologists and historians. However, one fact is certain – for well over a century now, none whatsoever has occurred. The Peranakan have either married among themselves, or far more commonly, they have married into the wider Chinese community. A result, Peranakan culture has been all but submerged by the Chinese community of modern Singapore.

Racially, the Peranakan are indistinguishable from the Chinese, and only the older generation of women still wear the traditional dress – a lace blouse or *kebaya*, worn over a sarong. In even greater decline is the Peranakan language – the elderly are the last to speak the pithy and often pungent patois of Hokkien and Malay, sprinkled with the odd word of English and Dutch. This is a tragedy, for the merging of Malay and Chinese cultures found immensely rich expression in Peranakan architecture, porcelain, clothing, jewellery and, most especially, cuisine.

Nonya cooking (for so it is called, since the women invented it) combines the finesse and blandness of Chinese cuisine with the rustic spiciness of Malay food. Many Chinese ingredients are used, such as dried mushrooms, fungi and anchovies, soy sauce and fermented soya beans – along with the spices and aromatic roots used in Malay cooking, such as lemon grass, kaffir lime leaves, galangal root and tamarind. Much use is made of coconut cream and also of pork, forbidden to the Muslim Malays.

Preparation of Nonya food was laborious, involving hours of pounding with a mortar and pestle. Even rice used to be ground by hand, when it was required for sweets. Yet a prospective bride was expected to have mastered the art, and indeed a marriage matchmaker would make a point of visiting her family home around ten in the morning, when the preparation of the rempah, or spice pastes, would have begun. By the rhythm of the pounding sounds coming from the kitchen, the matchmaker could tell whether the cook was competent or not. Then there would be the fateful day when the prospective mother-in-law came for lunch. A comment that the food was *chayer* (watered down) or, worse still, *tak alus* (coarse), was as good as announcing the marriage was off.

Such cooking was only made possible by hired kitchen help and by the fact that the Nonya wife virtually never left the house, let alone went out to work. As a result, Nonya cooking went into sharp decline after the Second World War, when servants were dropped, the restrictions were loosened and wives began to have careers. A nostalgic yearning for the food remains, nevertheless, and since the 1980s there has been a marked resurgence in Nonya cooking, this time led by the Singaporean and Malaysian restaurant trade.

Ayam Lemak Putih (Singapore Nonya chicken curry)

You find chicken curry too hot? This recipe has no chilli at all (the name means, literally, 'rich white chicken'. You dislike curried chicken because the skin goes flabby? This recipe delivers a crispy skin!

1 large onion, roughly chopped
4 cloves garlic
3 tbsp ground coriander seeds
1 tbsp ground cumin
800 ml (1½ pt) coconut cream
5 tbsp oil
1 chicken weighing about 1.4 kg (3 lb)
6 whole star anise
1 tsp salt
2 tbsp Thai fish sauce
3 slices galangal
2–3 stalks lemon grass, bruised

First make a curry paste, or rempah:

Pulverize in a food processor the onion, garlic, coriander and cumin. Add 3 tablespoons of coconut cream to the rempah, pushing the pulse button to mix it to a smooth paste.

Heat the oil in a wok, and gently fry the rempah for a few minutes, moving it from side to side, until the fragrance has been released. Add the chicken and fry it until the surface is coated with rempah. Add the rest of the coconut cream, along with the star anise, salt, fish sauce, galagal and lemon grass.

Bring the mixture to the boil, then lower the heat and simmer for 25–30 minutes, turning the chicken once or twice but cooking most of the time with the leg and breast side down, so it is submerged in the sauce. Do not cover the dish, or the coconut cream may separate.

Pick out and discard the lemon grass and star anise before serving.

Remove the chicken and place under the grill for about 10 minutes, turning on all sides until the skin is evenly crisped and browned.

Cut into four pieces (a leg or breast each) and serve with the curry sauce over plain rice, with a small bowl of thick soy sauce for dipping.

Ironically, Nonya cooking is more accessible today than it ever has been, owing to modern kitchen technology. Electric coffee grinders pulverize in minutes the hard spices which formerly took hours with a stone rolling pin and slab known as a *batu giling*, while blenders take only seconds to grind chillies, garlic, salt and belachan (shrimp paste) into sambals. The grating of coconut, which formerly had to be performed on a knuckle-dusting *parut* (a miniature bed of nails) is now done by shopkeepers on custom-made grinding machines, and sold by the kilo at the local market.

Ah, say the older generation, Luddites to the end, these machines don't do the same job. A blender doesn't heat a sambal like the old pestle and mortar did, so the flavour of the belachan is not fully integrated. (So, we reply, heat it in the microwave first!) As for the mechanized coconut grinders, they say, they heat up the coconut too much. It won't keep and quickly turns sour in the tropical heat (so use it immediately or refrigerate it!). It's the same reactionary response you hear from elderly peasant cooks the world over, from Italy to Mexico.

Unfortunately, much Nonya cooking is beyond the reach of the average Western cook, for we do not have access to the aromatic herbs, buds and roots so central to its flavouring. While lemon grass, galangal and daun kesom (Vietnamese mint) are sometimes to be bought from Asian stores, there are many, many more herbs growing in the domestic Nonya garden which we never see, such as bunga kantan (pink ginger bud) and daun kado (an aromatic creeper).

Here, however, is a Nonya dish with easily obtainable ingredients, including an unusual English influence – Worcestershire sauce – which surely everybody has in their kitchen cupboard.

Inchee Kebin (Nonya-style fried chicken)

1 large chicken, cut into 8 pieces
2 tbsp lemon juice
1 tbsp soy sauce
1 tbsp curry powder
1 tsp ground coriander
2 tsp sugar
1 tsp salt

DIPPING SAUCE
6 tbsp Worcestershire sauce
1 tsp mustard powder
1 red chilli, ground or ½ tsp chilli powder

GARNISH
oil for deep frying
20 kerupuk (prawn crackers)

Wash and thoroughly dry the chicken pieces, then marinate for 2 hours in a mixture of the lemon juice, soy sauce, curry powder, coriander, sugar and salt.

Meanwhile, mix together the dipping sauce ingredients and leave aside in a small bowl.

Heat oil in a wok and deep fry the kerupuk. Set these aside.

Using the same oil, deep fry the chicken pieces until cooked. Drain on kitchen towels, and serve with the kerupuk and the dipping sauce.

Thailand

A bottle of fish sauce is not one of those things you produce when a finicky guest has pleasantly surprised you for once, by having savoured every last forkful of your Thai chicken curry, then asked what was the magic ingredient. Just one prolonged whiff of this staple condiment of South-East Asia may cause your squeamish guest to scream that he or she feels like bringing that curry back up again, for its aroma is definitely on the lusty side, and the flavour is equally compelling.

Nevertheless, use it you must if you are the least bit serious about reproducing at home the food you have enjoyed at Thai or Vietnamese restaurants. Thai recipes rarely require more than a tablespoon or two of this fish sauce (or nuoc mam as it is called in Vietnam), yet without this subtle background flavouring the dish simply will not be the same.

There is no substitute for it, though thankfully the product is readily available from Asian food stores nowadays, and in a wide choice of brands. They are by no means all the same. Even the best brands are cheap in comparison to most condiments and since price equates largely with quality, it is worth spending a little extra and buying a good brand.

The basic manufacturing process – placing layers of small fish and salt in tanks or barrels and allowing the mixture to ferment for about three months – is the same wherever the sauce is produced, whether it be Thailand, Vietnam, Laos, the Philippines or Burma. Like wine, however, it is amazing how the same simple fermentation process can produce either a product of great finesse and complexity or, at its worst, a load of worthless plonk.

The best fish sauce is made by simply decanting off the liquid which forms naturally in the vats, then allowing further maturation in earthenware pots out in the sun, the contact with pottery absorbing unwanted odours. Second-grade fish sauce is made by pressing the fermented fish to extract more of the liquid, while the very worst is made by adding water to the mush to eke out still more.

Other more technical factors also determine quality, such as whether pineapple juice has been added to speed up fermentation (and profits), the amount of salt used (generally about 25 per cent) and the choice of fish. Laotians claim their use of freshwater fish produces a superior product to that of Thailand, where saltwater fish are more common. But then, being a landlocked people, they would.

The product is an excellent way of using up huge quantities of tiny fish which are not much use for anything else, and in the absence of refrigeration, it has provided a way of preserving seasonal gluts. Fish sauce also supplies essential protein to South-East Asian peoples, whose diet consists mainly of rice, fruit and vegetables. Modern nutritional studies tend to suggest that by trial and error over the centuries these societies discovered this for themselves, without the aid of science.

Fish sauce is not as alien to the Western tradition as we may think. The finest garum, the celebrated condiment of ancient Rome, was made from the viscera and blood of mackerel, and then fermented in the sun. A strikingly close modern-day relation is the pissala of southern France. Pissala is also made by fermenting small fish (anchovies) in barrels with salt, the difference being that herbs and spices are added to the mixture, and it is stirred and then mashed at the end of the operation to produce a paste rather than a liquid.

Thai Chicken and Peanut Curry

225 g (8 oz) peanuts or peanut butter
3 tbsp vegetable oil
1 tbsp Thai red curry paste
500 g (1 lb) chicken meat, diced
400 ml (¾ pt) coconut cream
2 tbsp sugar
2 tbsp fish sauce
10 kaffir lime leaves or lemon verbena, lemon grass or finely pared lime peel
basil leaves (optional)

If using whole peanuts, roast and then grind in a food processor to a paste.

Heat the oil in a wok and stir in the curry paste. Turn heat to low, then add the chicken and stir until the curry is blended through the meat. Add the coconut cream, ground peanuts (or peanut butter), sugar, fish sauce and kaffir lime leaves.

Simmer for 10–12 minutes, until the chicken is just cooked. Garnish with fresh basil leaves if desired, then serve with rice.

Turkey

The walnut tree, which has been prized for its beautiful mottled wood as much as for its nuts, is native to an extensive region stretching from south-eastern Europe, through Central Asia and as far east as the Himalayas, where wild walnuts can be found growing at altitudes as high as 2500 m (8000 ft).

The ancient Greeks pressed the oil from walnuts, and in past centuries the French, Swiss and Italians also used this oil very often as a flavouring, until it became prohibitively expensive. It has also been used as a thinner for artists' paints.

The Romans imported their walnuts at great expense from Persia and would generally eat them at the end of a meal with fruit. On 24 August AD79, some priests were about to settle into a feast of walnuts at the Temple of Isis, in Pompeii. They never got them to their mouths.

The Romans dubbed the nut juglans, or Jupiter's acorn, and considered it a model of the human head. The outer green skin (which encloses the shell while it is still on the tree) symbolized the scalp, while the walnut shell symbolized the skull. Smash this open, and out spills the knobbly oval kernel, a perfect miniature model of the human brain. It was believed that eating these symbolic brains was a cure for headaches.

Walnuts were also a fertility symbol in ancient Rome. A bridegroom would scatter them over the floor of the nuptial chamber after the wedding feast, or the guests would shower them over the bride and groom like confetti. In Romania the walnut has exactly the opposite meaning: the bride places a roasted walnut in her bodice for every year she wants to remain childless.

At various stages in European history walnuts have tided the peasantry over periods of famine. Up until the end of the eighteenth century, walnuts ground and soaked in water formed the staple 'milk' of the lower classes. During a particularly savage famine in 1663, the peasants of Dauphine in France, having eaten all their walnuts, ground up the shells with roasted acorns and made the meal into 'bread'. Only slightly more appetizing was the self-imposed diet of a Cathar *parfait* (a preacher of the heretical sect in twelfth-century France), who would live for days on end on the warm water in which a walnut had been boiled.

The most common use of walnuts in Western cooking seems to be in cakes, biscuits and confectionery. Occasionally they creep into salads (such as combining with apples, celery and mayonnaise in the classic Waldorf Salad) or as the main ingredient in the much-maligned vegetarian nut cutlet (with a protein content of about 20 per cent).

In Middle Eastern cookery, however, walnuts have a pride of place. In ancient Persian cookery, walnuts (along with almonds and pistachio nuts) were ground into rich creamy sauces to accompany meat, poultry or vegetable dishes, a practice still common in Turkey.

Circassian Chicken

To make this Turkish dish truly authentic you would not roast the chicken but boil it, something I always hesitate to do, since so much of the chicken flavour seems to disappear into the water. However, if you do wish to remain true to the original recipe, boil the chicken for about an hour, and place an onion and some tarragon in with the water to add flavour. Reduce the cooking water and use for the chicken stock in the recipe.

1 chicken
salt and pepper
butter
125 g (4½ oz) walnuts
125 g (4½ oz) white bread (4 toast-sized slices)
approx 450 ml (¾ pt) chicken stock
1 small clove garlic
1 tbsp paprika

Rub the chicken with salt, pepper and a little butter inside and out and roast at 180°C/350°F/Gas Mark 4, allowing 55 minutes per kilo (25 minutes per pound) plus an extra 20 minutes or so. Raise heat to 200°C/400°F/Gas Mark 6 for the last 10–12 minutes to crisp the skin, and baste.

Meanwhile, make the sauce. Crack open the walnuts, weigh, and then either pass through a mincer three times, pulverize in a blender, or chop with a knife and pound with a mortar and pestle. If any oil comes out of the walnuts, carefully collect and set aside.

Soak the bread in enough chicken stock to soften it. Add to this the ground walnuts, crushed garlic and paprika and mix thoroughly, either by hand or in a blender. Add more chicken stock as necessary to thin the sauce.

Just before the chicken is ready, place the sauce in a pan and heat through. Cut the chicken into 4 portions. Pour the sauce over and decorate with a little extra paprika mixed with any walnut oil you have saved (or a little ordinary oil). Serve with rice.

In Turkey, this dish is often served cold. In this case, strip all the chicken meat from the bones and slice into neat strips. The bones can now be boiled in a little water to make the stock for the sauce. The chicken strips are presented on a platter covered with the cooled sauce, and decorated with paprika and walnut oil as above.

SERVES 4–6, depending on the size of the chicken.

Fish and Seafood

Hong Kong

If you can picture a street full of last-minute shoppers on Christmas Eve, and then double it, then this will give you an idea of the street crowds on an average day in Hong Kong.

The overcrowding is so chronic that should a lorry driver be unloading a stack of cartons on to the footpath, then this will create such a bottleneck that you have to queue up in order to shuffle past. The irony of this situation, however, is that by taking a 20-minute ferry ride you can reach one of the many outlying islands and find it virtually deserted.

I did this one evening, when I took the ferry to the tiny fishing village of Sok Kwu Wan, perched on the fringe of the shore at the bottom of the steep hills of Lamma Island. The village used to support a fleet of fishing boats, but nowadays, in order to meet the demands of a huge market in Hong Kong, the local fisherfolk have turned to fish farming instead.

Out of a network of piers jutting out from the bay are a maze of tiny cages teeming with fish. The baby fish are brought over live from Thailand, fed on oatmeal and other artificial nutrients, and can reach full maturity in six weeks.

The ferry tied up at the wharf alongside several motorized junks belonging to wealthy local Chinese and to large Hong Kong trading hongs (companies) provided for the pleasure of their middle management executives. Then there was a mad race between the ferry passengers to reach the most popular of a series of seafood restaurants along the shore in order to secure a table.

The seafood served here was among the freshest I have ever tasted. The reason is simple: the fish, crayfish, prawns and crabs are all kept in tanks and tubs fed with a constant supply of oxygen bubbling through a length of garden hose, and taken out and cooked to order.

Course after course of seafood followed: steamed prawns with pepper-flavoured salt, squid with chilli sauce, sweet and sour pork, and oysters battered and deep fried. For me, the star of the meal was:

Braised Crab with Ginger Sauce

2 fresh crabs, washed and cleaned
50 g (2 oz) cornflour
400 ml (14 fl oz) vegetable oil
2 spring onions, sliced

1 small red onion, diced
100 g (4 oz) fresh root ginger, sliced and gently crushed
200 ml (7 fl oz) chicken stock
2 tbsp Chinese rice wine
3 tsp sesame oil
1½ tsp sugar
1 tsp salt
¼ tsp white pepper

Cut the crabs into six pieces (do not shell) and sprinkle with half the cornflour.

Heat the oil in a wok and deep fry the crab pieces for 2–3 minutes, then remove and drain on absorbent paper.

Pour off three-quarters of the oil and add the spring onion, red onion and ginger. Stir fry for 50–60 seconds and add the stock, wine, sesame oil, sugar, salt and white pepper.

Bring to the boil, return the crab to the wok, cover well and simmer gently for 4 minutes.

Mix the rest of the cornflour with a little cold water and stir into the sauce. Cook a further minute before transferring to a serving platter. (If you are using cooked crabs, add at the end of cooking and barely re-heat with the sauce before cooking.)

In the West you have made it if you drive a Mercedes-Benz. In Hong Kong, where a Mercedes is about as exotic as a Toyota Corolla, the measure of success is whether you can afford seafood. The Chinese set huge store by eating well, and despite Hong Kong being the largest fishing port in East Asia, the demands of a huge population mean the price of fresh seafood is staggeringly high.

One should not be fooled by the ragged appearance of the fishing junks, high pooped and blackened with age, moored in disorderly ranks at the port of Aberdeen. The huge profits to be made from fishing mean that the seemingly humble fisher folk sitting on the stern mending their nets, are in many cases millionaires. In the old days they hoarded gold, but now, since this pays no interest, they invest in real estate.

Having haggled over the price at the Lei Yun Mon market and bought his fish (preferably from a vendor who recognizes him as a regular) the customer, typically a besuited businessman, summons his family and proceeds to one of the adjacent restaurants where the fish is sent into the kitchen to be cooked. Again, however, he would be sure to go to a restaurant where he is known, for whether by design or pure accident amid the confusion of a busy restaurant kitchen, the fish that is sent in may not be the same one which comes back to the table.

At one of these places, I ate garoupa steamed with nothing more than spring onion, ginger, parsley and oil. This is very traditional, and typifies the Cantonese attitude that not many ingredients should be added when cooking seafood, so as to let the natural flavour speak for itself. The cooking of lobster is equally minimal.

Fried Lobster Balls

1 large lobster, weighing about 1.8 kg (4 lb)
salt and pepper
oil for frying
4 thin slices fresh root ginger
1 spring onion, chopped into 6 pieces
4 thin slices carrot

GARNISH
sprigs of parsley
1/2 cucumber, thinly sliced

Remove the meat from the lobster, keeping the shell intact. Slice the meat into pieces (i.e. rough 'balls'), season with a pinch of salt and pepper, then sauté in hot oil. Set aside. At the same time, steam the empty lobster shell until it turns red.

In a wok, stir fry the ginger, spring onion and carrot. Add the lobster meat at the end of cooking and heat through.

Have ready a large oval presentation platter. Put the lobster body at one end and surround with sprigs of parsley. At the other end, place the lobster tail, flap-end up. Decorate the platter with overlapping slices of cucumber. Spoon the cooked lobster 'balls' into the centre and serve immediately.

India

Oil from the coconut is the main cooking fat used in southern India. It used to be made at home by boiling freshly grated coconut in water and skimming off the oil as it rose to the surface. Although coconut oil has a pleasant flavour, many people find it difficult to digest and other vegetable oils are beginning to take its place.

Coconut cream is also much used in Indian cooking, mainly in the south. Interestingly enough, while India and Polynesia may be oceans apart both geographically and culturally, their method of making the cream is almost identical, right down to the implement used for extracting the flesh from the coconut.

In both cultures, this consists of a low rectangular stool with a serrated metal blade at one end. You sit on the stool and work the halved coconut around the sharp edge to scrape out the meat. In India, there is also a more sophisticated gadget consisting of a propeller-like blade which is cranked with one hand while the halved coconut is held in the other. Boiling water is poured over the grated coconut and it is left to soak for 10 minutes. The coconut is then put in muslin cloth and squeezed and wrung to extract the coconut cream. In Samoa, the fibres of the tau aga tree are used in place of muslin cloth. These look very much like unravelled and matted binder twine.

Blenders and food processors have meant that we too can make our own coconut cream without a huge amount of effort (*see* pp. 39–40), although tins of ready-made coconut cream are often a convenient substitute.

Machli Molee (fish in coconut cream)

3 steaks or fillets of a firm, meaty fish, totalling about 750 g (1½ lb)
1 lemon
salt
1 tsp ground turmeric
6 small dried chillies
3 tbsp desiccated coconut
3 tbsp oil or ghee
1 large onion
4 cloves garlic, crushed
1½ tsp grated fresh root ginger
1 tbsp ground cumin
1 tbsp ground coriander
375 ml (⅔ pt) coconut cream

Rub the fish on both sides with the juice from half the lemon. Sprinkle with salt and then rub in the turmeric. Set aside.

Soak the dried chillies in water for 10 minutes or so. Place the desiccated coconut in a pan without any oil, and lightly brown it, stirring often to avoid burning.

Heat the oil or ghee in a pan and fry the onion, garlic, ginger, cumin and coriander together for 3 minutes. Finely chop the chillies or grind with a pestle and mortar and add, along with the coconut cream. Allow to simmer for 5–10 minutes before adding the fish steaks and the desiccated coconut. Simmer gently until the fish steaks are cooked, allowing 7–8 minutes. Stir in the juice of the remaining half lemon before serving.

SERVES 3.

If your vision of paradise is a golden beach fringed by coconut palms, with clear blue sea and an abundance of pineapples, papayas and bananas, then Goa, in southern India, is one place to find it.

At Colva Beach to the south, where there is 40 km (25 miles) of uninterrupted white sand, you can sit in a cane armchair at one of the little beachfront cafés built out over the sand, sip a cold beer and munch a plate of prawns, while a few paces away the local fishermen mend their nets, or beach their lumbering great outrigger canoes.

These boats, which are rapidly being replaced by motorized trawlers, are some 8 m (25 ft) long, and look like something from the Middle Ages. The timbers of their hulls are sewn together with rope and sealed with tar.

With a supply of fresh fish and seafood literally at their front doorsteps, these modest cafés are among the best anywhere for sampling the famed Goan cooking, particularly the seafood specialities.

Fish Caldeirada

This dish encapsulates that truly magic heart of Goan cooking – the merging of Continental and Indian culinary styles which evolved over 451 years of Portuguese colonial domination. Here, Indian spices add a new dimension to an old Portuguese peasant dish of fish cooked in broth.

A steak or even a fillet from any firm-fleshed fish will do. For each portion you will need:

oil
1 small onion, sliced
3–4 cloves garlic, chopped

pinch of whole cumin seeds
2–3 cloves
2 small pieces of cinnamon stick
1/2 beef stock cube
1 fish steak

Cover the bottom of a pan with a smear of oil, add the onion and garlic and fry them until a light golden brown. Add the cumin, cloves and cinnamon, along with 125 ml (1/4 pt) or more of water and the stock cube (real beef stock, nicely reduced and concentrated, would, of course, be preferable if you happen to have any on hand).

Place the fish steak or steaks in the pan, cover tightly and cook over a low heat for 10–15 minutes until the fish flakes easily and is cooked through.

In Goa, where fishing is a major industry and coconut palms are everywhere, there are many fish and coconut dishes. One delicious example is grilled mackerel stuffed with fresh coconut chutney (Bhangra Chatni), shown to me by the wives of some Goan fishermen I had accompanied on a fishing trip early one morning.

Grilled Mackerel with Fresh Green Chutney

4 small mackerel (or other small fish), about 400 g (14 oz) each
3 cloves garlic
1/2 small onion
1–6 fresh chillies (according to taste), roughly chopped
flesh from 1/4 fresh coconut, roughly chopped, or 50 g (2 oz)
    desiccated coconut
2 handfuls of fresh coriander leaves
1/4 tsp ground cumin
juice of 1 lemon
1/2 tsp sugar
1/2 tsp salt

Scale and gut the fish, leaving as small a slit as possible. Rinse the gut cavity, and make the pocket larger by separating some flesh from the centre bone with a sharp knife. Score the fish with three gashes on each side.

Drop the garlic and onion into a food processor, followed by chillies, coconut pieces and remaining ingredients. Grind into a light green paste.

Stuff into the fish and grill or barbecue on both sides.

Indonesia

When Columbus brought the first chilli pepper back to Europe in 1493, he probably never dreamed that within a hundred years the plant would sweep across Asia and eventually become the most widely used spice in the world.

The fiery peppers were taken to Asia by the Portuguese, who established them in their colony of Goa in India and throughout the spice islands of South-East Asia. Later, the Dutch East India Company dubbed them chillies, one of the Mexican names, in order to avoid confusion with common black pepper.

The 150-odd varieties of chilli vary wildly, not only in shape, size and colour, but more importantly in the intensity of heat. Even chillies within the same batch can vary. Chilli heat is measured in Scoville Heat units. The sweet red pepper rates 0, and the birds-eye chilli rates 30,000 or more.

Long and thin in shape, yellow, bright green or scarlet in colour, the birds-eye chilli is the most popular variety in the great cuisines of Thailand, Malaysia and Indonesia. It is known in Indonesia as the *cabe rawit*, which incidentally is also their nickname for the type of person we would call a firebrand.

In Indonesian cooking, the birds-eye chilli is often blended with milder varieties, such as the large red variety from the island of Lombok near Bali. The word *lombok* in Javanese means, appropriately enough, chilli pepper. A similar taste to a Lombok chilli can be obtained by mixing fresh birds-eye chillies with sweet red peppers.

For this dish, a speciality of Lombok, a small variety of bream known as mujair is used, whose nearest relation would be snapper. Bass or bream would also work well. While for the sake of authenticity the fish should be deep-fried, this is not practical for a fish the size of snapper, so I suggest grilling it instead.

Ikan Cabe (Lombok snapper)

1 whole snapper or similar fish, weighing about 1.5 kg (3–3½ lb)
4 cloves garlic, crushed
2 tsp salt
1 stalk lemon grass or 1 tbsp dried lemon grass
1 sweet red pepper, roughly chopped
2 fresh red bird's-eye chillies, deseeded
walnut-sized piece of fresh root ginger, peeled

juice of 1 lime or lemon
1 tsp brown sugar
3 tbsp oil
1 medium onion, finely sliced

Clean, gut and scale the fish. Do not cut off the head, but cut three diagonal gashes across the body.

Mix the garlic with 1 teaspoon of the salt and 1 tablespoon of water, and spread over the fish.

Pound the lemon grass until flat. If this is not available, infuse dried lemon grass in 150 ml (¼ pt) of hot water.

Turn on a food processor or blender and drop in the red pepper, chillies and ginger, followed by 150 ml (¼ pt) of warm water (or the water in which the dried lemon grass has been infused). Add the lime or lemon juice, the remaining salt and the brown sugar. Failing a food processor or blender, use a mortar and pestle.

Heat the oil in a frying pan and sauté the onion until transparent, then add the blended ingredients, and the flattened lemon grass.

Meanwhile, grill the fish on both sides.

Simmer the sauce for 7–8 minutes while the fish finishes cooking. Before serving the sauce, pick out and discard the lemon grass.

Pour the sauce over the cooked fish, and serve the plain steamed rice and vegetables.

Strangely, for an island people surrounded by water, the Balinese have never been great seafarers. If anything they avoid entering the water and, as I sprinted down to the surf in Bali, I noted the quizzical expressions on the faces of some locals, who seemed to be asking themselves whether I was brave or merely stupid.

These looks I found vaguely disturbing, as they reminded me of those I had received once before from fishermen on Kovalum beach in India, moments before a murderous shore-break caught me in its foamy grip, spinning me into underwater cartwheels and almost drowning my companion. Thankfully, the worst thing that happened to me in Bali was coming face to face with a giant stingray, but that in itself explains the Balinese fear of the sea.

The sharks, sea snakes, barracudas and other diminutive monsters which lurk in these tropical waters confirm a Balinese spiritual belief that the sea is *tenget*, or magically dangerous, the underworld home of evil spirits. Even the sea shores are said to be under the influence of Jero Gede Macaling, the fanged giant who lives on the small barren island of Nusa Penida. Toward the end of the rainy season, when malaria and tropical fevers are rife, this monster is said to come ashore in Bali in the form of a fireball, releasing evil forces which bring on the illnesses.

On the other hand, the lofty volcanoes of Gunung Agung and Batur which dominate the centre of the island are considered the abode of the gods. Balinese temples commonly include shrines to these great mountains, and the temple compound is situated on the side of the village nearest the mountain. By contrast, profane places such as toilets and cemeteries are on the side of the village facing the sea.

The lowlands, or middle ground between the mountain tops and the sea are, in traditional Balinese terms, the right and proper abode of human beings, and accordingly, one should not tempt fate by climbing the mountains or venturing out to sea.

Nevertheless, humans need sustenance and there is plenty of that to be had from fish, so fishing villages do exist in coastal areas such as Kusamba and Candidasa. Fishing is done from beautiful sailing craft known as *prahu*, or prows, whose bows are shaped with long trunks like the elephant fish (*gadja-mina*), with 'eyes' on the sides to help them to see at night, which is when most of the fishing is done.

It was at a *warung* in one of these villages that I first had deep-fried fish with this wonderfully tasty Balinese sauce, which I have since discovered also goes equally well with tempeh, tofu, even potatoes.

Ikan Bali (Bali-style fish)

2 tbsp dried tamarind
2 tbsp dried lemon grass
4 tbsp peanut oil
16 shallots or 6 small onions
2–3 fresh chillies, finely chopped
walnut-sized piece of fresh root ginger, grated
1 tsp ground galangal (optional)
6 cloves garlic, finely chopped
2 tsp brown sugar
1 tsp terasi (preserved shrimp paste)
4 tbsp kecap manis
750 g–1 kg (2 lb) fish, either fillets or steaks

First prepare the sauce. Break the dried tamarind into tiny pieces and place in a saucepan with 375 ml (⅔ pt) water and the dried lemon grass. Bring to the boil and simmer for 5 minutes, then leave for another 5 minutes to infuse. Squeeze the mixture with your fingers, then rub through a sieve, discarding the lemon grass and any pith and seeds of the tamarind. Set the strained juice aside.

Heat the oil in a saucepan and fry the shallots or onions until lightly browned. Add the strained tamarind juice, together with the fresh chillies, ginger, galangal (if using), garlic, sugar, terasi and kecap manis.

Cook the fish. Traditionally it is deep fried, but for my heart's sake I tend to grill it.

Heat the sauce through thoroughly, then pour over the fish.

Malaysia

Palm oil features scarcely at all in the pantry of the Western home cook, yet if you have ever eaten a packet of potato crisps, had a take-away chicken and french fries or fish and chips, chances are you have unwittingly consumed it.

Increasingly, food manufacturers who use a deep-frying medium are looking to palm oil as an alternative to animal tallow, because it is doubly attractive in terms of both health and cost.

Palm oil is lower in price than other oils, even soya bean oil, contains only 50 per cent saturated fat compared to 80 to 90 per cent for butter and is said to have many of the same health-giving properties as olive oil. It is believed to enhance coronary blood flow and reduce the risk of some cancers. Far from raising blood cholesterol, as claimed during a smear campaign by the American Soybean Association some years ago, palm oil is now thought to reduce it.

From the cook's point of view, palm oil performs very well as a deep-frying medium. It has a mild, almost neutral taste which does not affect the flavour of whatever is being fried, there is virtually no foam produced when it is boiled, it is not as sticky as other oils (when spilled on to a bench top, for example) and it has a longer shelf life.

The only inconvenience is the oil solidifies when stored at a temperature below 23°C (74°F). In Malaysia, the source of virtually all the palm oil seen in the West, this is not an issue, as temperatures there rarely drop below this at any time of the year, so it can be kept in a bottle on the kitchen shelf without any fears of it going hard.

I visited one such kitchen in Kuala Lumpur, where palm oil was used to deep fry a whole pomfret – a much-valued fish reserved for honorific meals in Malaysia. Here is the recipe as demonstrated to me. While palm oil was used throughout, any mild-flavoured oil such as soya bean can be substituted.

Ikan Goreng Kichap

1 whole fish (any firm, white-fleshed fish will do)
ground turmeric
salt
oil
1 fresh red chilli
1 fresh green chilli
2 cloves garlic, crushed

2 large onions, sliced
2½ tbsp soy sauce
2 tsp sugar
2 tbsp tomato sauce (ketchup)
green tops of 10–15 spring onions, sliced

Clean the fish but leave on the head and tail. Rub with turmeric and salt. Deep fry in oil until cooked, then set aside.

Cut the chillies into just 3–4 pieces, so that diners who do not like chilli can pick them out and put them on the side of the plate.

Heat 3 tablespoons of oil and fry the garlic, onions, chillies. Lower the heat, then add the soy sauce, sugar, tomato sauce and 4 tablespoons of water.

Turn up the heat, stir well, then pour this sauce over the cooked fish. Sprinkle with the spring onion tops.

SERVES 4–6.

The palm originally came from Africa to Bogor in Indonesia over 150 years ago and from there the seed crossed to Malaysia. The oil comes from date-shaped berries which grow in huge clusters at the base of the palm fronds. They are harvested with long aluminium poles and mechanized loading grabbers, steamed to soften their outside pith, then crushed for their oil. In its crude form, this oil exudes a smell considered offensive by both Asians and Europeans, yet was being eaten 5000 years ago by the ancient Egyptians. In central Africa they still eat a traditional dish in which chicken is cooked with the crude crushed fruit of the palm tree. In Guinea, the Ivory Coast and Nigeria the fruit is also boiled and drunk as an aid to digestion.

Anybody who drives down the highways of Malaysia will realize how vital the palm is to their economy. Oil palm plantations account for a third of Malaysia's cultivated area, and the oil is the third most important revenue-earner after petrol and timber. It is the number one agricultural commodity, accounting for 10 per cent of Malaysia's foreign exchange earnings.

The industry is reaping the benefits of massive plantings, as a result of a Malaysian government decision in the late 1950s to diversify away from rubber. The first commercial planting had been made in 1917 by British colonial masters, who sent the crude oil to Europe for refining. Later, in the 1960s, the Europeans were surprised when Malaysia began the develop its own refineries. At first, the technology was imported, but nowadays the Malaysians themselves export their refining technology to the Middle East and the rest of Asia.

Singapore

Everywhere in South-East Asia it seems, regardless of the local language or culture, the diet centres around seafood and fish. For South-East Asians are island dwellers, whose civilizations were largely built along the riverbanks and coasts.

On the fringes of the Straits of Johore which separate Singapore from Malaysia, you can still see kelongs, or villages built on stilts extending 500 metres into the water, where for thousands of years the locals lived by dipping nets to the water to catch passing shoals of fish. Today these villages are decaying and deserted, as neither their nets nor the primitive *perahus* they sailed out into the South China Sea could reap sufficient fish to satisfy the citizenry of Singapore, who annually consume some 65,000 tonnes – about 24 kg (50 lb) per head of population. This lags slightly behind Japan's 30 kg (66 lb).

But the Singaporean ways with fish I find more interesting, since they concentrate all the flavours of Asia into one cuisine. Take chilli crab, for example. This ranks as Singapore's national dish and is quite literally a melting pot. It draws chillies from the Indian community, mixes them with Malay lemon grass, galangal and dried shrimp paste, and tosses them together with the crab in a Chinese wok, with ginger and garlic. Even English colonial cooking gets a look in, with lashings of tomato sauce, and slices of white bread served with the final dish, to mop up all that amazing sauce.

This chilli crab recipe comes from the Regent Singapore, a luxury hotel built around a sunfilled atrium, which blends modern elements with traditional Chinese carpets, wood panelling and one of the finest collections of Nonya antiques in Singapore. The hotel also features a Maxim's restaurant, based on the Paris original, with ornate Art Nouveau gold-framed mirrors and stained-glass accessories.

Chilli Crabs

750 g (1½ lb) crabs
5 fresh red chillies
10 dried chillies
1 tbsp belachan (dried shrimp paste)
1 stalk lemon grass
4 slices galangal
4 candle nuts (or macadamias, cashews or almonds)
6 tbsp oil
5 shallots, minced

3 cloves garlic, crushed
walnut-sized piece of fresh root ginger, minced
a little chicken stock
1 tbsp tomato sauce (ketchup)
2 tbsp sugar
1 egg, beaten
50 g (2 oz) peanuts, roasted and ground (optional)

Clean the crabs, then cut them into 4–6 pieces.

Make a rempah (flavouring mixture) in a food processor, or with mortar and pestle, by grinding together all the chillies, the belachan, lemon grass, galangal and nuts.

Heat the oil in a wok until very hot. Fry the shallots, garlic and ginger for 2 minutes, then add the rempah and stir fry for a few minutes longer.

Add the crabs and stir fry, adding a little chicken stock. Cook until the crabs turn red. Pour in the tomato sauce and sugar. Simmer for 5 minutes.

Add the beaten egg, stirring to mix with the sauce (it will curdle, but this is intentional). Finally, toss in the peanuts, if using. (If you are using cooked crabs, add at the end of cooking and barely re-heat with the sauce before cooking.)

Garnish on a plate with Chinese lettuce, and serve with white bread. There is no way to eat this dish but with your fingers.

SERVES 1.

Visitors to Singapore, noting the proliferation of Indian hawker food stalls and banana leaf restaurants, might be surprised to learn that Indians comprise only 6.8 per cent of the population. The Indian influence is thus out of all proportion to their numbers, yet their famous cuisine has melted so effortlessly into the local pot, probably because most early immigrants were from the southern tip of India, where the diet has much in common with South-East Asia. Both have rice rather than wheat as staple grains, and enrich their food with coconut cream rather than dairy products. The southern Indians added to the local range of spices, and were in turn introduced to the wonderfully fragrant Asian lemon grass, galangal root and pandan leaves.

With its vegetarian slant, Singapore's Indian food reflects the devout Hinduism of the Tamils, Telugus and Malayalees from the tropical palm-fringed state of Kerala. Initially these were convicts, though later others came freely to seek their fortunes as clerks, traders, teachers and *chettyars* (money lenders). Together with much smaller numbers of Muslims from the north of India, they settled in Little India, the part of town set aside for them by Sir Stamford Raffles.

A visit to Little India today is a fascinating, if shrinking, taste of India itself, right down to the colonnaded British colonial buildings which barely distinguish it from Delhi, Bombay or Calcutta. Crossing an invisible barrier, Singapore's Chinese majority population is suddenly replaced by Hindu men wearing dhotis and the three parallel lines of ash across their foreheads, symbols of Lord Shiva.

The smoke of burning incense and bidi cigarettes competes with the scent of jasmine, as roadside garland makers string up garlands for weddings and funerals and tailors work their sewing machines out on the pavement. Women shop for saris and chunky gold jewellery in the Chinese-owned shops which cater to their tastes and a few fortune tellers still ply their trade, allowing a pet parakeet to step out from a cage and choose a card or numbered bamboo stick, from which they will look up the fortune in a well-thumbed book.

This is also the last part of Singapore where you will see shops stacked floor to ceiling with charcoal, the traditional but virtually extinct cooking fuel of Indian kitchens, and the large open sacks of dried chillies, grains and rice in the shop doorway of the *mamak*, or old-fashioned provisioner, who today has largely been driven out of business by the large air-conditioned 'cold storage' food stores.

Stepping into a coffee shop on Serangoon Road, the illusion of being in southern India is complete. South Indian vegetarian food is served on stainless steel trays on plain benches, with tea and coffee in equally austere stainless steel beakers, supplied with little bowls to pour from one into the other in order to cool the drink down.

Like countless thousands of its counterparts in south India, the dining room is done out hospital morgue style, with spanking white tiles extending across the floor and up the walls, and a garlanded portrait of the money god, Ganesh, auspiciously positioned on the wall behind the cashier.

Not that the prices here are steep. On the contrary, that slightly cross-eyed labourer dressed in turban and dhoti can be seen breakfasting on iddlies, a partially fermented and steamed lentil and rice cake, for just a few Singapore dollars (today being pay-day, his next stop may well be the toddy shop around the corner). This and other south Indian vegetarian breakfast fare, such as the paper-thin rice pancakes known as dosai and the fried savoury doughnuts known as vadas, is indistinguishable from that served in southern India.

Other Singapore Indian dishes, however, are purely local inventions. Undoubtedly the most famous is fish head curry, a dish created in the 1950s by an immigrant from Kerala. You will find plenty of fish curries in Kerala, but never one using only the head. The dish spread like a scrub fire through all the cheap 'banana leaf' restaurants (where a clean banana leaf is placed on the table in front of you and all your food is dished up on it) with the result that today, fish heads in Singapore are quite expensive. Singapore shops now sell packets of made-up fish head curry spices (fenugreek, cumin, fennel and husked black gram dal) which some chefs use as a final garnishing, and special fish curry powder which is not that different from an ordinary mild curry powder, except that star anise and fenugreek are often included in the mix.

Fish Head Curry

1 large fish head, weighing around 1 kg or 2 lb (any variety)
10 cloves garlic, peeled
walnut-sized piece of fresh root ginger
walnut-sized piece of fresh turmeric root or 1 tsp ground turmeric
2 medium onions, roughly chopped
4 tbsp oil
2 tbsp curry powder
20 curry leaves
1 small aubergine, sliced
8 okra, stalks removed and cut in half lengthwise
400 ml (¾ pt) coconut cream

Wash the fish head, scaling it if necessary, and blanch in boiling water for 3 minutes before immersing in a basin of ice cold water.

Drop the cloves of garlic into a running food processor, along with the ginger, turmeric and onions. Process until the mixture forms a paste.

Heat the oil in a large pot, then add the spice paste and fry for 3 minutes, until the fragrance is released. Add the curry powder and curry leaves and stir for 2 more minutes.

Add the aubergine and okra to the pot, with 500 ml (scant 1 pt) of water, and simmer for 5 minutes. Add the fish head and coconut cream and simmer, uncovered, for 10–15 minutes until the fish head is cooked.

Serve with plain white rice.

Thailand

Although the fish cake may be regarded as another inheritance from the traditional cookery of Britain, the dish probably dates back no further than Victorian times, when stodge ruled supreme. Mrs Beeton's recipe is typical. Pick the meat from the bones of any cold fish, she tells us, then stew it in a pint of water for 'about two hours' (well, it just wouldn't do to serve half-raw fish, would it now?) before mincing it up into a cake with breadcrumbs and cold potatoes.

As our grandmothers discovered, the resulting dryness could be alleviated to some extent by adding some stiff white sauce to the mixture, and its bland flavour boosted with anchovy sauce. But even de luxe versions of the fish cake such as Cutlets Victoria (in which mushrooms and cream are added to the mixture) seem to belong to a bygone era.

However, just as we are about to read the last rites over this fusty, mildewed recipe, along comes the Thai fish cake! Forget the mashed spud and mince the fish *raw*, our brilliant Thai friends urge us, and mix in all those scrummy herbs and pungent roots which in the past few years have become so freely available.

The beauty of the Thai fish cake, in my view, is that it flatters the roughest, cheapest fish you can buy from your fishmonger. Indeed, there seems to be little point in using anything other than cheap fish, despite the insistence of connoisseurs that only firm-fleshed fish be used, in order to give the finished cakes a springy texture. Shark, huss, conger eel and ling would appear to fit the bill perfectly, given they are all very firm-fleshed and not too dear, although a medium-textured fish such as gurnard is also suitable. As the fish is to be minced up anyhow, you don't have to worry about spoiling its appearance in the process of cutting out all those annoying little bones.

Tod Ma (Thai fish cakes)

In Thailand these fish cakes are beloved of those humble roadside stall holders, whose specialities form the backbone of Thai cuisine, and upon whom even the poshest restaurants depend for their inspiration. In Bangkok, I even saw an itinerant peddler cooking them to order in a gas-fired wok set into a rickety blue plywood cart mounted on bicycle wheels.

1 stalk fresh or frozen lemon grass
2 cloves garlic
walnut-sized piece of fresh root ginger
1 fresh red chilli (size and strength according to personal taste)
2 tbsp chopped coriander leaf (and root, if possible)
$\frac{1}{2}$ tsp salt
1 tbsp Thai fish sauce
1 egg
500 g (1 lb) raw fish
8 thin green beans, very finely sliced
4 spring onions, very finely sliced
oil for deep-frying

Slice the lemon grass (before it thaws, if using frozen). Set a food processor running full speed, then drop in the lemon grass and grind to a wet powder. Follow with the garlic, ginger, chilli, coriander, salt, fish sauce and the egg. Process until smooth.

Cut the fish into strips, add to the flavouring ingredients in the food processor, and process until smooth. (Without a food processor, you will have to crank the fish through a mincer several times, then pound the flavouring ingredients with a pestle and mortar.)

Mix the slivers of carrots and spring onions into the fish by hand.

Take about a 4 tablespoons of the mixture at a time and, with oiled hands, shape into round cakes about 6 cm (2–2$\frac{1}{2}$ in) in diameter and 1 cm ($\frac{1}{2}$ in) thick.

Heat enough oil for deep-frying in a wok, and fry the cakes for about a minute only on each side. Have the oil on medium high rather than the highest heat; if the cakes cook too quickly, they will toughen. Drain on absorbent paper.

Invariably, the tod ma are accompanied by a relish:

SWEET-SOUR CUCUMBER RELISH
225 g (8 oz) sugar
1 tsp salt
185 ml (6 fl oz) white vinegar or rice vinegar
1 medium cucumber, finely diced
1 medium carrot, finely diced
1 shallot or 3 spring onions, finely sliced
handful of chopped coriander leaf
75 g (3 oz) roast peanuts

Heat the sugar, salt and vinegar with 3 tablespoons water in a pot, and boil for about a minute.

Mix together the chopped vegetables and pour over the sweet-sour dressing. Just before serving, sprinkle with the coriander and peanuts.

Turkey

As I mentioned earlier, traditional enemies Greece and Turkey have remarkably similar cuisines. Dolmas or dolmades, filo or yufka, ouzo or raki – it doesn't really matter whether you use the Greek or the Turkish name, it is still the same thing.

As might be expected, each country accuses the other of stealing its ideas. The Greeks point out that theirs is a very ancient civilization which was using sophisticated cooking utensils by 1000BC, and knew how to bake twenty kinds of bread by the fifth century BC.

However unpalatable it may be to both Greeks and Turks, a number of famous dishes claimed by them both actually originated elsewhere, often from other countries conquered by the Turkish Ottoman warriors. The famous dish known as moussaka, for instance, is neither Greek nor Turkish but was first developed in Baghdad during the days of the Caliphs, from a medieval Arab dish called mukhlabah, which consisted simply of minced meat and fried aubergine topped with cheese.

Baklava and kataifi – the famous sweet pastries common to Greek and Turkish cuisines, also originated elsewhere. Kataifi is of Arab origin (the name is derived from the Arabic *ataif*), and while baklava may have migrated to Greece from Turkey, the Turks themselves only acquired the recipe in the late fifteenth or early sixteenth century, following the conquests of Cilicia and Cappadocia by the Ottoman armies. In fact, baklava is of Armenian origin, the name being derived from *Bakh*, or Lent and *halva*, or sweet. Traditionally the Armenian Christians made their baklava with forty layers of pastry – one for each day of Lent – and ate it on Easter Sunday after Mass.

It was undoubtedly the Greeks who gave the Turks one of their staple foods – olive oil – since this is still almost unknown in Central Asia, the original homeland of the Turkish-speaking tribes. It is also true that during the formative period of Turkish-Islamic culture in Anatolia from the eleventh century onwards, there were substantial cultural borrowings from expatriate Greeks who were living there.

Having eaten fish as a staple for thousands of years, the Greeks in Anatolia taught the Turks their names for the different varieties, which survive as Greek loanwords in Turkish. They also taught the Turks to cook many fish dishes, and these too, still bear Greek names.

On the other hand, the Turks might reply that most of the typical features of their cuisine are of pre-Anatolian origin, and that the etymological evidence is weighted in their favour, since there are far more

Turkish loanwords in Greek relating to food than there are Greek loanwords in Turkish. The Greek answer to this is that during the period of Ottoman rule, when Greece was occupied by the Turks for nearly four hundred years, they were forced to refer to their dishes in the Turkish language. Since no record or description of dishes appears in ancient Greek literature or history, however, this claim cannot be proven.

Although the following recipe was given to me by a Turk, I suspect it is an adaptation of a Greek method of cooking fish.

Mussels Plaki

4 dozen fresh mussels
2 small onions, chopped
80 ml (3 fl oz) olive oil
1 large carrot, diced
1 large potato, diced
200 g (7 oz) chopped celeriac or celery
4–6 cloves garlic, chopped
1 tsp sugar
2 tomatoes, chopped
1 tbsp tomato concentrate (optional)
handful of parsley, chopped

Scrub the mussels well to remove the beards and any grit. Place them in a sink and cover with warm water. When they begin to open, shake the salty water out of each and place in a large pot. Add 125 ml (¼ pt) water, cover the pot tightly, and steam over a high heat until the mussels open wide.

Remove them from their shells and set the mussels aside. Strain the cooking liquid and reserve.

Gently fry the onions in the olive oil until transparent. Add the chopped vegetables and garlic. Sauté for several minutes, then add 250 ml (9 fl oz) of the mussel liquor and the sugar.

Cover the pot, reduce the heat, and simmer until the vegetables are tender. Add the tomatoes and tomato concentrate.

Take from the heat, add the parsley and mussels, and allow to cool. Serve cold.

SERVES 8.

Nuts, Dal and Dairy Products

China

While soya beans are praised by nutritionists for their high protein content (about 35 per cent – more than any other unprocessed foodstuff), they have also been castigated by gourmets for their lack of flavour. In the right hands, however, these little brown bullets can be transformed into the white jelly-like substance we all now know as tofu.

Discovered over 2000 years ago, tofu has always been an important source of protein for the Buddhists of China, Japan and Korea. It is made by soaking soya beans in water, reducing them to a pulp, simmering them briefly, then placing them in a cloth to press out the soya bean 'milk'.

A coagulant is added which separates the milk into curds and whey, in much the same way as adding rennet to cow's milk will turn it into junket. Finally, the soya bean curds are placed into a settling container and pressed with a weighted lid to extract the remaining whey.

Tradition has it that tofu was first discovered by Lord Liu An, a Chinese Taoist philosopher and politician, in 164BC. It is likely the curdling process was either taught to Liu An or an earlier Chinese by the neighbouring Indians or Mongols, or that it was discovered by accident, perhaps when sea salt was used to season a soya bean porridge and the natural magnesium chloride caused the mixture to curdle.

When Boddhisatva, the founder of Zen Buddhism, came to China from India in AD520, he praised tofu for its 'lovely white robes', and indeed it was Zen Buddhist missionaries who introduced it to Japan in the eighth century. The Japanese Zen Buddhists popularized tofu by opening restaurants in their temple compounds, and during the Kamakura period (1185–1333) it was adopted by the samurai, eventually replacing freshwater fish as the favoured delicacy of the shogun himself.

The Japanese also refined the tofu-making process, creating a softer, whiter variety.

Ma Po Doufu (Ma Po tofu)

The full title of this dish is Chen Ma Po Doufu, after its creator 'old pock-marked Madame Chen', the semi-mythical creator of many traditional dishes in the Chinese province of Sichuan. Some say, however, that Madame Chen was a historical figure, the wife of one Ch'en Fuchih, who in the 1860s ran a successful restaurant in the large Sichuanese provincial town of Chengtu.

Variations of the dish are to be found as far afield as Japan, where lotus root is commonly added. There is, indeed, a great deal of flexibility in the ingredients.

3 cups tofu, diced into ½ cm (¼ in) cubes
250 g pork, diced into ½ cm (¼ in) cubes
4 tbsp lard or oil
1½ tbsp hot (chilli) bean sauce (see p. 253)
1 cup chicken or pork stock
walnut-sized piece of ginger, chopped
3 cloves garlic, crushed
3 tbsp cornflour
1 tsp salt
1 tbsp mirin or dry sherry
1 tbsp soy sauce
2 tsp sugar
1 tbsp sesame oil
3 spring onions, chopped
½ tsp ground Sichuan peppercorns

Heat the lard or oil in a wok, stir-fry the diced pork for about 2 minutes, then add hot bean sauce, ginger and garlic. Stir-fry a further minute, then pour in the stock.

Add the tofu, taking care not to break up the cubes. Lower the heat a little, and simmer to reduce the amount of liquid by half.

Turn up the heat again and add the cornflour (mixed to a paste with ¼ cup cold water), salt, mirin, soy sauce, sugar, sesame oil and spring onions. Stir gently until the mixture comes back to the boil and thickens to a custard-like consistency. Add extra cornflour paste if necessary.

Sprinkle with the Sichuan peppercorns and serve over plain white rice.
SERVES 3–4.

India

Whether it is toasted and added whole to rice pilafs or ground and added to velvety smooth sauces and confectionery, there is little doubt that the almond is the favoured nut of Indian cookery.

A native of the Middle East, the almond was introduced to India by the Moghuls centuries ago and is now extensively cultivated in the far northern state of Kashmir. There, the young seeds of the almond tree are eaten as part of a salad, or as a dessert.

Since the almond is high in oil (up to 50 per cent) the Brahmin caste of northern India regard it as brain food. Thus, in the hope of fostering intelligence, the taking of a hot almond milk drink is as much a morning ritual in northern India as café au lait is in France. It is especially popular with the men and is often fed to children too.

It is made by stirring four parts milk to one of finely ground almonds over a moderately high heat, sweetening to taste with honey, and perhaps flavouring it with cardamom. Finally, the milk is poured from one container back into another for a minute or so, until it turns frothy. It is a common drink sold by street vendors, especially popular in view of the slight theatricality involved in making it.

Sabji Korma

2 large potatoes, cut into 2–3 cm (1 in) cubes
1 small aubergine
1 small or 1/2 large cauliflower, broken into florets
6 tbsp clarified butter
2 onions, finely chopped
1 tbsp ground coriander seeds
1/2 tsp ground fennel seeds
1/2 tsp ground turmeric
1/4 tsp cayenne pepper
75 g (3 oz) ground almonds
3–4 large cloves of garlic, crushed
2 tbsp grated fresh root ginger
handful of finely chopped fresh coriander leaves
250 ml (9 fl oz) tomato purée
1 tsp salt
1 tsp paprika
1 1/2 tsp cumin seeds
3 tbsp sesame seeds

Cut the aubergine into slices 2–3 cm (1 in) thick. If it is old and therefore possibly bitter, sprinkle the slices with salt and leave for 30 minutes before washing off the salt. Cut the slices into cubes.

Heat the butter in a large, heavy saucepan and add the onions. Fry, stirring frequently, until light brown. Add the coriander seed, fennel seed, turmeric and cayenne pepper. Mix the spices with the onion and fry for several minutes longer.

Now add the ground almonds, garlic, ginger, coriander leaves, tomato purée, salt and paprika. Turn the heat to low and cook for a further minute or two, stirring constantly to prevent the mixture sticking.

Stir in 1 litre (1¾ pt) water, then add the prepared potatoes and aubergine. Lower the heat, cover the pot and simmer these vegetables for 15 minutes.

Now add the cauliflower and simmer for a further 10 minutes, leaving the lid off the pot so the sauce can partially evaporate away and thicken.

Meanwhile, toast the cumin seeds in a dry pan and grind with a mortar and pestle or in a blender. Add to the dish at the end of cooking. If possible, leave the dish off the heat for 30 minutes to allow the flavours to merge, before reheating and serving.

At the last minute, toast the sesame seeds in a dry pan and sprinkle over just before serving.

SERVES 4–6.

India's export of cashew nuts now outstrips even that of Brazil, the cashew's original home.

The story of the cashew in southern India goes back to the fifteenth century when the tree was introduced by the Portuguese to their tiny colonial territory of Goa. Other useful South American importations followed, notably the pineapple and the papaya. Stands of the cashew tree, which is not unlike the walnut in appearance, are still to be seen everywhere in the sandy coastal areas of Goa and neighbouring Kerala, competing for space with the coconut palms for which both states are better known.

The name cashew comes from the Portuguese *caju* – itself derived from the Arawak Indian word *acaju*, meaning 'to pucker the mouth'. This is a reference to the astringent orange fruit, from which the cashew nut dangles almost as an afterthought.

While this fruit is edible raw, it is more commonly sweetened and turned into jams and drinks. In both Brazil and Goa it is also distilled into a spirit. I can personally attest to the potency of the Goan version, a murky, rather evil-looking brew known as feni which, due to a perennial shortage of glass in India, is sold in a bizarre variety of containers, including medicine bottles!

The cashew nut itself is encased within a kidney-shaped shell. Between the layers of this shell lurks a powerful highly astringent brown oil which will blister the skin on contact. Anybody who tries to bite through the shell of the cashew is in for a nasty surprise.

The oil has a multitude of uses, however. In the past, in India, it has been rubbed into floor boards to ward off white ants, and it has also been used to burn off warts and other unwanted skin growth. Modern uses include the production of plastics and lubricants, and also as an insecticide, which is hardly surprising since the reason for it being there in the first place is to protect the cashew nut from marauding insects.

Needless to say, the cashew nut is put to many uses in south Indian cooking, both in curries and as a confection. One very popular dish is cashew nut halva, in which ground cashews and fresh coconut are cooked in a sugary syrup until semi-solid, then cooled and cut into diamond shapes.

The green, unripe nuts are also eaten (usually fried) along with the ripe specimens we see here. Cashews are not, however, very suitable for baking, since they tend to soften, and with most dishes, it is advisable to add them only at the very end.

Aubergine Ambot with Cashews

200 g (7 oz) red lentils
½ tsp ground turmeric
1 medium onion, finely diced
1 large or 2 small aubergines, salted if necessary, and diced
6 tbsp oil
¼ fresh coconut, grated, or 30 g (1 oz) desiccated coconut
2 tsp ground coriander
1 tsp ground cumin
salt to taste
pinch of asafoetida (optional)
2 ground red chillies or ½ tsp chilli powder
½ tsp mustard seeds
juice of 2 limes or 1 lemon
15–20 cashews, roasted and roughly chopped

Boil the lentils and turmeric in 1 litre (1¾ pt) water until the lentils disintegrate.

Fry the onion and aubergine in 4 tbsp oil over a fairly high heat until the onion turns opaque. Add this to the lentils along with the coconut, ground coriander, cumin and salt to taste. You might also add a pinch of asafoetida if you happen to have it, particularly if you find lentils indigestible.

Cook, covered, over a low heat until the aubergine is soft.

Finally, heat the remaining oil in a pan and add the chillies (or chilli powder) and mustard seeds. Fry over a high heat until the mustard seeds stop popping, and add to the lentil and vegetable mixture along with the lime or lemon juice.

Serve with the chopped cashews sprinkled over. Accompany with plain-boiled or coconut rice.

One thing which impresses me most about the cooking in India is the amazing variety wrought from the most basic foods.

All over India the leguminous pulses (dried peas, beans etc.) known collectively as dal, are a staple food and provide almost the only source of protein for the poorer vegetarian Hindus. What could easily become a bland and repetitious diet, however, is enlivened by endless combination of spices and the use of different varieties of pulse. It has been estimated there are sixty-odd varieties of dal grown in India, although only about eight are commonly used.

The most important is the chickpea, or chana dal, which forms more than half the total pulse crop of India. The Indian chickpea is smaller and darker than the variety commonly seen in the West, although they do have a larger chickpea, kabuli gram, which is sometimes classified as a separate species.

Chickpeas are either cooked whole into a simple purée (sar) or are hulled and split into a yellow dal. In India much of the crop is ground down into a fine creamy yellow flour, known as besan. According to Hindu legend, chickpea flour was once used by Shiva's wife to make a statue. Shiva then struck off its head, which so infuriated his wife that he had to replace it with the head of the first thing that happened to pass – an elephant. Thus the elephant-headed god Ganesh came into being.

Chickpea flour may difficult to obtain, but the more common flour of split peas, sold as 'pea flour', can be substituted.

Pakora (vegetable fritters)

Pakoras are one of the great Indian snack foods. Almost any vegetable can be used for this batter, such as florets of cauliflower, leaves of spinach or silver beet, slices of green pepper, sliced onion or thin slices of potato. This mixture is sufficient for the slices of 2 medium potatoes.

250 g (9 oz) chickpea or split pea flour
1 tsp ground cumin
1 tsp ground coriander

1 tsp ground turmeric
1/2 tsp cayenne pepper
1/2 tsp salt
1/4 tsp bicarbonate of soda or baking powder
oil for deep frying

Mix the flour with the spices and salt, then stir in enough water (about 250 ml or just under 1/2 pint) to make a fairly thick batter. Dip in pieces of sliced vegetable, then drop into hot oil and deep fry, turning occasionally, for 6–8 minutes, until reddish brown.

Second only to chickpeas in importance in India, is the pigeon pea (*Cajanus indicus*), a small, orange pulse, somewhat resembling the common split pea. In India it is known as tur or arhar dal; in southern India as tuvaram. Originally from Africa, it was taken to India in prehistoric times. Since the plant is easily killed by frost, it is not grown in northern India and hence found mostly in the cooking of the hotter south and west in Gujarat and Bombay. This is the dal of the famous dhansak, or mixed dal dish of the Parsi religious minority, and of the rasam and sambhar of the south.

The red kidney bean was introduced to India from its native America, but was soon adapted into Indian cooking and rechristened rajma dal. Black-eyed beans (*Vigna sinsensis*), kidney-shaped and white in colour, are widely used in India under the name of lobia dal (also spelled lombia, lobhia or lobya). A closely related species is the Madras, or horse, gram, which is widely grown for animal feed in southern India, where the poor still gather the pods for food.

One of the most attractive-looking dals is the yellow moong dal. This is the green gram (*Phaseolus aureus*), better known in the West as the mung bean, used for sprouting. Whole, it is a tiny cylindrical green bean, while hulled and split it reveals yellow seeds.

Moong dal appears mostly in the cooking of central and southern India, where it is often fed to invalids on account of its lightness and digestibility.

Moong Dal

400 g (14 oz) skinned and split mung beans
1 1/2 tsp ground turmeric
3–4 tbsp ghee or oil
4 cloves garlic, crushed
4 medium onions, chopped
walnut-sized piece of fresh root ginger, grated

2 tsp ground cumin
2 tsp ground coriander
$\frac{1}{2}$ tsp ground fenugreek
salt

Wash beans and soak in water for an hour. Boil with the turmeric until soft. The water should easily cover the beans, but how much you use depends on individual taste. Some people prefer a thin, soup-like consistency, others a much thicker mixture. It is sometimes said the dal should be thicker than pea soup but thinner than porridge.

When the dal is soft and almost ready, heat the ghee or oil in a pan and fry the garlic and onions until soft. Add the ginger, cumin, coriander and fenugreek. Fry for several minutes, stirring constantly. Stir this mixture into the dal. Add salt to taste and serve hot.

SERVES 4–6, depending on what else you serve with it. Dals are usually served as part of an Indian meal with rice, chapattis, one or two vegetable dishes, perhaps a mutton or chicken dish, and with side dishes such as raitas (relishes) or chutneys.

Easily confused with a rare black variety of mung bean is black gram (*Phaseolus mungo*), which is the same size and shape and, to add to the confusion further, can also come in a green coat. However, once the black gram is hulled and split the difference is immediately obvious: the seed is off-white rather than yellow in colour. This is the urad dal (also spelled urhad, urhid, or urd) of Indian cooking. Often there will be tiny bits of black husk left in the dal, although in India the more expensive dhuli urad is available, with every trace of husk washed out.

Urad dal is eaten all over India, particularly in the Punjab and most often in the winter months. This is because it is a fairly heavy dal, not easily digested, and not readily broken up into a mush with boiling.

Considerably cheaper and rather less esteemed than urad dal are muttar, the common yellow or green split peas, and lentils, or masoor. Despite disagreement among botanists as to whether this tiny, round, flat, salmon-coloured grain is the same species as the European lentil, the common lentil available at most supermarkets can safely be substituted in all Indian recipes. It is often found in Bengali cooking and that of India's Muslims.

Regardless of whether your evening meals alternate between chicken vindaloo, gado-gado and calzone with sun-dried tomatoes, it is a fair bet your breakfasts remain totally traditional: porridge or cereals, perhaps the occasional bacon and eggs, followed by toast, and a pot of tea. The great British breakfast.

In 1925 an Englishman, V. H. Mottram, published a book entitled *Food and the Family*, in which he attempted to give a physiological explanation as to why this breakfast should be part of the natural order of things for the whole of humanity.

After twelve hours' fasting, he insisted, the body needs the immediate energy provided by easily digested carbohydrates like porridge, which pass rapidly through the pylorus into the small intestines, leaving behind in the stomach the eggs and bacon to be duly digested and so provide 'the sense of satisfaction which no breakfast, except the British and the American, can give'.

It is obvious the jingoistic Mr Mottram never travelled through certain countries of the East where breakfast is equally satisfying, yet comprises a full frontal assault of protein: Turkey's potent beyaz peynir cheese and olives, for example, or Japan's miso and seaweed, or Indonesia's meaty, fiery nasi goreng.

Perhaps these examples are unfair, for there are, it is true, a good many cultures which do prefer a breakfast menu high in bland carbohydrates. But surely the reason for this has less to do with digestion than with our palates: our sense of taste is most acutely sensitive first thing in the morning.

The pity of all this is that a good many excellent but very spicy ethnic breakfast dishes are ignored. One of these is the south Indian vada. This is part of a family of dishes based on a batter of ground lentils and rice, left overnight to partially ferment and take on extra fluffiness.

Vadas, and the related iddlies and masala dosa, are practically the mainstay of any south Indian café. While they are normally eaten for breakfast, however, vadas can also appear dressed with yoghurt and chutney for tiffin or dinner. Known as dahi vada in the south, dahi boorah in the north, and dahi bada in the east or west, the dish reaches its apotheosis in the sophisticated cuisine of the prosperous Marawadi caste of Bombay:

Dahi Bada

150 g (5 oz) split mung beans
150 g (5 oz) urid dal
walnut-sized piece of fresh root ginger
1 tsp caraway seeds
1 tsp salt
1 large green chilli
$\frac{1}{2}$ tsp baking powder
3 tbsp chopped raisins
2 tbsp chopped almonds
2 tbsp chopped pistachios

YOGHURT MIXTURE
500 ml (18 fl oz) plain yoghurt
3 tbsp desiccated coconut or dried coconut threads
1/4 tsp salt
1 tbsp roughly ground coriander seeds
1 tbsp roughly ground cumin seeds

TAMARIND AND DATE CHUTNEY
50 g (2 oz) dried tamarind
225 g (8 oz) dates, stoned and finely chopped
2 tbsp jaggery or brown sugar
1/2 tsp garam masala
1/4 tsp salt
1/2 tsp chilli powder

Wash the pulses in a sieve under a running tap, massaging them until the water runs clear. Cover them with water and soak for 5 hours. Drain.

Set a food processor running with the metal blade and drop in the ginger, 1 caraway, salt and chilli. Add the pulses and grind to a smooth paste with 125 ml (4 fl oz) of water. The action of the food processor should aerate the mixture. If time permits, cover and leave in the airing cupboard or other warm place for 6 hours, until the mixture begins to ferment, and rises even further.

Before deep-frying the vadas, fold in the baking powder, raisins, almonds and pistachios. Do this very gently with a spatula or rubber scraper, so as not to disturb (and hence deflate) the mixture any more than necessary.

Heat sufficient oil for deep-frying in a wok or saucepan. When almost boiling, drop in round patties of the mixture. An experienced Indian cook can dip into the mixture and shape patties by hand, but newcomers can scoop up the mixture with a soup spoon and scrape it into the oil with another soup spoon, in the way one would make French quenelles. Deep fry six at a time for 3 minutes, then flip over and fry the other sides for 3 minutes.

Drop the vadas into a large bowl of lukewarm water as they are done. Allow them to sink to the bottom of the bowl and remain there for about 15 minutes. Remove and gently squeeze them between your two flat palms, to extract the water.

Refrigerate while you prepare the yoghurt mixture and the chutney:

Ideally, you should make your own fresh yoghurt which is closer to true Indian dahi, being noticeably less sharp or sour. Otherwise use any mild unsweetened commercial yoghurt. Mix in the coconut salt. Toast the coriander and cumin seeds in a frying pan without oil, or for 2 minutes on high in a microwave. Pour the yoghurt into a wide bowl and sprinkle with the coriander and cumin seeds.

For the fresh chutney, break the tamarind into small pieces and cover with boiling water. Leave until lukewarm, then squash the fibrous bits of tamarind with your fingers until the water turns thick and brown. Pass the liquid through a sieve into the bowl of a food processor fitted with a metal blade. Press the tamarind well with a rubber scraper and discard the fibrous matter.

Add the dates, jaggery or brown sugar, garam masala, salt and chilli powder. Process until the mixture is smooth.

To serve, place the vadas on top of the yoghurt, then dribble over the chutney.

For the vegetarian Hindus of India, milk is the one animal product that can be enjoyed in the knowledge that no creature has had to suffer for it.

There are nearly 200 million cattle and buffaloes in India, one-third of all the cattle in the world, whose work in the fields and yield of milk is far too valuable to consider killing them for their meat. Not that any orthodox Hindu would dream of doing so anyway, for they are enjoined by the ancient Vedic scriptures to treat all forms of life as sacred, especially the cow because of its association with Krishna, Lord of the Gopis (girl cowherds), who grew up under the protection of the milkmaid Yasoda.

As a child, Krishna had as his closest companions the herd-boys and herd-girls, whom he was able to summon with his magic flute, along with the cattle that had wandered. But he was also very mischievous. He teased the herd-girls constantly, stealing their clothes while they were in the river swimming, and their pots of curds and butter while they were sleeping.

Krishna devotees compare milk to divine nectar which one can drink to become immortal. It is said that in Krishna's abode in the spiritual sky there is a cow called the Surabhi cow, which can give a limitless supply of milk.

A few such cows might not go amiss in modern India, where for all the herd numbers, milk is still so precious that it is almost impossible to buy it undiluted. Everywhere in the streets of Indian cities are milk vendors who are judged by the amount of froth they can work up on top of a glass of milk. This they do by repeatedly pouring the milk from one stainless steel cup to another, increasing the distance between the two until the milk appears like a stream of elastic. A very old joke tells of the bumpkin newly arrived in Delhi from the North-West Frontier (today the Afghani-Pakistani border region), who ordered some sweets and 'two yards of that white stuff'.

While Indians are acknowledged as masters in the use of milk in sweetmaking, strangely their commercial cheese-making industry has only begun recently.

For a very long time, however, they have been making a simple pressed curd cheese known as panir in their own homes, just as we will have to do, since panir is not commonly available in the West. It is however very easy and rather fun as well. Strict vegetarians should also note that this is one way of obtaining cheese which has not been made with rennet (which comes from calves' stomachs). Here's how.

Panir

Bring 1.2 l (2 pt) milk to the boil, stirring to prevent it sticking to the bottom of the pot, then reduce the heat to low and stir in lemon juice until the milk separates into white clotted curds and thin bluish whey. You will need any-where from one to four tablespoons of lemon juice, depending on the acid-ity of the particular lemon. Continue to stir gently, scraping the bottom of the pan, until the whey is almost clear.

Place a colander lined with muslin over a large bowl. Pour the contents of the pot into the colander, separating the curds from the whey (which will drip down into the bowl and should be saved).

Draw up the sides of the muslin and press the curds into a small ball, squeezing out excess moisture. Twist the ends of the muslin and then place a weight (e.g. a pot with heavy objects inside) of about 4 kg (9 lb) on top of the ball of curds in the colander. Leave at least 30 minutes or until the cheese is firm. It is now ready to be used in many Indian recipes, such as:

Muttar Panir (curd cheese with peas)

1 batch panir (see above)
3 tbsp ghee or butter
3 medium onions, chopped
2 cloves garlic, crushed
walnut-sized piece of fresh root ginger, chopped
1 tsp ground turmeric
1/4 tsp chilli powder
2 tsp freshly ground black pepper
1/2 tsp garam masala (optional)
3 tomatoes, mashed
300 ml (1/2 pt) whey (see above)
500 g (1 lb) green peas
salt to taste
1 tbsp chopped fresh coriander leaves (optional)

Cut the slab of panir into cubes and fry them in the ghee or butter until lightly browned on all sides. Remove and set aside.

Add the onions, garlic, ginger, turmeric, chilli, ground pepper, and garam masala (if using) to the pan. Fry until the onions are lightly browned, then add the tomatoes and 4 tablespoons of the whey. Cook for a few minutes longer, then return the panir cubes to the pan. Add the rest of the whey and bring to the boil. Add the peas and cook (if they are frozen they will only need to be brought to the boil). Add the coriander before serving.

Nowhere else in the world have so many races and cultures met and coalesced, in the course of time, as in India. Her toleration prompted her to give shelter to all faiths, and the all-embracing nature of Hinduism in the days before it was stiffened by caste rules enabled it to absorb foreign elements with ease.

In turn, the immigrants could not help but be influenced by the dominant culture, and so while they brought national dishes and dietary customs with them, these began to take on the stamp of the Indian kitchen, with its mastery of spices and seasonings.

So it was with the Parsis, followers of the ancient prophet Zarathustra, who, as we have seen, fled from Iran to India in about the eighth century AD to escape persecution by invading Arab Muslims. Immediately, their diet began to change. Out of respect for the Raja of Sanjan, the Hindu ruler who had given them refuge in what is now the state of Gujarat, the Parsis gave up eating beef. The shiny black hats resembling a cow's hoof still worn by some orthodox Parsis are said to be a mark of this respect.

Parsis tend to be hearty eaters of other meats, however, particularly poultry and mutton or lamb, although the more devout abstain during the month consecrated to Vohu-Mano, the 'guardian angel' of animals. The use of spices here reveals the Hindu influence.

Dahi Ni Kadhi (yoghurt curry)

500 ml (18 fl oz) plain yoghurt at room temperature
2 tbsp oil or ghee
1/2 tsp mustard seeds (preferably black)
1 tbsp pea flour
1 cm (1/2 in) fresh root ginger, grated
2 cloves garlic, crushed
1/2 tsp ground turmeric
1 tsp ground cumin
1/4 tsp salt
1 tsp fresh chopped coriander leaves (optional)

Heat the oil or ghee in a pan and fry the mustard seeds over a low heat until they splutter and pop (you will need to cover the pan to stop them jumping out).

Add the pea flour and stir fry for 1 minute, then add the ginger, garlic, turmeric, cumin and salt and stir fry for several minutes. Remove from the heat and allow the mixture to cool a little.

Stir the yoghurt into the spice mixture and simmer over a low heat for 3 minutes, until it is warmed through. Do not boil or you risk curdling the curry.

Sprinkle with the fresh coriander and serve over rice, or as a sauce for potatoes.

Indonesia

In its unadorned state, tofu is rather an offputting substance. Not only does its flabby white mass wobble like the stomach of a Pommie sunbather, but its flavour is subtle to say the least. Bland though it may be by itself however, tofu is the perfect vehicle for other flavours. In the past I often marinated it, but in Indonesia I learned an even better technique of forcing the accompanying flavours to impregnate the tofu, which is to simmer the cut pieces in a small amount of highly flavoured liquid.

Tofu is, of course, Chinese in origin (*see* p. 125), but since the Chinese have been in Indonesia for as long as the substance itself has been in existence, it is well ingrained in Indonesian culture. Known there as tahu, it is found mainly in the larger towns where there are large concentrations of Chinese. It is estimated there are over 11,000 tofu shops to serve the population of 130 million Indonesians.

Most Indonesian tofu is firm in texture, similar to the extra-firm varieties usually found in the West. The only difference between this and the softer variety is that, having been coagulated into a solid mass and the whey drained off, the bean curd is pressed longer with a heavier weight. Unlike Chinese-style tofu which is almost always coagulated with calcium sulphate or magnesium chloride, the tofu makers of Indonesia make a coagulant from whey which has been left overnight to ferment. The leftover whey, with its sawdust-like soya bean fibres, is also made into a type of tempeh (*see* pp. 140–2).

Another peculiarly Indonesian innovation is to simmer cakes of tofu in turmeric until they turn bright orange. As in China and other parts of South-East Asia, tofu is also fermented, salted or deep-fried. In Java, where tofu is especially popular, itinerant hawkers sell deep-fried cubes with a couple of chillies perched on top. Alternatively, larger pieces come with a spicy vegetable filling.

Tofu chips are made by drying strips of tofu in the sun. After having been grilled, they are eaten as a snack or form a topping for gado-gado (*see* pp. 169–70).

This tofu recipe, which was demonstrated to me in Bali, employs a basic list of condiments and a simmering technique which can be applied to a wide variety of meats and vegetables. A tumis made with shrimps or kangkung (water spinach) is popular in Bali. Even the dragonflies which the children delight to catch can be turned into a tumis.

Tumis Tahu

300 g (10 oz) cake extra-firm tofu
1 bunch spring onions, cut in half lengthwise
2 tbsp coconut oil
4 shallots or 1 small onion, finely chopped
3 cloves garlic, finely chopped
1–2 fresh chillies, cut lengthwise into very fine slivers
1 tomato, sliced
2 daum salam leaves or 8 curry leaves
1 tsp ground galangal (optional)
1 tbsp soy sauce
1 tbsp kecap manis
1 tbsp tauco or Chinese black bean paste

Cut the tofu into slices about the size of a domino, and then halve each of these to form small fingers. Cut the spring onions in half lengthwise and then across in two or three places (ideally they should be the same length as the tofu fingers).

In a large frying pan, heat the coconut oil, and then fry first the shallots and garlic, then the chilli, then the tomato, daum salam or curry leaves and galangal (if using). Add the tofu and fry, carefully separating the pieces. Add half each of the soy sauce and kecap manis.

Now add the spring onions, turn the heat up, and cover the pan. After 8–10 minutes the spring onions turn bright green. Turn mixture carefully and add half a tumbler of hot water.

Remove the pan cover and allow the liquid to reduce, adding the remaining soy sauce and kecap manis. Add a little water (maximum half a glass) as the mixture dries out. There should always be some sauce on the bottom of the pan, but do not add too much water or you lose the flavour which is impregnating the tofu. About 3 minutes before the end of cooking add the tauco or black bean paste. Serve with rice.

Before you write off soya beans as tasteless and boring, you should sample the delicious nutty flavour of a pressed beancurd cake known as tempeh.

Tempeh (pronounced TEM-pay) is perhaps Indonesia's greatest culinary gift to the world. It consists of soya beans which are soaked, boiled, hulled, and then fermented and bound together with a dense cottony *Rhizopus* mould or culture. Although commonly made at home or in cottage industries in Indonesia, most Westerners would be unlikely to go to the trouble of making their own.

Tempeh contains no cholesterol, is low in fat and is highly digestible.

The tempeh-making process greatly reduces the complex sugars (oligo-saccharides) that in other bean dishes and products are believed to cause flatulence.

In Indonesia, tempeh is a staple source of protein, eaten by choice by all social classes. For vegans (that is, vegetarians who abstain not only from meat but also eggs and dairy products) tempeh is a godsend since it supplies rich amounts of vitamin B12 which would otherwise be lacking in their diet. Vitamin B12 is necessary for the formation of red blood cells and the prevention of anaemia. Tempeh is also a good source of other B vitamins and also of minerals, especially iron.

Although tempeh can be baked or steamed, deep-frying seems to bring out the flavour best. It is usually sliced into large pieces before frying. I have also successfully grilled it over the barbecue, having marinated it first in a mixture of soy sauce, ground toasted sesame seeds, ginger and garlic. Tempeh absorbs other flavours particularly well.

Tempeh Bachem (simmered and deep-fried tempeh)

This tempeh dish is one of the most popular in Indonesian cooking, especially in central Java, where it is sold at street stalls. The Indonesian word *bachem* means 'to simmer in a small amount of liquid'. In this case coconut cream is used, which is absorbed into the tempeh before it is deep fried.

4 shallots or 1 small onion
250 ml (9 fl oz) coconut cream
½ tsp salt
3 tbsp brown sugar
300 g (10 oz) cake of tempeh, cut into six equal slices or fingers
oil for deep-frying

Place the shallots or onion into a food processor and pulverize (or mince by hand).

Transfer to a saucepan along with the coconut cream, salt and brown sugar (in Indonesia palm sugar is used, but our brown sugar is very similar in flavour).

Bring to the boil, stirring, then add the slices of tempeh. Reduce the heat and simmer for 15 minutes, uncovered, until the liquid has greatly evaporated.

Heat some oil for deep-frying in a wok, saucepan or deep-fryer (coconut oil is most authentic but of course any other can be used). Shake off excess sauce from the slices of tempeh and deep fry for 4–5 minutes, until nicely browned all over. Drain on absorbent paper and serve with the coconutty sauce remaining in the pan.

This dish can be eaten by itself or accompanied by rice. It is very rich and filling and serves 3 as a main course, or 6 as a snack or hors d'oeuvre. For extra flavour, a couple of teaspoons of ground galangal or tamarind paste is sometimes added to the simmering mixture.

Unfortunately, the history of tempeh is vague. The first written reference to it did not occur until about 1815, when passing mention was made of tempeh in a Javanese classic, *Sorat Centini*, which narrates the wanderings of two students in search of truth. However, even by the most conservative estimates, tempeh is much older than that, dating back at least several centuries, if not as far back as about AD 1000, when soya beans may have been one of the articles of trade introduced to Indonesia with the opening up of trade with China.

Although tempeh may have been developed from a technique for pressing cakes from residues of coconut after the oil has been extracted, it is thought more likely it was an Indonesian adaptation of a Chinese technique used in the making of soy sauce, where soya bean mash is inoculated with moulds such as *Aspergillus oryzae*. The adoption of the distinctive *Rhizopus* mould many have been simply due to its thriving in the Indonesian climate.

But, whatever its origins, tempeh only became really popular in Indonesia and elsewhere this century. During the Second World War, it was widely used in Japanese prisoner of war camps in Indonesia and New Guinea, and many POWs owed their very survival to it. So too, in the future, with a bit of foresight and planning, could the protein-starved peoples of the Third World.

Japan

In Japan, professional tofu making is recognized as a craft as surely as any other; the mastering of the technique is seen as a spiritual path, or Way, a fulfilment in itself quite apart from any financial reward. At the same time, however, tofu has always been made in Japanese homes by amateurs, so perhaps I may be forgiven for presuming to describe the technique here in only a few paragraphs.

Necessary equipment includes an electric blender or food processor, a large pot, a bowl, a cup, a sieve, a ladle, a piece of muslin or other coarse weave cloth.

You will also need a settling container. In Japanese farmhouses, this consists of an oblong wooden box about 18 x 10 cm and 10 cm deep (7 x 4 x 4 in), with holes drilled into the sides and bottom and a lid which slides down into it. If your cabinet-making skills are not up to making one, I suggest my own improvisation: take a large empty tin of the sort used for bulk tinned fruit (I scrounged mine from a cafeteria), keep the lid, and with a can opener pierce some holes in the bottom and in the sides near the bottom. Line it with a large square of muslin.

Home-made Tofu

300 g (10 oz) dried soya beans
4 tbsp fresh lemon juice or 2 tsp nigari or 2 tsp Epsom salts (see below)

Soak the soya beans overnight in about 1.5 litres (2½ pt) of water. Drain them and place about half of them in a blender with 500 ml (scant 1 pt) hottest tap water. Process for a couple of minutes at top speed until thoroughly puréed.

Meanwhile, have 1.75 litres (3 pt) of water boiling in a large saucepan over a high heat. Pour the puréed beans into the boiling water, cover the pot and turn off the heat underneath.

Purée the remaining beans in the same way and add to the pot.

Line a colander with a square of muslin and place the colander over a large pot. Tip the soya bean mixture into the colander and let the soya 'milk' drip into the pot.

Draw up the four corners of the muslin, twist them, and with a potato masher or jar, press out as much moisture as possible. Open up the cloth, fluff up the solids a little, then pour 750 ml (scant 1½ pt) boiling water over, stir and press again.

Place the pot of soya milk on the stove and bring to the boil over a high heat, stirring across the bottom frequently to avoid sticking. Reduce heat and simmer for 7–8 minutes.

While the milk is simmering, prepare the coagulant.

The most convenient coagulant to use is lemon juice, which yields a mildly tart tofu. A sweeter result can be got from nigari, the traditional Japanese coagulant, which is sometimes available from some healthfood shops. More readily available are Epsom salts, which can be bought from any chemist.

Place your chosen coagulant in a measuring jug and make it up with water to 250 ml (9 fl oz). If using Epsom salts or nigari, stir until the crystals are dissolved.

Take the pot off the stove. Pour in a third of the coagulant, stirring back and forth five or six times, making sure the spoon reaches the bottom. Stir another half dozen or so times. Wait until all movement stops, then sprinkle another third of the coagulant over the surface.

Leave the mixture for several minutes, then slowly stir the top centimetre or two of the surface for 20–30 seconds, while you pour the last of the coagulant over any uncurdled milky areas.

Leave for 3 minutes (6 minutes if using Epsom salts) for the curdling to take full effect. There should now be billowy white curds and a clear yellowish whey on the surface. Slide a spatula down the side of the pot in several places to free any uncurdled soya milk which may have been trapped at the bottom.

Take a sieve and press it down into the pot so that it fills up with whey. Ladle this out and pour over the muslin which you have used to line your settling container, so that it clings to the side. Repeat the ladling until most of the whey is removed, then transfer the curds and any remaining whey into the settling container.

Cover with the lid of the settling container. Fold the excess muslin over the top, and place a brick or other heavy object on the lid to weight it down. Leave for 20 minutes, then remove the weight and immerse the settling container in cold water. Leave for 5 minutes to firm up, then remove the cake from the cloth, and it is ready to eat.

Tofu is very nice eaten simply as is, perhaps with a little miso (fermented bean paste) or soy sauce or shoyu (Japanese soy sauce) mixed with ground toasted sesame seeds, lemon juice and grated root ginger. It can also be grilled, deep fried or steamed, as in a traditional Japanese dish known as gizeidofu.

Gizeidofu (steamed tofu roll)

500 g (1 lb) tofu
1 egg
1 carrot, very finely diced and blanched
5 Chinese dried mushrooms, soaked in hot water and finely chopped
1 tsp sugar
1/2 tsp salt

Wrap the block of tofu in muslin and squeeze to extract excess moisture. Mix with the remaining ingredients.

Roll the mixture into an cylindrical salami shape, then wrap in muslin. Steam for 25 minutes. In Japan, this is usually served cold, although I have found it is also nice eaten hot.

The Japanese also use tofu to make some fascinating savoury steamed custards, or chawan mushi, which have no real equivalent in the West. Here is a Buddhist temple version:

Chawan Mushi

175 g (6 oz) cake tofu, cut into small cubes
2 tbsp tamari or soy sauce
1 tsp sake (substitute dry sherry)
4 large button mushrooms
1 tsp sesame oil
1 tsp honey
500 ml (18 fl oz) stock (see below)
4 eggs
4 leaves spinach, shredded, or small bunch watercress
peel of 1/2 lemon, finely shredded (yellow part only)

Sprinkle the tofu cubes with 1 tablespoon of tamari or soy sauce and the sake (or sherry) and leave to marinate while you prepare the other ingredients.

Wipe clean the mushrooms, cut a cross in the cap of each, and trim the stems. Simmer for several minutes in a little water mixed with the sesame oil, honey and the remaining tamari or soy sauce.

Meanwhile, prepare the stock. Made properly in the Japanese fashion, this involves bringing a little kombu (Japanese dried kelp) to boil in the water, but I have made this dish by mixing the hot water with Marmite to taste.

Lightly beat the eggs (do not allow them to become fluffy) and stir into the cooled stock.

Divide the tofu between 4 cups or small Chinese bowls (in Japan they have special, lidded chawan mushi cups). Place a mushroom in each bowl. Divide the shredded spinach or watercress between the cups. Pour in the stock mixture and top each cup with the liquid from the mushrooms. Finally, sprinkle a little lemon peel over each serving.

Cover each bowl with foil and either place in a steamer, or in a pot with hot water coming halfway up the sides of the bowls. Steam for 12–15 minutes until the custard is just set – it will not be very firm.

Macau

If an eight-armed creature were to land on Earth from outer space, the joke goes, the Hindu would drop to his knees and worship it, while the Chinaman would scratch his head, searching his memory for a suitable recipe. This carnivorous reputation particularly adheres to the Cantonese, about whom the northern Chinese have a saying: if it has four legs but is not a table, and if it has wings but is not an aeroplane, the Cantonese will eat it.

Setting out to explore the food culture of Macau, where the population is about 94 per cent Cantonese, I braced myself for local specialities such as yellow worms baked with eggs, orange peel and garlic. In fact, what I discovered was some delightful vegetarian food at the Pou Tai Un Temple where, in accordance with the Buddhist monastery tradition of extending hospitality to travellers, the monks run a restaurant.

Situated on the island of Taipa, down several flights of steps at the feet of the temple's giant bronze Buddha, the leafy restaurant courtyard presents a tranquil contrast to the traffic noise of downtown Macau. Only the distant chanting of monks is audible, punctuated with rhythmic hoe strokes of the old Chinese woman planting the temple vegetable garden. She told me her garden used to supply all the needs of the temple restaurant. Nowadays, however, the restaurant is so famous they must also buy in from outside to meet the demand for specialities such as mashed purple taro in pastry crescents, deep-fried beancurd sheet filled with water chestnuts, or a dish which encompasses an astounding array of braised vegetables.

The chefs are professionals, hired by the head monk who pays them only a little less than they would earn in an outside restaurant, but insists that they regard each other as equals, and that there be no traditional kitchen hierarchy. So humble were the two chefs I spoke to that they only reluctantly supplied their names. I commented to the younger of the two that the kitchen staff all seemed middle aged or elderly.

'Yes,' he agreed, 'most of us have been here for ten years at least. We all live together here in the temple. It's a life that doesn't seem to appeal to young people, but we find it peaceful.'

'By that he means boring!' chipped in my Cantonese interpreter.

Boring is precisely how critics describe vegetarian food, especially tofu. Yet these temple chefs wrought wonders with the stuff, recognizing its role as the bland vehicle for tasty sauces. I was given the following recipe.

Sichuan-style Tofu

6–8 dried Chinese mushrooms
1 cake firm tofu, cut into 1 cm (½ in) cubes
1 large leek
3 tbsp oil
8 button mushrooms, cut into quarters
2 cloves garlic, crushed
2 tsp fermented black beans
1 tbsp chilli bean sauce
2 tbsp rice wine or sherry
1 tsp light soy sauce
2 tsp cornflour

Soak the dried mushrooms in a small bowl of boiling water for 30 minutes. Save the water, but remove the mushrooms and squeeze out excess liquid. Cut each into quarters.

Blanch the tofu cubes in boiling water for 3 minutes, remove and set aside.

Slice the leek lengthwise into quarters, then cut into 2 cm (1 in) lengths.

Heat the oil in a wok, add the leek and the button mushrooms and stir fry for 5 minutes. Add the Chinese mushrooms, tofu, garlic, black beans, chilli bean sauce, rice wine or sherry and soy sauce. Stir the ingredients to combine, but gently, to avoid breaking up the tofu. Add about 500 ml (scant 1 pt) of the water used to soak the mushrooms, then cover the wok if possible, and leave the mixture to simmer gently for 10 minutes.

Before serving, mix the cornflour to a paste with a little cold water and stir into the sauce in the wok. Bring to the boil to thicken. Serve with plain steamed rice.

Vegetarianism flourished in China with the introduction of Buddhism during the Eastern Han dynasty (AD76–720), but its origins are much older and probably stem from the Chinese obsession with the link between food and health. In the *Zuo Zhuan* (Historical Annals by Zuo), which pre-dates Buddhism by a least a century, we read: 'They are debased who indulge in meat.'

Yet most Chinese yearn very much to indulge. After wrestling expedience with their Buddhist conscience, they came up with the concept of the part-time vegetarian. Such part-timers eat vegetarian food on the first and fifteenth day of every month on the Chinese calendar. Another custom, still observed by 90 per cent of the Chinese in Macau, is to eat vegetarian food at the beginning of the Chinese New Year, the idea being that the start to the year is auspicious if no animal is killed.

Middle East

'Bullet-sized peas quite beyond the powers of digestion,' wrote Alexandre Dumas of the chickpea.

'As for garbanzos [chickpeas], they sounded in our bellies like pieces of lead in a basque drum,' sniffed Théophile Gautier after a tour of Spain in 1848.

However disparaging these and succeeding generations of Frenchmen may have been about the chickpea, it remains the basis of some truly outstanding dishes from other parts of the world, particularly the Middle East, Spain and India.

The chickpea is thought to be of Caucasian origin, but its cultivation goes so far back that the plant is unknown in its wild state. We know from Homer that they were eaten in ancient Greece, but they were known in Egypt and India even before that. In AD711 they were the staple ration of the Arab army which successfully invaded Spain and when the Spaniards in turn conquered South America nine centuries later, chickpeas went with them under the name of garbanzos. Today they are grown in all temperate climates.

The name has nothing to do with our feathered friends from the farmyard but is a corruption of the old English 'chich pease'. This is a translation of the French *pois chiche* which in turn comes from the Latin name, *Cicer arietinum*. The word *arietinum* refers to the ram's head symbol of Aries (if you look at a chickpea from both sides you will see the set of curly horns).

Chickpeas need to be so soaked in water at least overnight, preferably for as long as 48 hours. They will need to boil from two to four hours to soften, and can rarely be overcooked. Add salt about five minutes before the end of cooking. If you have a pressure cooker this is where it comes into its own, because the chickpeas will be done in only about 45 minutes.

Hummus

Strictly speaking this dish should be called Hummus bi tahina, since *hummus* is simply Arabic for chickpea. Ready-made tahina, or sesame seed paste, can be bought from health food stores (make sure it has been made from toasted sesame seeds and also that it is fresh – stale tahina has a most unpleasant aftertaste) but provided you have a blender it is really not much trouble to make your own. Simply toast the sesame seeds in a heavy pan (do not use oil or butter), shaking the pan and stirring them until they are an even brown, then place in the blender and reduce to a paste (a pestle and mortar will suffice if you have no blender).

Proportions of ingredients for hummus are flexible.

150 g (5 oz) dried chickpeas, soaked
1 tsp salt
50–75 g (2–3 oz) tahina or sesame seeds
2 cloves garlic, crushed
4–6 tbsp lemon juice
cayenne pepper
oil (optional)
paprika

Boil the chickpeas until soft, adding salt about 5 minutes before the end. If not using shop-bought tahina, toast and grind the sesame seeds while the chickpeas are cooking.

Drain the chickpeas and save the water. Place chickpeas, tahina, garlic, lemon juice and a pinch or two of cayenne in a blender, turn on to full speed and add just enough of the chickpea water to set the mixture moving about in the container. You may have to do this in two batches. If you have no blender, use a mortar and pestle. A little oil (either soya bean, olive or sesame oil) makes a nice addition.

Turn out into a bowl and decorate with lines of paprika. Serve with bread as a dip or as a first course.

Felafel (chickpea fritters)

Although felafel are said to be an Israeli invention (they have been called the 'Israeli hotdog' since they are often sold on the streets there), they show very obvious Arab influences.

50 g (2 oz) cracked wheat
150 g (5 oz) dried chickpeas, soaked and boiled
salt
juice of 2 lemons
1 large clove garlic, crushed
black pepper
½ tsp ground cumin seeds
½ tsp ground coriander seeds
oil for frying

1. Crawford Market, Bombay, India *(see p.7)*

2. Satay hawker, Melaka, Malaysia *(see p.42)*

3. Making roti canai on the terrace of the Regent Hotel, Kuala Lumpur, Malaysia *(see p.180)*

4. World's longest popiah at the first
Singapore Food Festival, 1994 *(see p.209)*

(see p.209)

5. Pasar Besar Buluh Kubu market, Kota Bharu, Malaysia

7. Market day for a smallholder's produce
(bananas, chillies, papaya, bitter gourd, kangkung),
Singaraja market, Bali *(see p.247)*

6. A cook slices shallots for Tumis Tahu, Ubud, Bali *(see p.140)*

8. Chillies on sale at Singaraja market, Bali

9. Family Altar offering, Galungen Festival, Bali

10. Planting tong ho (garland chrysanthemum) at the
Pou Tai Un Temple vegetable garden, Macau *(see p.147)*

11. Singaraja market, Bali

Barely cover the cracked wheat with water and leave to soak for 15 minutes. Completely drain off the water.

Add salt (to taste) to chickpeas 5 minutes before the end of cooking, then drain completely when cooked.

Place chickpeas, lemon juice, garlic clove, a few grindings of black pepper, cumin and coriander in a blender and reduce to a paste. Do not add any extra liquid to the mixture (it must hold together during frying), so the blending will have to be interrupted frequently while you unclog the machine. Alternatively, pound the mixture with a mortar and pestle. Mix in cracked wheat and adjust seasonings to taste.

Roll into small balls a little larger than a walnut, allow to dry at room temperature for an hour, then fry in hot oil. Although they are supposed to be deep fried, these balls have an annoying tendency to disintegrate unless the mixture is just the right consistency. A beaten egg helps to bind the mixture, although this is not traditional (if you can say that about a dish which cannot date back any further than 1948).
MAKES 10–12 BALLS.

The warm, spicy scent of cumin pervades every Eastern cuisine from Morocco to India, yet until recently most Western cooks barely used this delightful seed. So neglected has cumin been in Europe that in at least two languages it is confused with caraway, a seed which is similar in looks, yet light years away in flavour.

In France, for instance, caraway is often called *cumin des prés*, which only goes to show how the French, for all their self-professed culinary mastery, fall down miserably in the area of spices. Similarly, an alternative Spanish name for caraway is *comene holandesa* ('Dutch cumin'). The Dutch are more partial than most Europeans to both caraway and cumin (using the former in candied form as a breakfast spread and the latter for flavouring Leydon cheese), as are their neighbours, the Germans (think of sauerkraut and Münster cheese). In Germany cumin baked in bread would not only magically keep a would-be robber in the house until the owners returned, but it would ward off thieving wood goblins as well. In Greece there was another reason for putting cumin in bread. The herb was credited with the power of inspiring fidelity: when a soldier or merchant was about to leave for a long journey, his lover might present him with a loaf of bread baked with cumin or force him to drink a cumin-laced glass of wine in the fond hope that it would cure his roving eye.

To both the ancient Greeks and the Romans, cumin symbolized greed and the Emperor Marcus Aurelius was nicknamed Cuminus for this reason. The Romans were never known to hold back on cumin; in fact, they were so fond of it they ground the seeds into a distinctly unsubtle paste to spread over bread. They believed that smoking the seeds helped to produce a desirable pallor in the face (from nausea, perhaps?) and according to Pliny, the pupils of the rhetorician Porcius Latro took it to induce a studious expression. Theophrastus advises that the planting of cumin be accompanied by abuse and curses, perhaps to ward off the effect of the evil eye which would otherwise damage the germinating plants.

Their descendants largely ignore cumin, despite the fact that the plant grows very well all around the Mediterranean, and it is only in North Africa and Western Asia eastwards that it regains its popularity, adding its warmth to vegetable, rice and meat dishes. It does occasionally appear in the Greek recipes such as the beef stew, stifado, soudzoukakia (Smyrna sausages), and I came across this unusual combination of chickpeas, cumin and apricots there. However, I doubt whether the dish really originated there, as the Greeks are not usually fond of mixing sweet and savoury like this and the recipe has the ring of their neighbours further to the east, in Turkey and Iran.

Chickpeas with Cumin and Apricots

300 g (10 oz) chickpeas, soaked overnight in plenty of water
1 large onion, diced
250 ml (9 fl oz) olive oil
1¼ tsp ground cumin
1 tsp dried oregano
1 tsp salt
200 g (7 oz) dried apricots
400 g (14 oz) tinned tomatoes
3–4 cloves garlic, crushed

Simmer the chickpeas in fresh water until soft.

Fry the onion in the oil until transparent, along with the cumin (cumin always needs to be heated in order to bring out its flavour), oregano and salt.

Add the apricots and tomatoes (including their juice), breaking them up slightly with a spoon. Simmer for 10–15 minutes until the apricots are soft, adding a little of the water used to boil the chickpeas from time to time as necessary. 5 minutes before the end of the cooking add the garlic.

Turkey

In London I have visited cheese shops, and in Bologna those that sell only game, but nowhere except Istanbul have I seen shops which sell nothing but nuts: hazelnuts, pine nuts, peanuts, pistachios, almonds, pumpkin kernels and chickpeas, all stored in row upon row of shiny metal containers, each with a little oval window to display the goods.

Usually you can detect these shops a block away, by the cloud of aromatic smoke wafting down the street from a pot of chickpeas being toasted out on the footpath. This is sort of a calling card, designed to lure customers. (My caterer father used to employ a similar trick at his coffee house in Nelson, New Zealand; every lunchtime he made a point of grilling bacon with the air extractor fan aimed strategically at passers-by!)

The Turks have a special gadget for roasting chickpeas, consisting of a charcoal brazier with a pot built into the top. Into this are poured the chickpeas, well drained and dried following a full week's marinating in olive oil. With a hefty, long-handled spoon, the shopkeeper stirs the chickpeas until tiny charcoal spots appear all over them. Then with a great flourish, a little door at the side of the pot is opened and the chickpeas spill down a chute into bags for sale to waiting customers. The end product is delicious, tasting more like a nut than the legume that strictly speaking it is. However, to open such a specialist shop in the West you would have to be, well, nuts. In Turkey the nut sellers survive because of a national obsession with taking titbits with the national drink, raki.

I cannot help wondering why anybody bothers to eat anything at all with raki, since everything ends up tasting of aniseed, despite the most vigorous sluicing of the palate with the glasses of water which usually accompany it. Nevertheless, I have been at meals in private homes in Turkey where raki has accompanied the entire meal from appetizers through to dessert.

These nut-filled dolmas can be eaten either as an appetizer or as a main course. They are usually served lukewarm rather than piping hot. The cabbage leaves, by the way, are authentic and not intended as a substitution for the vine leaves commonly assumed to be *de rigueur* for this dish.

Lahana Dolmasi

1 cabbage, left whole
3 medium onions, chopped
6 tbsp olive oil
200 g (7 oz) long-grain rice
4 tbsp raisins
1 tsp ground allspice
½ tsp chilli powder
2 tsp salt
4 tbsp roughly chopped almonds
4 tbsp pine nuts
juice of 1 lemon
2 tbsp freshly chopped parsley
2 tbsp freshly chopped mint
2 tbsp freshly chopped dill

Remove the outside leaves of the cabbage and place it in a large pot of boiling water. Boil vigorously for 5 minutes, then carefully remove the outside leaves, keeping them intact. Boil the heart for another 5 minutes. Separate the remaining leaves.

Sauté the onions in the oil until soft. Add the rice, raisins, allspice, chilli powder, salt and 450 ml (¾ pt) water. Cover, bring to the boil, lower the heat and simmer until the rice is cooked and the water has been absorbed.

In a dry frying pan, lightly toast the almonds and pine nuts. Stir these into the cooked rice mixture, along with the lemon juice and chopped herb leaves.

Cut the large central ribs from the cabbage leaves, then place about a tablespoon of the mixture on each (use more or less according to the size of the leaf). Fold the cut flaps over, then fold the two sides of the leaves in, and roll up the parcel into a cylinder.

As far as I am concerned, these are now ready to eat as they are, perhaps accompanied with yoghurt sauce (½ teaspoon salt, 1 clove crushed garlic and 1 tablespoon dried mint mixed with 500 ml (18 fl oz) plain yoghurt).

However, the traditional Turkish practice is to immerse these dolmas in water and subject them to a further hour's boiling. Food technologists tell us that the amount of hydrogen sulphide produced in boiled cabbage doubles in the fifth through to the seventh minute of cooking. After a whole hour's boiling, the hydrogen sulphides, ammonia, mercaptans and methyl sulphides will have reacted with each other to form even more pungent trisulphides. So by all means stew these dolmas for another hour, if in your cooking you seek the aroma of rotten eggs.

Vegetables and Salads

China

Sesame oil has to be one of China's more delectable contributions to our store cupboard, yet it remains strangely neglected. Just a teaspoon or two is enough to send a delightful sesame fragrance wafting through a dish of plain steamed, vegetables, and it is great for marinades, too.

Strangely for an oil, however, it is not particularly suitable to use for frying. It is true the Muslims of north China do use it like this, but the oil loses its fragrance when heated (which is why most chefs add it only at the end of cooking) and it also smokes and burns at quite a low temperature. Besides which, it is just too strongly flavoured and expensive to use in any great quantity.

The sesame oils produced in China, Japan and Korea are all made from toasted sesame seeds which accounts for the dark amber colour and the nutty flavour. In China some sesame oil is still produced with small hand grinders, and is greatly sought after by Chinese gourmets who prize its superior fragrance and disdain the products of the large government-run mills.

These Oriental sesame oils are not to be confused with the sesame oils produced elsewhere in the world. Such oils are made from the untoasted seed, meaning they are bland and odourless, and for this reason much used in the manufacture of margarine. Since over half the weight of a sesame seed is in its oil, it is especially suitable for pressing and it is estimated that commercial sesame plantings amount to some two million hectares (five million acres) worldwide.

In India, this untoasted sesame oil is known as gingelly oil and is greatly favoured for its long keeping qualities, even in a humid tropical climate. It is, however, rather looked down upon by those who can afford to cook with ghee. On the other hand, toasted sesame seed oils have a tendency to turn rancid rather quickly, which is a good reason to buy only small bottles.

Sesame and asparagus seem to have a natural affinity – in this recipe, thin-stalked asparagus will absorb the marinade better. If you wish, you can also add some strips of gherkin, cucumber or lightly steamed carrot to the finished dish.

Sesame Marinated Asparagus

500 g (1 lb) asparagus (thin if possible)
2 tbsp sesame seeds
2 tsp honey
1 tbsp sesame oil
2 tsp wine vinegar
1 tsp soy sauce
½ tsp dry mustard powder

Wash the asparagus and snap the tough white end off each stem – the point at which the stem breaks will be where the tough stringy part ends. A more fiddly but economical alternative is to peel the bottom part of the asparagus, which will get rid of the strings as they are concentrated near the surface of the stem.

Cook the asparagus for about 6 minutes, either in a microwave (covered, with a little water to allow the asparagus to absorb the moisture) or standing upright in a tall pot, with the water level falling short of the delicate tips (which will cook in the rising steam).

Meanwhile, toast the sesame seeds in a dry pan, shaking it often until the seeds are lightly browned. Tip out the seeds, set aside, and return the pan to the heat. Melt the honey and then blend in the sesame oil, wine vinegar, soy sauce and mustard powder.

Drain the cooked asparagus well, then pour the marinade over while both are still warm. Leave at room temperature for at least 2 hours but no more than 6 hours. Rotate the top stalks to the bottom from time to time.

Refrigerate about half an hour before you are ready to eat, and sprinkle with the toasted sesame seeds before serving.

India

Some years ago a pile of exotic vegetables caught my eye at an Indian greengrocer's in London. Despite their grotesque appearance – their knobbled skins looked like a case of chronic acne – I decided to give them a try. Back in my flat, still ignorant of what they were, I simply boiled them up and chomped into one. I immediately spat it out again in disgust, wondering who could enjoy such mouth-burning bitterness.

I suspect this experience is common to many Westerners, which explains why the aptly-named bitter gourd, or karela, remains a leper in our vegetable repertoire. Only on a later trip to India did I learn that the karela needs careful preparation to reduce the bitterness sufficiently to render it edible.

Although the bitter gourd is now grown commercially in the West, the main market still appears to be among Chinese and Indian communities. This is true certainly of the United Kingdom, where they were introduced as long ago as the sixteenth century but never met with much enthusiasm; bitterness, it seems, is not a quality much appreciated by the Anglo-Saxon palate. Rudyard Kipling, in 'Mowgli's Songs Against People' in *The Second Jungle Book*, regards the bitter gourd as a sort of malignant triffid:

> I will let loose against you the fleet-footed vines –
> I will call in the jungle to stamp out your lines!
> The roof shall fade before it,
> The house-beams shall fall;
> And the Karela, the bitter Karela,
> Shall cover it all!
> In the gates of these your councils my people shall sing.
> In the doors of these your garners the Bat-folk shall cling;
> And the snake shall be your watchman,
> By a hearthstone unswept;
> For the Karela, the bitter Karela,
> Shall fruit where ye slept!

The karela is a climbing annual (*Momordica charantia*) noted for its pretty yellow flowers and five-fingered leaves. It has been cultivated in kitchen gardens in China and India for thousands of years. Right across northern India, from the Punjab to Bangladesh, karela are considered a delicacy. Punjabis stuff them with nuts and fry them whole; Bengalis turn them into stews. They are preserved by slicing and drying, a process which mutes the bitterness, and the resulting chips can then be deep-fried as an Indian equivalent of our potato crisps.

It is also a medicinal plant. According to the ancient Auruvedic system of medicine, still widely respected and practised in India today, the karela is an anti-diabetic and a stimulant to appetite.

Specimens to look for are the small fruits, slightly immature and firm to the touch, with white seeds. By the time it has turned yellowish and soft, it is not really worth bothering about.

As I have said, preparation is vital: peel them and slice lengthways. With a teaspoon scoop out the seeds and pith and discard. Cut the green flesh into small pieces and place them in a colander under a running tap. Grab handfuls and gently squeeze them to extract the bitter juice. They can now be either soaked in salted buttermilk for 15 minutes or, better still, sprinkled heavily with salt, and left in a colander for at least an hour (preferably as long as three). The acrid-smelling liquid which slowly leaches out during this time should convince you of the wisdom of this operation. Repeat the washing and squeezing before cooking.

Imported canned karela is also available from Asian food stores. They should be added to a dish only at the last minute.

This recipe, which I picked up in Bombay, is as delicious as its poetic name suggests. Even without the karela, the nut sauce stands alone as a wonderful topping for any vegetable or mixture of vegetables. With karela, however, the flavour of the dish is extraordinary, as it embodies the Oriental principle of balancing the four tastes – sweet, sour, salty and bitter.

Kareli Cha Panchamrit (bitter gourds with five nectars)

175 g (6 oz) peanuts
75 g (3 oz) sesame seeds
40 g (1½ oz) cashew nuts
5 tbsp dried tamarind
80 ml (3 fl oz) oil, plus 1 tbsp
500 g (1 lb) bitter gourds, prepared as described above
50 g (2 oz) dried coconut threads (or desiccated coconut)
150 g (5 oz) loosely packed soft brown sugar (or grated jaggery)
2 tsp garam masala
¼ tsp salt
black pepper
1 tsp black mustard seeds
3–6 broken dried red chillies (according to taste)

Roast separately the peanuts, sesame seeds and cashew nuts, until all are a very light tan colour. Grind all these nuts to a coarse powder in a food processor or with a mortar and pestle.

Break the tamarind into small pieces and cover with boiling water. Mash the lumps with a spoon to break up further, and leave 5–10 minutes, then strain out the pith and stones, leaving the juice.

Heat the oil and fry the pieces of bitter gourd until they lose their colour and begin to brown at the edges. Add the nuts, tamarind juice, coconut and sugar and sprinkle with garam masala, salt and a few grinds of black pepper. Mix in 500 ml (scant 1 pt) of water, then cover the pan tightly and simmer, stirring occasionally, for 10 minutes.

Just before serving, heat 1 tablespoon of oil in a small frying pan and add the mustard seeds and chillies. When the mustard seeds turn red, remove and stir into the karela mixture. Serve hot.

This dish is guaranteed to confound dinner guests. It is too rich to eat in great quantities and is best served in conjunction with rice, chutneys and other Indian dishes.

Despite half a century of independence, Calcutta retains more than a faint echo of its imperial past. Dalhousie Square may have been renamed DDB Bag and the more prominent statues of Queen Victoria hauled off into exile in obscure corners of public parks, but the English churches and crumbling colonial palaces survive, their Corinthian pillars blackened with fungus and the fumes from passing double-decker London buses (leaning precariously like the Tower of Pisa on their shot suspensions).

Equally evident are the living British institutions – the gentlemen's clubs, the race meetings, the dozens of cricket matches simultaneously in progress on the maidan on a Sunday afternoon, and the genteel stores where the assistants use hilariously antique expressions such as: 'I'll be with you in a jiffy.'

Then there is the Fairlawn, one of the more unusual hotels of the world. It is not just that this 200-year-old mansion is a storehouse of Raj memorabilia, although all that is extraordinary enough: framed photographs of Darjeeling circa 1920, teak furniture, cane armchairs, Chinese vases, cabinets full of strange sea shells, Oriental carvings and brass Buddhas. Rather, it is the atmosphere of sitting in the upstairs lounge at an Anglo-Indian writing bureau beneath a forest of swishing fans and a skylight breaking through the gloom, listening to the cawing of an army of crows outside interspersed with Sandhurst-accented cries of: 'Bearer! Bearer! Take this luggage to room 13.'

The gong sounds for lunch. You cross the cool marble floor inlaid with black tiles and descend the staircase, a potted aspidistra on each step forming a sort of indoor hedge all the way down. In the dining room the guests are seated six to a table and formally introduced. At ours there are a couple of haughty Germans, an Englishwoman now resident in New York, and an Indian whose family settled in Jamaica three generations ago from Uttar Pradesh. 'I am here to discover my forgotten heritage,' says the intense, bespectacled young man.

An elderly, bow-legged waiter appears by my side, bearing a tray containing a pastry-topped pie with a mashed potato base and a curried mutton filling. The gold peak in his braided turban signifies he is the head waiter; he has been in service here for forty-five years. Another waiter bears a beetroot and cucumber salad and a pumpkin in white sauce. Then to follow, a prawn curry, rice, yoghurt raita, dal, mango chutney, lime chutney and this interesting potato dish:

Peanut Potatoes

4 medium potatoes
50 g (2 oz) peanuts, roasted then ground (or use peanut butter)
2 tbsp oil
walnut-sized piece of fresh root ginger, grated
1 tsp cumin seeds
1 tbsp ground coriander seeds
$\frac{1}{2}$ tsp garam masala or curry powder
salt
chilli powder
2 tbsp grated coconut or desiccated coconut
handful of chopped fresh coriander leaves

Boil the potatoes until nearly cooked, then peel and dice them.

Heat the oil in a frying pan and sauté the ginger and cumin seeds. When the seeds begin popping, add the potato and fry until browned. Toss with the peanuts, ground coriander and garam masala (or curry powder). Season to taste with salt and chilli powder, then decorate with grated coconut and coriander leaves.

Each year around August or September the Hindus of the southern state of Kerala celebrate the festival of Onam, which commemorates a trick played by Lord Vishnu on a mythological southern Indian king named Mahabali. Angered at Mahabali for allowing his subjects to worship him as a god, Vishnu appeared before him in the form of a Brahman youth named Vamana ('the deceiver') and demanded of him a favour. Declining the king's offer of the royal vegetable gardens,

Vamana asked instead to be given all the land he could cover in three paces. The king assented, and Vamana then immediately puffed himself up into a giant and traversed the entire kingdom in three steps.

King Mahabali was banished to the underworld, but every year around Onam time his spirit is allowed to reappear to see how his subjects are getting on. Since fruit and vegetables grew especially well during his reign, the streets and markets are stacked high with fresh produce and flowers. On the final day, a clay image of Vishnu is moved in procession from the household to be ritually immersed in a nearby river, accompanied by fireworks, singing, dancing, and of course, feasting.

One dish which is traditionally served at this time is this Keralan classic, Aviyal. Often it is prepared at temple feasts in vast brass urns measuring some 3 m (10 ft) across.

Aviyal (Keralan mixed vegetables with coconut and yoghurt)

The list of vegetables used for this dish is flexible, which is why we can retain its authenticity in the West, even though we do not have ready access to exotic Keralan vegetables such as ash gourd, drumsticks (a long hard fibrous bean with an asparagus-like flavour) and jack-plum seeds (which taste a little like chestnuts). Suggestions include: carrots, green beans, green peppers, aubergine, courgettes, celery, cucumber, choko or pumpkin.

1 coconut
1 tsp cumin seeds
1 clove garlic (optional)
2 fresh green chillies, sliced and deseeded
2 large potatoes, peeled and cubed
750 g (1½ lb) mixed vegetables (see above), cut into pieces approximately 5 cm (2 in) across
4–6 curry leaves
1 tsp ground turmeric
1 tsp salt
1 plantain or under-ripe banana, sliced
half a green mango, peeled and cubed
250 ml (9 fl oz) plain yoghurt
1 tbsp coconut oil
3–4 tbsp chopped fresh coriander leaves

Break open the coconut, remove the water (although not traditional, this can be used to boil the vegetables later) and break up the shell into smaller pieces for easier handling. Prise the flesh away from the shell with a flexible table knife. Reserve half the flesh for some other use, and slice the hard brown outer rind from the other half. Break into smaller pieces and set aside.

Turn on a food processor and drop in the cumin, garlic (if using) and chillies. Grind them, then add the coconut pieces and grind these to a paste also. Alternatively, grate the coconut on a grater, and grind the condiments with a mortar and pestle.

Place the potatoes in a large pot with the curry leaves. Barely cover with water, sprinkle with the turmeric, and parboil.

Keep adding the rest of the vegetables according to how long they need to be cooked, ending up with those such as capsicums and celery, which barely need any cooking at all. Add more water as needed during cooking, and towards the end, add the salt.

When the vegetables are nearly ready, add the plantain or banana and the mango.

Before serving, add the coconut mixture, yoghurt and coconut oil. Mix well and allow to heat through.

Serve sprinkled with coriander leaves.

Provided some starchy filling vegetables have been used, this could provide more or less a complete meal for two people, accompanied perhaps by rice and chutneys.

Having spent two days travelling on a succession of barges through the canals, lakes and backwaters which intersect Kerala, I now understand why its name translates as 'Land of the Coconut'. Everywhere I looked, there appeared to be little else but a wild profusion of coconut palms, so it is not surprising that coconut dominates the cooking of this region.

Kerala Coconut Chutney

walnut-sized piece of fresh root ginger
5 fresh green chillies
flesh from 1/2 fresh coconut
1/2 tsp salt
1 tbsp tamarind paste
1 tsp oil
1/2 tsp mustard seeds
1 tsp cumin seeds

Peel the ginger and drop into a running food processor along with the chillies, then the coconut, salt and tamarind paste (from which you have picked any seeds and large pieces of pith). Grind at full speed to make a paste. Alternatively, chop the ginger and chillies very finely and grate the coconut by hand.

In a small frying pan, heat the oil and add ½ tsp mustard seeds. Cover the pan and wait until the seeds begin popping. Add the cumin seeds and cook a little longer, then add to the mixture in the food processor and process with the pulse button to blend the spices in.

This is a fresh chutney, served as a side dish.

In 1977 I spent a week as a guest of the Sikhs at their holiest shrine, the Golden Temple in Amritsar.

If the Golden Temple is now associated with its storming by the Indian Army in 1984, it was, back then, the very picture of tranquillity. The dazzling copper-gilt dome, set in the middle of a vast tank of water attracted a continuous stream of pilgrims, fulfilling the wish of all pious Sikhs to visit the temple before they die.

Inside the temple, or Harimandir, priests played the harmonium and chanted hymns and prayers for peace and brotherhood in front of the Sikh holy book, the Granth Sahib, which lay opened on a burgundy shawl. Incense burned among garlands of flowers at each side, and the golden walls gleamed with the reflection of an oil lamp. I followed the procession circumambulating the inner shrine and, on leaving, was blessed by a kindly white-bearded old priest, who handed me a marigold.

Apart from harmonizing Islam and Hinduism, one of the main aims of Guru Nanak (1469–1538), the founder of Sikhism, was to abolish the destructive Hindu caste distinctions. To this end Guru Amar Das, one of his successors, founded the institution of the *langar*, or common kitchen.

Some of the most rigid Hindu caste distinctions refer to food. For example, a highborn Brahman considers it polluting even to eat food in the presence of low castes, let alone have it prepared by their hands. By serving vast gatherings with food cooked in one communal kitchen, therefore, these distinctions are broken down. The kitchens also further the Sikh ideal of service to others, and today the poor and needy can still obtain free meals from Sikh temples all over India.

At the Golden Temple, the catering was done on an awesome scale, with giant sacks of dal being emptied into cauldrons the size of a paddling pool and cooked up twice a day.

Before the food was distributed, the pilgrims and other guests formed lines and sat down to chant the holy mantra, 'sathya nam, wai guru', as the food was brought in. It was simple fare – just chilli-hot dal and chapattis (flat wheaten bread) – but there was as much as anybody needed.

Accommodation at the temple inn was similarly spartan, but again, it was free. It was there I met a wild-eyed young French-American who told me he was destitute. Having been robbed of $500 at the temple inn four months previously, he had been there ever since. At one point the temple authorities had offered to train him as a temple guard, and given him a turban and ceremonial sword. However, he lacked the discipline to make the requisite study of the Sikh holy scriptures and when set before a panel of elders, failed an oral examination dismally. This led to him being stripped of his turban, robes and sword and unceremoniously thrown back into the street! He was, however, allowed to continue living at the temple inn.

On my last day in Amritsar he decided to accompany me to the railway station, where be clapped his crazy eyes on some baggage scales by the counter. Without further ado, he stripped off all his clothes and jumped on to the scales, to open-mouthed gasps of horror from a gathering crowd of curious but typically modest Indian onlookers.

Back on the street, worried by what the scales had read, he begged a piece of rotten apple from a street vendor and then picked up an onion from the gutter and ate it raw on the spot, without so much as wiping off the dust. Later I took him to a Sikh restaurant and fed him a proper meal.

The Punjab is famous the world over as the home of the tandoor, or charcoal-fired clay oven, from which emerges the celebrated tandoori chicken and breads such as naan and tandoori roti. Although Punjabis tend to eat more wheat than rice, both grains thrive here. Indeed, so fertile is the Punjab that it contributes over half the wheat and rice for India's public distribution system's food pool, a fact which complicates the political situation greatly.

Cattle also thrive here, leading to generous use of ghee (clarified butter) and milk products, as in this traditional Punjabi recipe.

Mutter-Alu

1 small onion
4 cm (1½ in) piece of fresh root ginger
2 tbsp ghee or butter
500 g (1 lb) potatoes, peeled and cubed
1 tsp ground cumin
1 tsp ground turmeric

1 tsp garam masala
$\frac{1}{2}$ tsp salt
1 large fresh chilli, finely chopped, or $\frac{1}{2}$ tsp chilli powder
500 g (1 lb) frozen peas
2 large tomatoes, diced
250 ml (9 fl oz) plain yoghurt
3 tbsp cashew nuts
handful of chopped fresh coriander leaves (optional)

In a food processor, grind the onion and ginger to a paste. Melt the ghee or butter in a pot and fry this mixture for a minute. Now add the potato cubes, along with the cumin, turmeric, garam masala, salt and chilli.

Stir fry for several minutes more, then add 125 ml (4 fl oz) water and cover the pot tightly. Cook until the potatoes are tender, stirring from time to time.

Now stir in the peas, tomatoes and yoghurt. Cook until these ingredients are heated through. Before serving, sprinkle with cashew nuts and coriander.

Indonesia

'I'm sorry,' the Balinese shopkeeper told me with a smile, 'I only speaking gado-gado English.' What he meant was that his grammar was jumbled, just as the famous Javan vegetable dish gado-gado is also a mixture, usually of whatever produce the cook happens to have around the kitchen.

For this very reason, gado-gado is most atypical of Indonesian cuisine, in which vegetables are rarely mixed together with the same gay abandon as, for instance, in Chinese cooking. Hence the common view that gado-gado shows a foreign influence, perhaps Chinese but more likely Dutch. This is because the dish originated in Jakarta, which in colonial times as Batavia was the centre of the Dutch administration, and hence one of the few regions of Indonesia where European culture made lasting inroads.

The peanut sauce which is the crowning glory of gado-gado is undeniably Indonesian, but interestingly, even this would not have been known there before the discovery of the peanut in Central America by Christopher Columbus. Dialect names indicate the peanut was brought to Indonesia by Portuguese and Spanish trading ships, and it has been an important crop in Java for at least two hundred years. Raffles mentions that in the early 1800s there were extensive plantations around all the major towns.

Gado-gado is one of Indonesia's great contributions to international cuisine, but one which has suffered some fairly awesome maulings at the hands of Western cooks. Fortunately, because of the proliferation of Asian food stores in the West which provide fresh chillies, tamarind paste and terasi (preserved shrimp paste), good cooks can much more ably produce an authentic Indonesian peanut sauce.

I was taught how to make gado-gado by a very entertaining Indonesian cooking teacher in a little village near Ubud in Bali. Here is the recipe as I recorded it, along with suggestions for unavoidable substitutions which I have made since. Note that soy sauce, neither kecap manis nor the ordinary salty kind, is not listed here. My cooking teacher was adamant these are added to peanut sauce only when it is to be used for satay. As for the chillies, since neither variety is easily available, just add finely chopped fresh red chillies to taste. The terasi will need to be briefly grilled or microwaved before using (*see* p. 261).

Gado-Gado

SAUCE
1 egg-sized ball of tamarind paste
200 g (7 oz) peanuts
coconut (or other) oil for frying
3 cabe lombok (mild red chillies about 8 cm (3 in) in length)
5 cabe rawit (fiery hot chillies about 2 cm (¾ in) in length)
2 tsp salt
3 large cloves garlic
1 tsp terasi (preserved shrimp paste)
2 limau (a tiny, wondrously aromatic little lime, related to the jeruk purut, or
    Kaffir lime; substitute 1 tbsp lime or lemon juice)
30 g (1 oz) palm sap sugar (ordinary brown sugar is a perfectly acceptable
    substitute)

VEGETABLES
150 g (5 oz) kangkung (a leafy green vegetable with tubular stems, which
    grows in watery areas all over Indonesia. An ideal substitute, very close in
    flavour, would be New Zealand spinach; otherwise, ordinary spinach will
    do)
200 g (7 oz) kacung panjang ('yard-long bean', the same as our ordinary green
    bean, only much longer. Substitute ordinary green beans cut into three).
50 g (2 oz) carrots, cut into 4 cm matchsticks
1 choko (or similar mild gourd or pumpkin)
200 g (7 oz) Chinese cabbage, cut into 4 cm (1½ in) lengths
1 medium potato
50 g (2 oz) beansprouts
½ small cucumber, peeled and sliced
2 medium tomatoes, sliced

GARNISH
2 eggs, hard-boiled and sliced lengthwise
3 shallots, sliced
8–10 kerupuk udang (prawn crackers)
oil for deep frying

Begin by making the sauce. Break up the tamarind into small pieces and
soak in 150 ml (¼ pt) boiling water. Allow to stand while you prepare the rest
of the sauce.

Fry the peanuts in oil until they are well browned. They need to be darker
brown than if you were cooking the peanuts to serve by themselves as a
snack. Take care, however, not to burn them, as this will turn them bitter.
Drain the peanuts and set them aside.

Grind the chilli, salt, terasi and sugar to a paste. In Indonesia this is done on a ulekan, a dish-like mortar, with a broad flat pestle, but a food processor does the job just as well, and much more quickly. Add the peanuts and leave the motor on until the mixture is ground to a smooth paste.

Strain the tamarind and add the liquid to the mixture, together with the lime juice. Place the sauce in a wok on the stove and work in 500 ml (scant 1 pt) of water slowly. Bring to the boil and add more water if necessary, until the sauce is thin and runny, but not too soup-like.

Prepare the vegetables. Either blanch, lightly steam or microwave the spinach, green beans, carrots, choko and Chinese cabbage, one after the other. Bruise the stalks of the Chinese cabbage in order to allow the sauce to penetrate better later. Boil the potato and cut into cubes.

Deep-fry the shallots until brown, remove and, in the same oil, deep-fry the prawn crackers. There is a bit of an art to this: have the oil hot but not smoking, and fry one kerupuk at a time, spreading it with two spatulas from the centre out to both sides, to flatten it as it fries. Flip the kerupuk over and fry very briefly on the other side. The operation is over in seconds, and the kerupuk should then be drained on absorbent paper.

In Indonesia the vegetables are often simply put in separate piles on a platter, with the bowl of peanut sauce, so each person can assemble the dish as they like it. However, one particularly attractive presentation I encountered in a restaurant in Bali was to have the cooked vegetables mixed together on an individual plate, the cucumber and tomato slices fanned around the sides, and the peanut sauce poured over liberally. On top was a circle of kerupuk chips surrounding a half hard-boiled egg in the centre. Optional extras for gado-gado include tofu (cubed and deep-fried) and tempeh (sliced and cooked with kecap manis until it is dry).

The leaf of the kaffir lime (*Citrus hystrix*) exudes such a mouth-watering sweet citrus scent that, for me, it was a case of love at first sniff. There is no other herb quite like it; lemon verbena perhaps would come closest, but that has a cloying, slightly medicinal edge not found in kaffir lime leaf.

In South-East Asian cooking it is used in every type of curry – beef, lamb, chicken, duck, fish, vegetable – almost always in conjunction with a coconut cream. It also goes into fish stuffings, chilli sauce for duck, and an unlikely sounding Thai marinated pork-skin salad.

Why then has kaffir lime leaf never reached the kitchens of the West? The name provides a clue. In European colonial days, any indigenous food which the great white rulers regarded with contempt was designated 'kaffir'. Thus we have 'kaffir beans' (blackeye beans), 'kaffir bread' (sago), and 'kaffir cherry' (the fruit of the gardenia). The kaffir lime was doubtless so named because the fruit is fairly undistinguished: a small, knobbly skinned lime, full of pips and meagre of juice. 'No damned good at all for a gin and tonic, eh what, old bean?' The Colonel Blimps, however, missed the point completely: it is the fruit's grated rind and the leaf which provide the magic cooking ingredients.

The dried leaf does not need reconstituting, but should be added to dishes only near the end of cooking. Far preferable, however, are fresh or frozen leaves which are sometimes obtainable. These too should be added towards the end of cooking – the flavour-giving oils contained in the leaf are volatile and dissipate quickly.

Curry of Summer Vegetables with Kaffir Lime Leaves

4 tbsp oil
500 g (1 lb) cauliflower, cut into florets
1–2 tsp Thai red curry paste, or garam masala or curry powder
2 carrots, sliced
100 g (4 oz) green beans, cut into thirds
3 sticks celery, sliced
200 g (7 oz) asparagus, cut into thirds
500 g (1 lb) spinach
250 ml (9 fl oz) coconut cream
10 kaffir lime leaves (or fresh citrus leaves or lemon verbena)
4 cloves garlic, chopped
1 tbsp Thai fish sauce
handful of chopped fresh coriander leaves and stems (optional)

In a large heavy pot with a close-fitting lid, heat the oil and sauté the cauliflower for several minutes, turning occasionally. Mix in the curry paste thoroughly. Add the carrots, beans, celery and asparagus, stir fry for another minute. Place spinach on top of the curry, add coconut cream, put on lid and cook for another 5 minutes. After the spinach has wilted, stir it in, along with the kaffir lime leaves, garlic and fish sauce. Cook, covered, on a low heat for a further 5 minutes.

Sprinkle with coriander before serving, and serve with plain boiled rice.

Japan

Shiitake is the great mushroom of Japanese cooking, and is also highly prized in China and Korea. It has an unusual Marmite-like flavour which is more pronounced than our ordinary cultivated or field mushrooms.

In Japanese, *shiitake* means 'mushroom of the shii tree'(*Quercus cuspidata*), an oak of central and southern Japan. The mushroom is more frequently seen growing out of the trunks of the shii than any other tree, but other dead hardwood trees play host to the shiitake in Japan, particularly other deciduous trees such as chestnuts and hornbeams. The wood provides the food for the growing mushroom.

The Chinese were the first to cultivate the shiitake some eight hundred years ago, and it was probably they who introduced the technique to Japan, where records show the wild mushrooms had been eaten at least as early as the year AD199. The early cultivation technique involved cutting notches in tree trunks at the edge of a forest, and then waiting patiently in the hope that the wind would blow the shiitake spores into the holes and bear fruit. In the 1920s, scientists discovered how to propagate the spawn by inoculating sawdust, and a new technique evolved whereby holes were drilled into the logs and filled with the sawdust.

For both Chinese and Japanese, it is a shiitake rather than an apple a day that keeps the doctor away. As early as the Ming dynasty (1368–1644) a famous Chinese physician named Wu Shui claimed shiitake could endow people with vigour and energy, and was effective in the treatment of brain haemorrhage. Recently, Japanese researchers have shown it reduces blood cholesterol and contains an agent which combats influenza and other viruses. In experiments with mice, there have also been indications that extracts of shiitake can combat cancerous tumours when administered under the skin (though not when eaten).

Shiitake might be recommended to vegetarians suffering carnivorous withdrawal symptoms, for in both taste and texture it resembles very tender beef steak. Besides having traces of Marmite flavour, it is also vaguely reminiscent of tamari (Japanese soy sauce) with which it harmonizes so well in cooking.

Distinctive though it may be, the flavour of shiitake is delicate and when cooking great care must be taken not to drown it with other strong ingredients. For this reason, when I set about devising this recipe I chose relatively bland ingredients, with the exception of the tamari which seems to accentuate the flavour. Puréeing the mushrooms also seems to bring it out.

Shiitake Vegetarian Pâté

1 medium potato
100 g (4 oz) shiitake mushrooms
1 small onion
30 g (1 oz) butter
1 tsp sesame oil (optional)
2 tbsp cream cheese
2 tsp tamari or soy sauce
2 tsp lemon juice

Peel and quarter the potato and boil until soft. Meanwhile, wipe the mushrooms and cut off the stalks. As these are very fibrous, cut them thinly across the grain into rounds (otherwise they will have to be discarded or used for stock). Chop the caps, and peel and chop the onion.

Fry the mushroom and onion in butter and sesame oil over a medium heat, stirring from time to time until the mushrooms are lightly browned.

Transfer this mixture and the cooked potato to a food processor or blender and add the cream cheese, tamari and lemon juice. Purée until smooth. Serve cold as a snack or hors d'oeuvre on plain cheese biscuits or wholemeal toast. Also delicious as a sandwich filling.

If you have ever paid the horrendous price for the so-called Chinese dried mushrooms which have been available from Oriental food stores for many years, then you will have already tried dried shiitake without knowing it. The Chinese have a number of names for the shiitake but one common one is dong-gu or donko. These can be used in the above recipe after soaking in warm water for about 15 minutes. You might also substitute ordinary button mushrooms, but double or triple the amount to allow for their milder flavour.

Any Japanese and most Chinese cookbooks will contain plenty of Oriental recipes using shiitake. In Japan, it is often used in tempura (*see* pp. 178–9) and sukiyaki. With a substantial Japanese lunch or dinner there will often be a single shiitake with each person's serving, rather than large quantities dominating any dish. Mushrooms are considered by some to be Japan's fourth basic food group (in lieu of dairy products) after meats, vegetables and grains.

In the seventh and eighth centuries, as closer relations with China developed, Buddhism took hold in Japan. Since Buddhist doctrine strictly forbids the taking of life, whether animal or human, one might expect the 85 million Buddhists of Japan to be vegetarian. In fact, this is not the case, for while the Japanese still eat more vegetables and far less red meat or poultry than we do in the West, Buddhist beliefs hold far less sway that they once did and today most Japanese families expect to eat some sort of seafood every day and meat such as chicken at least once a week, if not more. Indeed, from its first introduction to Japan in about AD530, Buddhist vegetarianism has fought and steadily lost a battle of attrition.

Tofu (beancurd) was introduced from China, and the Japanese invented natto (whole fermented soya beans) at some time in the eighth century. These foods – along with miso (fermented soya bean paste), vegetables and grains – formed the basic diet of the ordinary Japanese peasant right up until the end of the Second World War. Occasionally, there might be fish or eggs available, but the chickens were almost never eaten, except for an occasional young one which would be served raw as sashimi.

With the nobility, however, it was a different matter. They loved to hunt, and thus game such as duck, deer and wild boar regularly appeared on their tables. The latter they euphemistically referred to as 'mountain whale', on the basis that Buddhist strictures against killing applied only to four-legged animals.

With the Meiji reforms in the nineteenth century, when Japan embarked on a programme of intensive Westernization, meat eating took a further hold. At that time, it was being seriously suggested that English replace Japanese as the official language, and that the high intake of animal protein in the West was responsible for the Western-ers' superior physiques and their high mental faculties. Accordingly, the slaughter of cattle for beef began, which had hitherto been unknown in Japan except for a small area round Nagasaki. Pork, too, was introduced into the Japanese diet and a breaded cutlet similar to wiener schnitzel was concocted.

Since the war, with the pervasive influence of Western convenience foods such as luncheon sausage, pizza and hamburgers, red meat has become even more common. One of the last bastions of vegetarianism in modern Japan are the temple kitchens of certain Buddhist sects, notably the Tendai, Nicherin, Shingon, and certain branches of Zen. In the Zen sect, the emphasis on ascetic discipline goes hand in hand with vegetarianism, though this does not necessarily mean the food served in Zen temples is spartan. On the contrary, a thirteenth-century text urges the cook in a Zen establishment to introduce variation in cook-ing techniques and to 'make every effort to enable the monastic com-munity to eat with enjoyment'.

The existence of this text, *Tenzo Kyokun*, written by the Zen master, Dogen, founder of the Soto branch of Zen, has no doubt helped to ensure the status of the *tenzo*, or cook, in a monastery or nunnery, for elsewhere we read: 'Tenzo duty is awarded only to those of manifest excellence – who exhibit deep faith in the Buddhist teachings, have a wealth of experience, and possess a righteous and benevolent heart. This is because tenzo duty involves the whole person.'

Zen cooks are urged to offer up love and gratitude to the Buddha in the course of their work and to put their hearts and souls into their cooking, regarding attention to every small detail as a step on the path towards Buddha-hood. A Buddhist proverb says, 'Even tiny drops accumulate into an ocean.' Even the simple task of washing rice, for instance, is to be seen as an act of samadhi, or contemplation. As Dogen says: 'When washing rice, focus attention on the washing and let no distraction enter.' Such principles have a universal application, regardless of the type of cuisine one happens to be preparing.

Since Japanese cuisine developed over a long period in isolation, many of the ingredients are virtually impossible to obtain outside Japan, and those that are, usually cost a small fortune. The ingredients for the following dressing should, however, be available in most Western kitchen cupboards. The dish was developed during the Edo period (1615–1854), when the Shoguns effectively ruled Japan and banished the offspring of the Imperial families to temples in Kyoto, where an elaborate cuisine was developed to cater for them.

Originally, this dressing was intended for Japanese cucumbers (much smaller than ours) which had been thinly sliced, salted and left for 10 minutes, rinsed, and finally squeezed to extract the moisture. However, I have used it with considerable success over lightly steamed spinach or broccoli, and with non-Japanese green vegetables such as courgettes and Brussels sprouts.

Sesame-mustard Dressing

2 tbsp white sesame seeds
1 tbsp rice vinegar or cider vinegar
1 tsp soy sauce
1 tbsp sugar
1/2 tsp hot mustard powder

In a frying pan, toast the sesame seeds – without any oil – over a moderately hot heat until light brown, shaking the pan constantly.

Grind the sesame seeds with a mortar and pestle or in a blender, then add the vinegar, soy sauce, sugar and mustard powder. Mix well and toss the vegetables in this dressing.

For a simple Japanese meal, serve this with boiled white rice (which may be cooked with thin slivers of root ginger) and miso soup (allow about 3 tbsp red miso paste to 750 ml or 1½ pt stock made with kombu – Japanese dried kelp) which has been heated, not boiled, with cubes of tofu.

The Chinese radish is fundamental to Japanese cooking, where it is known as daikon (literally 'giant root'). Indeed, it is estimated that daikon forms up to one-quarter of Japan's total vegetable crop. In India, a virtually identical vegetable is known as mooli, and both root and leaves are eaten.

There are many Japanese recipes for cooking daikon but I prefer the mild pungency of the raw vegetable (something which is lost when it is heated). In Japan, raw grated daikon is one of the most common garnishes. The Japanese even have a special grater with a tray at the bottom to catch the juice. There is also a very elegant Japanese technique, quite difficult to master, of peeling a continuous sheet by working a long sharp knife around and around the full length of the daikon. The sheet is then rolled up tightly and cut into thin shreds, which are then placed in iced water to curl before being arranged in neat piles to serve as a condiment. In China, where it is thought to have originated, this is how the daikon was first used. Sixth-century records tell us it was used as a seasoning instead of pepper and ginger.

We know the radish had reached Japan by the fourteenth century, as it features in this story recounted by the Zen monk and diarist Kenko:

> Once, in Tsukushi province, there was a certain prefect of police whose name escapes me. Believing in the marvellously health-giving properties of the radish, he had for many years eaten two grilled every morning. One day enemies attacked his house on every side when there was nobody to defend it. Two warriors suddenly appeared and fought without regard for their lives, putting all to flight. 'Gentlemen,' the completely astounded man asked them, 'since I have never had the honour of seeing you before, might I ask who you are who have fought so remarkably?' They replied, 'We are those in whom you have put so much confidence for so many years, the radishes you have eaten every morning, come now to serve you.' Saying this, they disappeared. Such is the virtue of profound faith.

It was a Zen master too, who in the seventeenth century used daikon to invent what is still one of Japan's most popular pickles, named takuan in his honour. This bright yellow-coloured pickle is still commonly made in Zen monasteries in Japan today. Most Japanese tend to buy takuan rather than make it themselves at home, for it is a lengthy process which involves sun-drying the daikon, pre-pickling it in brine, and then pickling it for several months in a mixture of salt and rice bran. As good a reason as any for not making it at home is that it emits an odour for the entire time it is curing.

Here is a much less involved recipe which also pickles the daikon slightly, which explains why the dish is much improved after a day or two in the fridge, and will keep up to a week tightly covered and chilled.

Red and White Salad

Since carrots form the 'red' part of this salad, the name involves a little artistic licence, the reason being that it is traditionally served at the Japanese New Year, when red and white are considered very auspicious colours. Since New Year in Japan is closely associated with the family, the root vegetables in this recipe symbolize that the roots of the family are also deeply set. Substitute ordinary red radish in this recipe if daikon is not available.

1 large daikon or 750 g (1½ lb) radish
225 g (8 oz) carrots
1½ tsp salt
125 ml (4 fl oz) rice vinegar or cider vinegar
2 tbsp caster sugar
2 tsp soy sauce

Peel the daikon or radishes and cut into rectangular blocks. Slice very thinly (this can be done quickly in the food processor, using the slicing attachment) and then cut again into tiny playing card shapes, about 4 x 1 cm (1½ x ½ in). Alternatively, cut into fine matchstick lengths. Peel and slice the carrots in same way.

Place the vegetables in a large bowl and sprinkle with salt. Leave for 20–30 minutes to extract excess moisture. Quite a significant pool of water will gather in the bottom of the bowl. Drain this off, then knead and squeeze the vegetables over the sink to extract more moisture, until the daikon turns translucent.

In a saucepan, heat the vinegar and dissolve the sugar in it. Take off the heat and add the soy sauce. Pour this mixture over the vegetables and mix well. If you happen to have any kombu seaweed, place a few pieces on top for extra flavour.

Leave the salad in the fridge until ready to serve. In an emergency it could be served in 30 minutes but it will not reach its peak of flavour for one or two days. It is served in small individual bowls, and can be garnished either with sesame seeds or with finely shredded lemon or orange rind.

All traditional rules of batter-making are turned upside down by the Japanese dish of tempura. The strands of batter which cling like hoar-frost to a vegetable fried tempura-style are a delight to both eye and palate, yet the method of achieving this effect would have enraged an authority such as Mrs Beeton.

The batter recipe in her *Book of Household Management* is sternly English in tone: flour, eggs, and a little melted butter and cream are to be stirred until smooth, with water added gradually. 'Beat well for 10 minutes,' she commands, then 'put aside for at least half an hour.'

Tempura batter is in direct contradiction to all this: flour and water are scarcely stirred at all, and certainly not until smooth; if there are lumps, that does not matter. Furthermore, Japanese cooks consider the very worst treatment of a tempura batter would be to let it stand for half an hour; it must be mixed immediately before use.

This is a healthy warning against dogmatism in the kitchen for, iron-ically, the basic idea of tempura is derived from the West.

Between 1543 and 1634, Spanish and Portuguese missionaries and traders in Nagasaki introduced battered and deep-fried prawns to the Japanese. The name tempura is derived from the Latin *tempora*, mean-ing 'times'. It is a reference to the *Quattuor Tempora*, the 'four times' of the year on Roman Catholic feast days (Ember Days) when meat was rejected in favour of fish – in this instance, battered prawns. In time, the Japanese developed the dish to include all vegetables and seafood – everything in fact, except poultry and red meat.

Tempura

selection of vegetables and/or seafood (*see below*)
plain flour for coating

DIPPING SAUCE
2–3 cm (1 in) piece of kombu (dried kelp)
1 tbsp katsuo bushi (dried bonito flakes) (optional)
1 tbsp sugar
3 tbsp soy sauce (preferably shoyu – Japanese naturally fermented soy sauce)
2 tbsp mirin (sweetened rice wine)

BATTER (ENOUGH FOR 6 PEOPLE)
oil for deep frying (*see below*)
400 ml (¾ pt) ice cold water
1 egg yolk (optional)
salt (optional)
pinch of baking powder (optional)
180 g (6½ oz) plain white flour

First prepare the vegetables and/or seafood. Choose all or any from the following list of traditional tempura ingredients, or add some of your own: sweet potato, sliced into thin rounds; carrots, sliced into thin sticks; green beans, cut into equal lengths; aubergine, sliced into thin rounds; mange tout, stalk ends removed; red and green peppers, sliced into squares; button mushrooms, whole; spinach leaves, whole; king prawns, shelled and de-veined; squid, cut into squares; fish fillets, cut into thin squares; small whole fish; scallops, whole; mussels, whole.

Now make up the dipping sauce. Prepare some traditional Japanese stock by bringing the kombu to the boil in 250 ml (scant ½ pt) water. Remove the kombu, then add the bonito flakes (if using). Allow to settle, then strain off the stock. Stir in the sugar, soy sauce and mirin (sweetened rice wine).

Heat some oil for deep frying in a pot or wok. Japanese cooks use special mixtures of vegetable oils for tempura, such as 75 per cent peanut oil, 20 per cent sesame oil and 5 per cent olive oil, but ordinary soya bean oil is fine.

Finally, when everything else is ready, mix your batter. Have the measured ice-cold water ready in a large bowl. Into this you may mix egg yolk if you wish. (I usually add some salt and a good pinch of baking powder also, but this is not traditional.) Now sift over the flour. Stir the flour into the water with a chopstick or wooden spoon, with light circular motions. Do not over-mix, and don't worry about the inevitable lumps.

Have a plate of plain flour ready. Using tongs, coat the vegetables or seafood first with flour, then twirl in the batter, and deep fry in the oil, in batches of about 6 pieces at a time.

Fry the pieces about a minute on each side until a light golden colour, and drain on absorbent paper. After each batch, remove particles of batter from the oil with a perforated spoon.

Serve the tempura as soon as possible. Indeed, it is best to set up your kitchen like a Japanese tempura bar, cooking the food in front of your guests and serving it as it comes. In Japan, tempura is a meal in itself, followed by plain steamed rice, Japanese pickles and miso soup.

Malaysia

Malaysia offers any amount of bland comfort food to the visitor, particularly at the sophisticated hotels, all steel and smoked glass, which now punctuate the skyline of the main cities. For the adventurer who wishes to experience the real food of Malaysia, however, it is necessary to walk through the air-conditioned marble lobby, past the smiling bellboys and the Filipino at the grand piano, and into the furnace-like heat of the street.

No more than a minute's walk in any direction you will find the inevitable hawker food stalls. These typify Malaysian culture at its ideal best – a delightful mélange of Malay, Indian and Chinese. The Malay is busy fanning his satay sticks over a little trough of charcoal, the Indian is peeling vegetables for his pasembor, or Indian salad, while from a short distance away comes the distinctive clunk-clunk sound of the Chinaman wok-frying broad, flabby koay teow noodles. Each is looking over his shoulder at the other, and not surprisingly, over the years, the hawkers have borrowed ingredients from one another's cuisine. The Indian noodle seller, for example, uses yellow Hokkien noodles, while the Chinaman, in turn, has adopted the Malay recipe for the spicy fish soup known as laksa. In recent years Thai influences have crept in, and tom yum soup stalls are everywhere.

Everybody eats from these hawker food stalls; it is a national pastime indulged in by everyone from street cleaners to business tycoons. In a society which places so much stress on saving face, it is refreshing to note that it is not considered in the least demeaning for the wealthy to patronize the street stalls. The fact is, as everybody knows, for certain dishes there is nowhere better.

Hawker food is the natural outcome of mass immigration and urbanization, where families can set up small business with very little capital, the parents doing the cooking and the children the serving. Word spreads by mouth, there is no need to advertise. Originally the hawkers balanced their wares in boxes at both ends of a pole slung across their shoulder, setting the load down before a prospective customer. Nowadays the poles and boxes have been superseded by sophisticated three-wheeler carts, propelled by pedals or an in-built motorcycle, protected from the elements by awnings and covered with gleaming stainless steel.

They may also take the form of a small permanent stall set up in a special covered hawker food centre. Rather than herd the hawkers wholesale into these somewhat soulless centres as the Singapore government has done, the Malaysians have struck an ideal compromise: the hawker food sellers are still permitted to ply their trade from carts which come in all shapes and colours, but their standards of hygiene are rigorously scrutinized. In Penang, where the hawker food is perhaps the most famous of all Malaysia, the carts gleam with polished stainless steel, and the hawkers themselves must undergo an annual medical checkup.

Here is a famous Indian hawker dish from Penang. The daikon, or mooli, is a substitute for the Malaysian sweet turnip called bangkuang.

Pasembor (Indian salad)

2 large potatoes, boiled
3 eggs, hard-boiled
1 cake tofu, deep-fried
200 g (7 oz) squid, cooked
300 g (10 oz) beansprouts
1 large cucumber, shredded
1 small daikon, shredded
100 g (4 oz) roast peanuts, crushed
2 tbsp sesame seeds, toasted

PRAWN FRITTERS
150 g (5 oz) self-raising flour
1/2 teaspoon salt
225 g (8 oz) small prawns or shrimps
oil for deep frying

SAUCE
4 tbsp dried tamarind
300 g (10 oz) sweet potato, boiled
2 tbsp dried chillies
10 shallots or 2 medium onions
3 cloves garlic
4 tbsp oil
3 tbsp brown sugar
1/2 teaspoon salt

Soak the tamarind in 750 ml (1½ pt) of boiling water for 15 minutes, massaging to break up the pith. Strain out the juice through a sieve and discard the pith. Either pass the sweet potato through a sieve, or purée in a food processor, with the tamarind juice.

Soak the dried chillies in water for 15 minutes, then grind to a paste with the shallots or onions and garlic. Fry this mixture in the oil, then add the tamarind/flavoured sweet potato, brown sugar and salt. Simmer for 20 minutes on a low heat, stirring occasionally. Cool.

Slice the cooked potatoes, eggs, tofu and squid. Briefly dip the beansprouts in boiling water, then douse in cold water and drain.

To make the prawn fritters, mix the flour into a batter with the salt and 8 teaspoons water. Stir in the prawns or shrimps. Heat some oil in a wok for deep frying, then drop spoonsful of the mixture into the oil and deep fry. Slice the fritters when cooked.

On a large platter, arrange the sliced prawn fritters, the potatoes, eggs, tofu and squid. Sprinkle the beansprouts and the shreds of cucumber and daikon over the top. Ladle over the sauce, then sprinkle with peanuts and sesame seeds.

Morocco

Pleasant as it is, I had always found mint tea rather insipid until I visited Morocco and discovered a superior way of making it.

Once you have been told how, it seems obvious: a handful of fresh mint leaves is added, along with sugar, to a pot of green China tea. The China tea provides the body, the mint the edge. Served piping hot it is ambrosial, I assure you, despite or perhaps particularly in the heat of the Moroccan sun. No wonder tea and sugar are two of North Africa's biggest imports. At home I make this tea with everyday black China tea, with good results.

Sometimes, a Moroccan may add the petals of half a dozen orange blossoms (or a tablespoon of orange blossom water) for extra fragrance.

In Morocco, tea is as much a ritual as it is in England. Apart from a bed, a Moroccan considers the most basic household effect to be a tea service consisting of a tray, teapot and thin tea glasses. These are among the first things a newly married Moroccan woman brings to her husband.

The Moroccan tea tray fits a Middle Eastern model in being a vast richly patterned brass disc on short legs. In a wealthy house the tray may be of copper or even silver, whereas in a poor home it is more likely to be of wood. Often, a family will paint a wooden tray, covering it with geometric patterns. Such is the devotion to tea that teapots are often taken on journeys, and you will often see them aboard Moroccan trains, wrapped carefully in a cloth bundle.

My first experience of Moroccan tea was at a café in Tangier. A great branch of mint had been rammed into a stained and rather grubby tumbler, but the waiter preserved great dignity, pouring green tea from a great height into our cups. Every so often, a newcomer would be greeted in the traditional manner – by an embrace with a kissing motion over the left shoulder. Many of the men were carrying packages of fruit, vegetables or meat, for in Morocco it is the men who do the domestic shopping, women being discouraged from appearing in public.

It was also at this café that I first enjoyed this rather famous Moroccan carrot salad:

Schlada Dsjada

While this is officially a salad, it has so much delicious juice that it is best served separately in small bowls, with a spoon.

12 medium carrots, cut into rounds
5 cloves garlic
few sprigs of parsley
½ red pepper
1 tsp ground cumin
½ tsp chilli powder
4 tbsp oil (preferably olive oil)
125 ml (4 fl oz) lemon juice

Boil the carrots in 600 ml (1 pt) water until barely cooked – the carrots should still be slightly crunchy. Allow them to cool in their own liquid.

Pulverize the garlic, either by chopping and mashing with the side of a knife, crushing with a pestle and mortar or in a food processor (have the machine running as you drop them in). Do the same with the parsley and red pepper. Add the cumin and chilli powder.

Place this paste in a small saucepan with the oil and heat. Add 250 ml (scant ½ pt) of the liquid from the carrots and bring to the boil. Add this to the carrots and their juice along with the lemon juice. Serve cold.

Since the spice and lemon juice preserve the carrot to some extent, this salad will keep up to a week in the refrigerator.

SERVES 6.

This more traditional salad is flavoured with harissa, the pungent spice mixture popular throughout the Middle East (see p. 232).

Spicy Moroccan Salad

½ small cauliflower, broken into florets
2 medium potatoes
1 carrot, cut into matchsticks
8 radishes, quartered

DRESSING
1 tsp harissa
½ tsp ground cumin
5 tbsp olive oil
juice and grated rind of 1 lemon
2 tbsp chopped parsley
1 tbsp chopped fresh coriander

Steam the cauliflower florets for 5 minutes. Boil or steam the potatoes and cut into cubes. Put into a large bowl with the carrot and radishes.

Mix together the dressing ingredients and toss the vegetables in it until well coated.

Pakistan

One of my most vivid memories of food in Pakistan is of a mountain of meat: of butchers' shops in the bazaars with earth floors and antique hanging scales, and bits of beast strung up everywhere on hooks, the exposed ends painted bright purple with preservative; of eating houses with cooks squatting out the front over troughs of smoking charcoal, turning shish kebabs of beef, lamb and chicken; and of customers seated on carpets spread with white sheets, before gigantic platters of biryani, a spicy rice dish with yet more meat. Then there was the wedding feast I happened to chance upon at the hotel I stayed at in Lahore, where guests were being served slices from vast boneless joints of spicy marinated roast beef.

This, of course, is a reflection of Pakistan's Muslim heritage, dating from the eighth century, when invaders from Arabia swept to the area, bringing a style of cooking which eventually developed into a synthesis of Middle Eastern and Central Asian. Pork was forbidden but meat of every other kind was eaten in abundance – beef, lamb, goat, chicken, deer, peacock, duck, partridge. There is a Pakistani saying, 'You cannot be a good Muslim unless you eat meat and plenty of it.'

To the south of Pakistan, however, is a largely vegetarian region known as the Sindh. Amazingly enough, the Sindhi people have remained staunchly Hindu despite twelve centuries of Muslim rule: in the eighth century, the Caliph of Baghdad sent an army who defeated the Rajput rulers, who in turn were defeated by another group of Muslims, the Moghuls. The latter ruled until the arrival of the British.

Naturally, the pilaus, biryanis and exotic mutton dishes of the Moghul Empire have influenced the cooking of the Sindh, as has that of the neighbouring Punjab. However, for all that, there exist a number of distinctively Sindhi dishes which have remained unchanged through the centuries. Among these is an original way with pea flour, a product which should be part of every busy cook's repertoire since it yields the flavour of split peas, chickpeas or lentils without all that lengthy soaking and cooking.

The Sindhis mix pea flour with spices, knead it with water and turn it into gianthia – a sort of pasta which is then either boiled or fried, and served with a vegetable curry.

Gianthia and Spinach Curry

250 g (9 oz) pea flour (preferably chickpea flour,
   but ordinary pea flour will do)
1 tbsp oil
1–4 green chillies (according to taste), finely chopped
1 tbsp chopped fresh root ginger
1 tbsp cumin seeds
$\frac{1}{2}$ tsp salt
1 onion, finely chopped
2 tbsp butter
500 g (1 lb) spinach, thoroughly washed and finely sliced
375 g (13 oz) tin chopped tomatoes in tomato juice
1 tbsp ground coriander seeds
$\frac{1}{2}$ tsp ground turmeric
1 tbsp chopped fresh root ginger
3 cloves garlic, chopped

In a large bowl, place the flour, oil, chillies, ginger, cumin seeds and salt. Add just enough water (about 4 tablespoons) and mix into a stiff dough. Roll out into a thin sheet, about 3 mm ($\frac{1}{8}$ in) thick. Cut into strips, then into 2–3 cm (1 in) squares.

Bring a large pot of salted water to the boil, then drop in the gianthias and boil for 20 minutes.

Meanwhile, fry the chopped onion in butter in a large pot or wok until light brown. Add the spinach, tomatoes and the juice, coriander seeds and turmeric.

Stir until the spinach is cooked, adding the cooked gianthias near the end, along with the ginger and garlic. Serve with rice.

SERVES 3–4.

Thailand

Thai cuisine challenges all our conventional notions of a salad. For a start, a Thai salad very often includes meat, tofu or seafood where we would expect only vegetables. A Thai dressing can also transform what traditionally in the West has been a rather bland affair into a riot of flavours, simultaneously cool, pungent and fiery.

All the great salads of Thailand can be tasted at wayside stalls, some of which are solely given over to a particular dish. One of these is the som tam stall, where a delicious sweet-sour green papaya salad is freshly made to order. Som tam literally translates as 'pounded and sour', which aptly describes the salad, as the ingredients are bruised with a pestle and mortar.

The papaya used is very under-ripe indeed – white, in fact. Papayas fruit all year round and are so prolific throughout South-East Asia that people can easily tire of their bland, sweet flavour. Thus, the papaya is often cooked green as a vegetable or used raw in salads.

Som Tam (green papaya, carrot and tomato salad)

1 small, unripe papaya
100 g (4 oz) green beans
1 large carrot, grated
2 tomatoes, sliced
2 tbsp roast peanuts, lightly crushed

DRESSING
2 cloves garlic
2 tbsp dried shrimps
$\frac{1}{2}$ small fresh red chilli or $\frac{1}{2}$ tsp chilli sauce
1 shallot or half a small onion
3 tbsp lime or lemon juice
1 tbsp brown sugar (or palm sugar)
1 tbsp Thai fish sauce

Peel, halve and remove the seeds from the papaya. Grate the flesh, either in a food processor or by hand, making the shreds as long as possible. (If the papaya is too ripe for this, cut it into small cubes.)

Steam the beans and cut into bite-sized pieces. Place with the grated carrot in a large bowl and gently pound with a pestle, just enough to bruise them. They certainly should not be turned into a mush!

Now make the dressing. With a metal blade in the food processor drop in the garlic, followed by the dried shrimps. Grind to a powder, then add the fresh chilli or chilli sauce, shallot or onion, lime or lemon juice, brown sugar and Thai fish sauce. Alternatively, pulverize all these dressing ingredients with a pestle and mortar.

Arrange the papaya, beans, carrot and tomatoes on a plate, then spoon over the dressing. Sprinkle the roast peanuts over the top.

Serve this with:

Laab Gai Chiang Mai (Thai chicken salad with mint and coriander)

2 chicken legs (thighs and drumsticks)
2 stalks lemon grass, sliced
2 tbsp fish sauce
2 tbsp lime or lemon juice
salt
4 tbsp finely sliced fresh mint leaves
1 tbsp finely sliced fresh coriander leaves
2–3 whole mint leaves
2 tbsp roasted rice (optional, see below)

Strip off and discard the fat and skin from the chicken legs. Cut away the meat from the bones and set aside. Place the bones in a saucepan and barely cover with water. Cover and boil to make a small amount of stock while you prepare the remaining ingredients.

With a metal blade fitted to a food processor, pulverize the lemon grass. Add the chicken meat and continue to process until it forms a ball of minced meat.

Remove the chicken bones from the pan and reduce the stock over a high heat until you are left with only about 3 tablespoons in the bottom. Now add the minced chicken meat and lemon grass, along with the fish sauce and lime or lemon juice. Simmer for only about 5 minutes, stirring and breaking up the chicken meat with a wooden spoon, until the meat has just cooked through and is still moist. Add salt to taste.

Allow the meat to cool, then stir in the chopped mint and coriander leaves. Serve in a bowl, and garnish with the whole mint leaves.

A more convenient, though unorthodox, way of making the salad is simply to chop leftover cooked chicken and add the remaining ingredients.

To make this salad completely authentic, you should add 2 tablespoons roasted rice. This is sold at Thai markets, and is nothing more than rice which has been dry toasted to a golden colour, then ground. I have not seen it for sale in the West, although it can be made at home if you have a food processor – and a little spare time.

Widely available nowadays are fresh coriander and the translucent Thai fish sauce which make it possible to create a delicious Thai variation of gado-gado (*see* pp. 169–70). Thai peanut sauce is heavier in both citrus and sugar, and strongly scented with fresh coriander, a herb which Indonesians loathe as much as the Thais love.

Yam Yai (grand salad Thai-style)

1 large cucumber
6 lettuce leaves
4 medium tomatoes, cut into wedges
1 head broccoli
1 onion, finely sliced into rings
100 g (4 oz) tofu
any left-over cooked meat or seafood, cut into bite-sized pieces
4 eggs, hard-boiled
1 small red pepper, cut into strips
green tops of spring onions (optional)
fresh red chillies (optional)

PEANUT SAUCE
4 cloves garlic
1/2 bunch fresh coriander (leaves, stems, roots and all)
200 g (7 oz) roasted peanuts
125 ml (4 fl oz) lemon juice
3 tbsp sugar
1 tsp salt
2 tbsp Thai fish sauce

Peel the cucumber, but leave on a few strips of green for colour, and slice thinly. Arrange the lettuce leaves around the edge of a platter. In the centre, place the tomato wedges and cucumber slices.

Blanch the broccoli until bright green, then cut into florets. Add these, along with the onion rings, tofu and cooked meat or seafood, to the platter. Arrange the eggs on top.

Into a running food processor, drop the cloves of garlic, one by one. Now add the coriander, peanuts, lemon juice, sugar, salt and fish sauce, together with 125 ml (4 fl oz) water. Blend at top speed to a smooth paste.

Dribble the dressing over the salad in a zig-zag pattern, then arrange the slices of red pepper over the top. For a truly decorative Thai effect, decorate with green tops of spring onions and fresh red chillies, both of which have been cut in several places from the top almost to the base, and then left in iced water to allow the 'petals' to curl out.

Turkey

Sitting round a table comparing notes with a group of Western travellers in an Istanbul hotel, it seemed everybody had a good word for the Turks and their hospitality. I have asked directions and been led through the streets personally; have been showered with little gifts of food and cigarettes aboard buses and in restaurants; I have had my beers and teas paid for, and within an hour of meeting one couple, was offered the free use of their holiday home. Perhaps the greatest honour of all, however, was being invited into a family home.

I was greeted at the door in true Turkish fashion with a handshake and a kiss on both cheeks from each of the family. When dinner was announced, I was ushered into the dining room, where a giant table had been laid out for a sumptuous Turkish feast.

To begin we had a lentil soup known as mercimek corbasi. Red lentils had been boiled with onion and stock and then passed through a Turkish kitchen utensil resembling a colander with extra fine holes. It was served at room temperature with a pepper grinder and a bottle of lemon juice passed around the table.

For the main course we had whole grilled fish, two per person, and each had a different type, one tasting like very rich mullet and the other rather like trout. They were fresh that day from the Bosphorus, the narrow sea passage which runs through Istanbul and separates Europe from Asia, and had so much flavour of their own that they needed no further embellishment than the fresh parsley which was served with it, along with lemon wedges and whole fresh green chillies. There were juicy, fresh carrots, grated with a little lemon juice and placed in a bowl alongside two other salads, one a fairly standard combination of lettuce, tomatoes, cucumber and spring onions, and the other a real masterpiece of Turkish culinary art.

Kirmizi Pancar (beetroot, garlic and yoghurt salad)

4–5 uncooked beetroot
2 tbsp olive oil
375 ml (13 fl oz) plain yoghurt
5–6 cloves garlic
salt to taste
lettuce leaves, lemon wedges, olives to garnish

Wash the beetroot and cut in half. If you are in a hurry, cut in quarters. Boil uncovered until the beetroot are tender when tested with a skewer. Remove them and save the cooking water. Peel the skins off the beetroot with a sharp knife, then grate on the large holes of the grater.

Stir the olive oil into the yoghurt. Crush the garlic with some salt and stir this into the yoghurt along with the grated beetroot.

Measure out two tumblers of the beetroot cooking liquid and boil until reduced to 125 ml (4 fl oz) or less. It should be a deep cherry colour. Allow to cool.

Just before serving, stir this into the yoghurt and beetroot mixture, doing so gradually to avoid curdling the yoghurt. The dish will turn such a bright shocking pink that you may have difficulty persuading your friends or family that the colouring is entirely natural!

Break up pieces of lettuce, coil them into cone shapes, and press the pointed end down into the mixture. Sprinkle over 4–5 black or green olives and arrange some lemon halves around the sides.

Note: I am sure you could easily substitute finely chopped tinned beetroot (in brine not in vinegar) and get the same effect. Use a little of the juice for colouring.

SERVES 6.

Perhaps I would have refused the third helping of this dish had I known what was still to come, for following the main course were traditional spinach pastries known as ispanak borek. These consisted of paper-thin sheets of yufka, the Turkish equivalent of filo pastry, which had been filled with spinach and rolled up, then coiled into the shape of a snail's shell and baked in the oven (*see* p. 20). They were served with pieces of beyaz peynir (literally 'white cheese'), very similar to Greek feta cheese.

In the Sultanahmet district of Istanbul, within the shadow of the magnificent Blue Mosque and just around the corner from the crowded noisy bazaar, lie a group of cafés known as the pudding shops. In the halcyon days before the Russians invaded Afghanistan and the Ayatollah Khomeini or General Zia were even heard of, these were the gathering places for the many young Westerners making the overland trip to India.

One lunchtime I was sitting in one of these pudding shops enjoying a meal of shish kebab, beans and a superb cold aubergine dish flavoured with olive oil, tomatoes, garlic and pine nuts. In walked a gigantic barrel-chested Turk and sat down in front of me. He had a bull neck, or rather, no neck, since it seemed to merge in with his cone-shaped head, the effect being accentuated by a short-back-and-sides and a crew cut on top. His enormous walrus moustache spread in a dead-straight line right across both cheeks, like a pair of well bristled hearth brushes. He was, in short, the classic Hollywood image of the Cruel Turk, except for his good-natured belly-guffaws as he joshed with the man behind the counter. This he alternated with a rather comic shaking of his shoulders in time with some wailing belly dancer-style music which was blaring from a nearby speaker.

Eventually he introduced himself in remarkably fluent English as Mohammed, and I asked the name of the delicious aubergine dish I was eating.

'Ah,' he said, 'that is a very famous Turkish dish – Imam Bayildi – the Priest Fainted. There is a story that once there lived here in Istanbul an imam [Muslim priest] who was very greedy both for food and money.

'One day he surprised everybody by announcing his marriage to the daughter of a humble oil merchant. But soon it became known about the town that the girl was a very good cook, and that as part of her wedding dowry her father would give the imam twelve pots of his best olive oil – very big pots,' he said, gesticulating with his hairy arms the outlines of a jar which Ali Baba or one of his forty thieves could have hidden in.

At this point his tea arrived in one of those curious Turkish tea glasses barely twice the size of a liqueur glass, along with several sugar cubes. These he broke into pieces and began placing with surgical precision into the gaps between his yellowed teeth. With great noise and obvious relish he slurped in the strong black tea through his teeth, before continuing:

'On the first day of their marriage the bride cooked a delicious aubergine dish, rich in oil, which the imam loved so much that every day for twelve days the same dish was put before him. On the thirteenth day, however, the aubergine dish did not appear, and the imam became very angry. When he asked his wife for an explanation, she began weeping and told him she had used up all twelve pots of olive oil. Hearing this, and realizing both the cost of the dish and its richness, the priest fainted!'

I have since discovered that there are other versions of this story. Some have it that the imam fainted because he was overcome by the wondrous perfection of the dish, others that he passed out through sheer overeating. Besides my Turkish friend's romantic tale, however, these versions seem rather prosaic. I know which I prefer to believe.

Imam Bayildi

This is a marvellous dish for late summer, for while it can be eaten hot, it is at its best when cooled (but not refrigerated).

2 large unskinned aubergines
6 medium tomatoes
6 tbsp olive oil
2 large onions, diced
4–5 cloves garlic, crushed
2–3 tbsp toasted pine nuts (optional)
2–3 chopped black olives (optional)
chopped parsley to garnish

If the aubergines seem old (and therefore in danger of being bitter), slice each in half lengthways and sprinkle liberally with salt. Leave for 15 minutes, then wipe off the beads of moisture.

Blanch the halved aubergines for 6–8 minutes in boiling water. Briefly blanch the tomatoes in the water used to boil the aubergines, then remove, peel and chop.

Scoop out the flesh from the aubergines and chop. Spread 2 tablespoons of the olive oil over the shells inside and out, place them in a baking dish and bake in a moderate oven for 20 minutes.

Meanwhile, fry the onions in the rest of the olive oil until soft but not brown. Add the crushed garlic, chopped tomato and aubergine flesh and fry for about 15 minutes over a low to moderate heat, uncovered, stirring from time to time to avoid sticking.

Just before the mixture is ready, add the pine nuts and olives (if you are using them) and heat them through. Remove the shells from the oven and pile high with the mixture. Sprinkle with chopped parsley and leave to cool.

Rice, Noodles and Pancakes

India

In Iran it is known as polo, in Pakistan pollau, in India pilau, in Turkey pilav, in Spain paella and in Italy risotto. But whatever you choose to call this delicious rice dish, the basic principle is the same: you cook rice in a rich stock and then mix through chopped meat and vegetables, perhaps also spices, nuts and dried fruit.

The similarity between the names is no coincidence, for all the Oriental versions, at least, can be traced to one source – the cooking of the Sassinad Persians in the tenth and eleventh centuries, who, along with poetry and miniature painting, took the cooking of rice to new heights of refinement.

Polo followed the spread of the rice plant from east to west into Turkey and the Arab world, and it is very tempting to assume that risotto and paella are legacies of the Arab conquests of southern Italy and Spain. It is true that both paella and risotto are made from round-grain rather than long-grain rice, that both are turned first in hot olive oil and that both are served wetter than an Eastern pilaf, but these are merely details; a basic Arab influence is not difficult to discern.

When the Moghuls from Persia invaded northern India and set up their imperial court there in the sixteenth century, the dish reached its apex. In Persia the use of spices had been largely confined to cinnamon and allspice, but suddenly India's rich array was available. Sensualists that they were, the Moghuls would have their rooms filled with the fragrance of saffron before a pilau was served. Well into this century, at princely wedding feasts in the fabulously wealthy state of Hyderabad, spicy spit-roasted sheep would be stuffed with pilaus in which entire chickens and eggs were buried.

On the southern coasts, pilaus were made from prawns and fish, while the Christians of Goa introduced that abomination of the Prophet, pork. The most delicious pilau of all comes from the devoutly Hindu vegetarian state of Gujarat, where dal and mixed vegetables are combined with a technique rare in India but common throughout South-East Asia, that of finishing the cooking of the rice in coconut cream.

Gujarati Vegetable Pilau

Basmati is regarded as the ideal rice for these festive Indian pilaus, but if, like me, you balk at paying a 400 per cent premium for it, you may like to experiment with Thai scented rice at half the price.

120 g (4½ oz) moong dal (split and skinned mung beans) or red lentils
500 g (1 lb) long-grain rice
1 tsp salt
4 cloves garlic
walnut-sized piece of fresh root ginger
1–4 fresh chillies (according to size and taste)
small bunch of fresh coriander leaves
500 g (1 lb) mixed seasonal vegetables, such as cauliflower, carrots, peas,
    potatoes, French beans, mushrooms, aubergine
3 tbsp ghee
1 tsp ground turmeric
1 tbsp garam masala
3 tbsp grated fresh coconut or dried coconut threads
    (or desiccated coconut)
400 ml (¾ pt) coconut cream
juice of 1 lemon or lime
150 g (5 oz) cashew nuts, fried

GARNISH (OPTIONAL)
strips of tomato
thin rings of fried onion

Soak the moong dal for one hour, then simmer until tender. If using red lentils instead, put them in a bowl with water to just cover them, and microwave them on medium power for 10 minutes.

Rinse the rice in a sieve under the cold tap. Transfer to a large heavy pot (with heatproof handles), barely cover it with water, add salt and cover tightly. Bring to the boil and simmer for about 8 minutes, until two-thirds cooked. Allow to stand off the heat, with the lid still tightly on.

Turn on a food processor and drop in the cloves of garlic one by one, followed in quick succession by the ginger, chillies and coriander leaves. Alternatively, crush them in a mortar and pestle.

Prepare the vegetables: cauliflower should be broken into tiny florets, carrots sliced into tiny sticks, French beans and mushrooms finely sliced, and aubergine diced small.

Heat the ghee in a pan, add the turmeric and vegetables (except peas if using frozen), and stir fry for 5 minutes. Add garam masala in the final minute. Remove from the heat and mix in frozen peas (if using), coconut, and the garlicky spice paste.

Mix the vegetables and the cooked mung beans or lentils through the rice and then stir in the coconut cream mixed with the lime or lemon juice. Cover the rice pot tightly and bake in a preheated oven at 180°C/350°F/Gas Mark 4 until the rice is cooked and has absorbed the coconut cream.

Before serving, sprinkle over the cashew nuts (these can also be cooked for 5 minutes in the microwave on medium power, with a little butter to coat them), and garnish if you wish with the tomato and onion.

Kedgeree is a prime example of how, with old age and distant travel, one recipe can eventually transmute into another. For, aside from the rice, this delightful Anglo-Indian jumble of smoked fish, rice and chopped eggs bears no relation to its parent Hindu recipe of the same, or similar name.

'Kitcheri', as it is commonly understood in Indian cookery, means a combination of dal and rice boiled together with spices such as cardamom, cloves, coriander, ginger and chillies.

When the British arrived in India in the seventeenth century, they adopted kitcheri as a breakfast dish, only, being the inveterate flesh-eaters they were, substituted the dal with flakes of fresh fish. In their defence, it does have to be said that, in the south at least, it was just as well to eat a freshly caught fish for breakfast, for without refrigeration the Indian heat would turn it bad within a day. At some time, the British dropped the spices and added hard-boiled eggs and eventually the word 'kitcheri' (which was from the Sanskrit *k'ysara*), was Anglicized into kedgeree.

During the eigtheenth century the recipe reached Britain and underwent another change. Smoked fish replaced the fresh, as kedgeree's rise to popularity happened to coincide with the appearance in the markets of Edinburgh and eventually London, of smoked haddock from the little Scottish port of Findon, of Finnan. To define just what constitutes the true kedgeree is a good way to provoke an argument, but at the risk of fraying the tempers of retired Indian army colonels, might I suggest its three essential ingredients are rice, smoked fish and hard-boiled eggs. Most people I think would also agree on onions, butter and chopped parsley.

Kedgeree

350 g (12 oz) smoked fish fillets (e.g. haddock, mackerel, ling, hake)
oil
1 large onion, chopped
175 g (6 oz) long-grain rice
2 eggs
1 tbsp butter
salt and pepper
2 tbsp parsley, chopped

Cover the fish with boiling water and simmer over a low heat without boiling for 10 minutes. Save the water.

Heat a little oil over the bottom of a heavy saucepan and fry the chopped onion until transparent, then add the rice and stir until it is lightly glazed. Either add 600 ml (1 pt) of the fish water and cook until it is absorbed by the rice, or boil the rice in plenty of water, drain and then rinse with hot tap water.

Meanwhile, hard-boil the eggs (allow 10 minutes) and flake the fish. Chop or slice the hard-boiled egg and mix into the hot rice with the fish, butter and salt and pepper to taste. Arrange in a pyramid-shaped pile and sprinkle the parsley over the top.

SERVES 3–4.

And that, according to the purists, should be all. But, as with all recipes, the golden rule about making a kedgeree is that there are no golden rules. You may, for instance, wish to enrich the above mixture with a raw egg and 150 ml ($^{1}/_{4}$ pt) cream. Beat these lightly together and mix into the kedgeree over the heat for about 90 seconds at the end of cooking, until the mixture is creamy. If the kedgeree is to be kept on a hot plate, this is especially recommended to prevent it drying out.

Curry powder appears in some recipes and this would appear logical in view of the place of its origin. Use up to a teaspoon for the above recipe, and add at the same time as the rice. This is recommended if you are using fresh or leftover fish rather than smoked fish.

Indonesia

Given that Bali has always been one big paddy field, it seems incredible that at one time rice was so expensive there that the common people could only afford to eat it mixed with very much cheaper corn and sweet potatoes. Then about twenty-five years ago the Indonesian government introduced a new strain of rice which can be harvested four times a year, as against twice for the traditional Balinese variety. The result is that rice is now a fraction of its former price and the practice of mixing it with corn and sweet potatoes is so out of fashion that these days it is almost back again as a novelty dish for the younger generation.

The trouble is, however, that this new 'miracle' strain of rice can only be grown with the aid of massive amounts of fertilizers and pesticides. These have killed off the tiny eels and other little fish which used to live in the rice paddy fields and at one time were integral to the peasant farmers' diet. Even more alarming is that the chemicals have also decimated a useful insect which used to inhabit the rice plants, attacking another insect, which now runs rife eating the sap in the roots of the plants and, surprise, surprise, itself now has to be kept in check with massive doses of a new insecticide. As one rather embittered Balinese pointed out to me, all these chemicals must be imported into Bali from Java, a situation which is doubtless considered very politically satisfactory by the Javan-dominated government in Jakarta. In fairness, however, it must be said that the Indonesian government is now attempting to clean up the mess, conducting research into what sort of chemicals are needed and how much. Regulations controlling their use have now finally been introduced.

From the gourmet's point of view, the sad thing is that this improved strain of rice is bland and tasteless, and is not a patch on the fragrantly perfumed old Balinese variety. Traditional Balinese rice is still grown in certain parts of Bali, but is now many times more expensive.

Another curiosity of rice in Bali is their roundabout way of cooking it: first it is soaked, then steamed, then steeped in its hot cooking water, and then steamed a second time. Finally, the rice is carefully spooned into another container to disperse any residual steam. This laborious process, which takes over an hour, certainly produces good fluffy rice with separate grains, but frankly the result is no better than from the good old absorption method.

While we are on the subject, let me dispel a myth I see perpetuated time and again in cookery books, which suggests using two parts water to one of rice. This is completely wrong, as there is far too much water, resulting in an excess by the time the rice is cooked, and hence the dreaded sticky goo. Use only 1½ times as much water as rice, bring to the boil and keep at a low boil, tightly covered, for 12 minutes or until the water is absorbed and the rice cooked.

Another cooking method is required for 'yellow rice', a festival dish eaten all over Indonesia to celebrate weddings and the birth of children. In Hindu Bali it is eaten on Banyu Pinaruh, the second day of a festival which honours Saraswati, goddess of the arts and scholarship.

Nasi Kuning (yellow rice)

500 g (1 lb) long-grain rice
400 ml (¾ pt) coconut cream
1 tsp ground turmeric
pinch of salt
2 whole cloves
3 curry leaves

Soak the rice in water for an hour. Transfer it to a colander and wash and drain it, then place in a saucepan with the coconut cream, turmeric, salt, cloves and curry leaves (in Indonesia, a daun salam leaf would be used). Bring to the boil and simmer, covered, for 5–6 minutes until all the coconut cream has been absorbed by the rice.

Stir, and then transfer to a collapsible steamer basket or Chinese steamer and steam for a further 20 minutes. (If you do not possess a steamer, place the lid on the pot tightly and leave on the lowest heat for another 10 minutes.)

In Bali this is eaten with green beans cooked with coconut cream, chilli, palm sugar and shrimp paste. The main thing is to avoid very strongly flavoured accompaniments as the coconut flavour of the rice is quite subtle.

Iran

There is something pleasantly addictive about rice; the more you eat it, the more you appreciate subtle differences between the varieties.

For most of us, rice means the long-grain type, cheap and perfectly serviceable, satisfying our demand for a rice which cooks into separate grains, pristine, white and individually self-contained. Of the long-grain varieties, the undisputed king is Indian basmati. Anybody who has drawn in the gorgeous nutty aroma from a bowl of steaming basmati will know that. The distinctive flavour is said to improve with keeping and basmati is wonderfully forgiving. Even at the hands of the worst cook, it turns out loose and fluffy every time. Much basmati is grown in Pakistan and in Bihar state in northern India ('Patna basmati'), but the best is from Dehra Dun in Uttar Pradesh, north India.

Considerably cheaper than basmati, and almost as tasty, is Thai fragrant rice. Sold also as jasmine rice, and incorrectly as Thai basmati, it, too, is becoming easier to obtain.

Either basmati or Thai fragrant rice is best for the following pilaf, as the spicing is confined to the meatballs, allowing you to savour the delicacy of the rice. But any long-grain variety would suffice.

Persian Pilaf with Carrots and Meatballs

500 g (1 lb) lamb or beef, minced
1 medium onion, finely chopped
½ tsp salt
1 tsp ground cinnamon
1 tsp paprika
6 tbsp butter
4 medium carrots, peeled and diced
1 tbsp sugar

In a bowl, mix the minced meat with the onion, salt, cinnamon and paprika. Roll into small balls about the size of a walnut. Melt half the butter and fry the meatballs for 10 minutes, until nearly cooked.

In another pot, melt the rest of the butter and add the carrots and sugar. Cover with a lid, and allow the carrots to simmer gently, stirring occasionally while you fry the meatballs.

Meanwhile, cook the rice. When the rice is done, spread half of it in a casserole dish. Arrange the meatballs over the rice in a single layer, and cover with the rest of the rice. Top the dish with the cooked carrots. Heat the dish through in the oven or microwave.

SERVES 3–4.

Risotto with Mushrooms

500 g (1 lb) mushrooms, sliced
4 tbsp butter
3 cloves garlic, crushed
750 g (1½ lb) arborio or ordinary short-grain rice
2 x 375 g (13 oz) tins chopped tomatoes in tomato juice
100 g (4 oz) parmesan cheese, finely grated

STOCK
1 kg (2¼ lb) beef bones
500 g (1 lb) cheap stewing steak, cut into pieces
2 onions, quartered
2 sticks celery
3 bay leaves
3 carrots

Put the ingredients for the stock into a large pot and cover with water. Simmer for 3–4 hours, partly covered. Strain off the liquid (there should be 600–900 ml or 1–1½ pt) – you can feed the meat to your pets.

Fry the mushrooms in the butter in a large pan or wok for 6–7 minutes, until they begin to exude liquid. Add the garlic to the mushrooms, take out of pan and set the mixture aside.

In the same pan or wok, tip in the rice and add 500 ml (scant 1 pt) of the stock and the contents of one of the tins of tomatoes. Stand at the stove and stir until the liquid is absorbed. Keep adding the stock by the cupful, and then the other tin of tomatoes. About 5 minutes before the end of cooking, add the mushrooms and heat through.

It is hard to say how long a risotto needs, but begin testing after 20–25 minutes. Take it off the heat when the grains are just firm in the centre.

Before serving, stir in the parmesan cheese, and at the table offer more parmesan to sprinkle over the top.

SERVES 4–6.

One of crowning glories of the Persian kitchen is the cooking of lamb. Marinated in yoghurt, skewered as kebabs or mixed with rice, dried fruit, nuts and spices, it reflects an ancient, highly sophisticated cuisine noted for its refined fusion of flavours.

Some of the sweetest, most succulent lamb to be found in Iran comes from the fat-tailed breed of sheep. The curious fan-shaped tail of this sheep, which can account for as much as a sixth of its body weight, was first reported by the Greek historian Herodotus (c. 485–425 BC), but for many centuries he was disbelieved. It is a perfectly genuine breed, as I can attest. There are some whose tails are so heavy they have to be supported on little carts with wheels. Like the hump of the camel, this tail is considered a prize part of the beast, and it yields a rich source of cooking fat.

The quality of this sheep is judged by the fatness of tail. At market places in Iran I have watched men feeling the tails, pushing them up gently, kneading them and weighing them in their hands. The story is told of a young boy who asked his father why he was doing this.

'So that I can decide which sheep to buy,' came the reply.

That evening, when the father returned home, the son said: 'The neighbour was over here today, father. I think he wants to buy mother!'

Lamb and Apricot Polo

When rice is mixed with other ingredients in Iran it is known as polo, a close relative of the Turkish pilav and the Indian pilau. The slight tang of apricot seems to have a special affinity for lamb.

500 g (1 lb) long-grain rice
salt and pepper
600–700 g (1¼–1½ lb) lamb leg steaks or chops
100 g (4 oz) butter
2 medium onions, finely diced
pinch of saffron (optional)
¾ tsp cinnamon
200 g (7 oz) dried apricots, cut in half
50 g (2 oz) seedless raisins

Wash the rice until the water runs clear. Place the washed rice in a large bowl, cover with plenty of water mixed with 2 tbsp salt. Leave for at least 2 hours, preferably overnight.

Trim all the fat and bone from the lamb. You should be left with only about 500 g (1 lb) of lean meat. Dice into cubes.

Melt half the butter in a pan and sauté the onions until they begin to turn a golden colour, then add the lamb and sauté for several minutes longer. If you are using saffron, grind it with a mortar and pestle and pour a table-spoon or so of boiling water over it. Stir well, and add to the pan, along with the cinnamon and salt and pepper to taste. Add water to just cover, then put on the lid and leave to simmer until tender. The traditional recipes call for around 1½ hours cooking, but this leaves the meat too dry for my liking and I prefer to cook it for only half that time – 45 minutes or so. Add apricots and raisins 10 minutes before the end of the cooking time.

When the lamb has almost cooked, bring 1.5 litres (2½ pt) of water to the boil. Drain the rice and dribble it slowly into the boiling water. Cover and boil briskly for 5 minutes, then drain.

Melt the remaining butter in the bottom of a heavy pan. Spread over a layer of rice, then cover this with the lamb mixture. (If there still seems to be plenty of sauce with the lamb, boil briskly with the lid off to reduce.) Spread the rest of the rice over the meat, then stretch a folded cloth across the top of the saucepan and jam it in place with the lid, making sure the edges do not hang down too close to the heat. The idea of this is to absorb the steam and thus cause the grains of rice to separate. Leave over a very low heat for 20–25 minutes.

To serve, spoon out the rice and meat mixture and pile on a platter. A golden brown crust of rice should have formed on the bottom of the pot. This is known as *tah dig*, and is considered a special part of the dish, offered first to guests. Lift it out with a fish slice, break it or cut into pieces, and arrange around the sides of the platter.

SERVES 4–6.

Malaysia

Situated at the two extremes of the bay of Bengal with favourable trade winds between, India and Malaysia have profoundly influenced each other's cuisines. As far back as the fourth century, Indian traders were active in the Kedah province of northern Malaysia. An intermarriage of food and ideas began, which was greatly accelerated in the nineteenth century when huge numbers of Tamil workers were brought from southern India to work the British plantations – first sugar and coffee, and then rubber during the boom of 1907 to 1928.

Today, Indians comprise 10 per cent of Malaysia's population, the largest Indian community overseas. They are still largely clustered around the former rubber-planting areas in the west of the Malay Peninsula, and particularly in the cities of Penang, Ipoh and Kuala Lumpur.

To walk around the markets of Jalan Masjid India, the hub of Kuala Lumpur's Gujarati Muslim community, is to be momentarily transported back to India. The scent of jasmine garlands being strung up around a flower stall mingles with the spicy aroma of vadas and pakora being deep fried next door. An old man fires up a mobile tandoori oven on wheels, while his daughter prepares nan bread and her husband, dressed in a longhi, bags up take-away plastic bags of wet curry. One stall advertises five different kinds of 'tosai', which is nothing more than dosai – the lacy South Indian pancake.

But wait – what is jackfruit doing in that curry? And what is authentically Indian about those bunches of petai – native Malaysian jungle beans? An Indian cook in Malaysia routinely adds the lemon grass and galangal to his curries, while into the very Moghul biryani goes Chinese star anise and the scented leaves of the Malaysian pandan (screwpine). The abundance of coconuts in tropical Malaysia has also meant that the rice for the biryani is enriched with coconut cream:

Nasi Biryani

Nasi here is simply the Malay word of rice.

10 cashew nuts
10 almonds
2 cloves garlic
5 cm (2 in) piece of fresh root ginger
1–2 fresh chillies

1 tbsp black poppy seeds
4 tbsp ghee or butter
1 large onion (in season, use shallots), finely sliced
5 cloves
3 whole star anise
1 cinnamon stick
1 kg (2¼ lb) chicken pieces
2 tsp ground turmeric
2 tsp salt
125 ml (4 fl oz) plain yoghurt
600 g (1¼ lb) long-grain rice
400 ml (¾ pt) coconut cream

In a food processor, liquidizer or with a mortar and pestle, grind together the cashew nuts, almonds, garlic, ginger, chillies and poppy seeds.

Heat the ghee or butter and fry the onions, along with the cloves, star anise and cinnamon stick, until the onions are transparent.

Add the chicken pieces, turmeric, the ground ingredients and 1 teaspoon of salt. Mix well, then cover the pot and cook for 10 minutes on a low heat, stirring intermittently. At the end of cooking, add the yoghurt.

Meanwhile, wash the rice in a sieve under a running tap, to extract the starch – it is done when the water runs clear under the sieve. Place in a large pot with the coconut cream, 375 ml (⅔ pt) of water and 1 teaspoon of salt. Cover tightly, bring to the boil, and cook on a medium low heat for about 10 minutes.

When all the liquid has been absorbed, make a well in the centre of the rice, and add the spicy chicken and yoghurt mixture. Cover well, and place in an oven preheated to 180°C/350°F/Gas Mark 4 for 15 minutes.

Very gently mix the rice and chicken together and serve on a large platter.

Singapore

Cajoled and herded at every move by a paternalistic government, the citizens of Singapore may at first appear compliant and lacking individuality. Any outsider who characterizes them as passionless, however, has failed to appreciate their almost fanatical love affair with food.

Wherever a group of Singaporeans gather, food is never far away. Either they are eating it, discussing it, or arguing about it – sometimes all at once. On virtually every street in Singapore, you will see a coffee shop, a restaurant, or a food centre with orderly lines of hawkers, who, since the earliest days, have fed an immigrant population too busy to cook for themselves.

These immigrants all stem from the cultures with hugely famous cuisines of there own – Chinese, Indian and Malay. Mix them together in one city and you have the makings of one continuous banquet, which now been formalized into the annual Singapore Food Festival.

At the inaugural festival in 1994, Singapore's multi-ethnic culinary culture was highlighted in month-long local street celebrations, which travelled each weekend from one ethnic area to the next, featuring music, contests, demonstrations and food stalls. Indian, Malay and the Chinese–Malay food mix known as Nonya or Peranakan were all honoured.

First up was the Chinese Weekend, held in the heart of Chinatown. A row of stalls selling trinkets led to the main arena, where chefs sweated over charcoal braziers, twirling rods packed with glazed chicken wings, frying up Singapore chicken rice, ladling out bowls of soupy laksa, and selling cups of 'bird's nest drink'.

Highlight of the day was the successful attempt to create Singapore's (and surely the world's) longest spring roll. Known as popiah, this is a lighter variation on the better known deep-fried spring roll, where the diner chooses from a wide array of ingredients, rolling them up in a fresh crêpe-like wrapper.

For this record-breaking popiah, 320 such wrappers were overlapped along a table that stretched over 53 m (175 ft). A team of chefs, coordinated by a head chef who ran back and forth bawling into a loud hailer, spread the wrappers with one ingredient after another, beginning with 1.5 kg (3 lb) of chilli paste and 2.5 kg (5½ lb) of crushed garlic until, two hours later, a solid tube of ingredients lay ready for a 99-strong team of volunteers to come forward and roll it, with much cheering and clapping, into the record popiah, authenticated on the spot by a surveyor from Singapore's Ministry of Law.

Popiah

The list of ingredients needed for making your own popiahs at home may seem equally record-breaking, but bear in mind that the dish is largely an exercise in shopping, chopping and assembly.

The only tricky part is making the popiah skins. At the small Singapore cookhouses which manufacture these crêpes, the professionals somehow manage to get the simple flour and water paste into the consistency of a ball of gluey dough, which they smear ever so lightly over a dry hot plate. We mere mortals can get by with a looser pancake mixture using eggs, which are a standard variation on the recipe.

POPIAH SKINS
5 eggs
375 ml (⅔ pt) cold water
½ tsp salt
2 tbsp oil, plus a little for frying
100 g (4 oz) plain white flour

GARNISHES
2 eggs
salt and pepper
10 cloves garlic, left whole
oil for frying
20 shallots, sliced
225 g (8 oz) tofu, finely sliced
2 handfuls of beansprouts, blanched
½ cucumber, cut into matchsticks
1 sprig fresh coriander leaves, chopped
leaves from 1 lettuce
125 ml (4 fl oz) hoisin sauce
3 tbsp chilli sauce
3 tbsp plum sauce (optional)
3 tbsp crushed fermented black beans

FILLING
300 g (10 oz) prawns
10 green beans, shredded
300 g (10 oz) lean pork
2 tbsp oil
2 tbsp soy sauce
400 g (14 oz) sweet potato, peeled and cut into matchsticks
½ tsp salt
400 g (14 oz) tinned bamboo shoots, cut into matchsticks

First, make the popiah skins. Beat the eggs and water together with a whisk or beater, but do not allow the mixture to become frothy. Add the salt, 2 tablespoons of oil and the flour and beat until smooth. Allow to rest for 30 minutes.

Smear a frying pan (preferably non-stick) with an oil-soaked paper towel, then ladle in just enough batter to make a very thin coating, swirling it around in the pan to spread it out further.

Cook over a low heat until the underside is cooked but still pale and the edges begin to curl. Turn over and cook on the other side for a few seconds only – the popiah skins should not be allowed to brown. Stack in a pile as they are cooked, and after you have finished, wrap in kitchen film to prevent them drying out.

Makes about 25 popiah wrappers.

Now prepare the garnishes.

Lightly beat the eggs with a little salt and pepper, and make three very thin omelettes. Roll them up and shred finely.

Fry the garlic cloves in 2 tablespoons of oil until light brown, then transfer to a small dish.

Fry the shallots in 2 tablespoons oil until brown and crisp. Remove and drain on absorbent paper, then place in a small bowl.

Deep fry the tofu, then drain and place in a small bowl.

Set out the rest of the vegetables and sauces in separate small bowls.

To make the filling, first lightly steam the prawns, beans and pork.

Shred the partly cooked pork and fry until cooked, then add the soy sauce, shredded sweet potato and salt. Continue cooking until the sweet potato is soft, then add the prawns, beans and bamboo shoots.

Transfer the filling while still warm into a serving bowl, and arrange, along with all the garnishes in their little bowls, around the stack of popiah wrappers.

To assemble, have your guests smear some chilli, hoisin and/or plum sauce over a popiah skin. Follow this with the filling and any of the garnishes which take their fancy.

To roll, fold over one edge, fold in both sides and roll up into a roll. Once assembled, they should be eaten immediately, otherwise the filling will begin to turn the popiah soggy.

Thailand

The noodle man is one of the great street sights of Thailand. By the time his rickety box-shaped cart mounted on three bicycle wheels comes into view along the leafy suburban lane, you will have already heard his call: the ring of a bicycle bell, the tap of a spoon against a bowl, or simply the cry of 'Gueyteow! Gueyteow!' (noodles! noodles!).

In no time the inhabitants of the houses come scurrying forth, crowd around and exchange gossip while the noodle man lifts a bunch of fresh noodles high in the air, plunges them into a pot of boiling water for a few seconds, then places them in a bowl with a ladle of broth, some pieces of chicken or pork, or a couple of squirts from the sauce bottle, and finally, a topping of the customer's choice: crushed peanuts, perhaps a dish of sugar and chilli vinegar.

This is brunch. For while rice may be at the centre of any Thai meal, noodles are the great snack food.

There are three main types of noodles used in Thai cuisine – rice, soya bean and egg. The latter – ba mee – are 'nests' of dried Chinese-style thin egg noodles.

Chiang Mai Noodles

Originating from Chiang Mai in the north of Thailand, this soup-stew shows a strong Burmese influence.

300 g (10 oz) fresh thin egg noodles
 or 200 g (7 oz) dried egg noodles or Italian-style vermicelli
oil for frying
1 large onion, finely sliced
4 large cloves garlic, finely sliced
1½ tsp Thai red curry paste
250 ml (9 fl oz) coconut cream
500 ml (scant 1 pt) stock
300 g (10 oz) chicken or pork, minced
3 tbsp Thai fish sauce
2 tsp mild curry powder
½ tsp ground turmeric
1 tsp brown sugar
juice of 1 lemon

Cook the noodles in plenty of boiling water.

Heat 1 tablespoon of oil in a wok and fry the onion until brown. Remove with a slotted spoon, add another tablespoon of oil and fry the garlic slices until these too are brown. Remove and set aside.

Heat 4 teaspoons of oil in the wok and fry the red curry paste for 30 seconds, then pour in the coconut cream and stock. Add the chicken or pork and cook for several minutes.

Add the Thai fish sauce, curry powder, turmeric, brown sugar and lemon juice, stirring between each addition.

Pour this over the noodles in a large bowl and serve immediately with the garnish of onions and garlic floating on top.

In Thailand, this dish is generally offered with little bowls of equal quantities of fish sauce and lemon juice, and chilli flakes marinated in warmed vinegar.

Thai Fried Rice

500 g (1 lb) long-grain rice
3 tbsp oil
salt
3 tbsp dried shrimps (optional)
1 large onion, diced very finely
3 cloves garlic, chopped
meat from 2 chicken legs or 300 g (10 oz) of any
    other cooked meat, cut into strips
1 red pepper, finely diced (optional)
1 tomato, finely diced (optional)
6 spring onions, chopped (optional)
5 tbsp tomato sauce
1 tsp brown sugar
3 tbsp Thai fish sauce (optional)
2 eggs, lightly beaten
4 tbsp chopped fresh coriander (optional)
1 small cucumber, finely sliced

Put the rice in a sieve and wash out the excess starch under running cold water, massaging the grains until the water runs milky and then clear. Place in a saucepan with 1 tablespoon of the oil, toss to coat each grain, then add a little salt and 750 ml (scant 1½ pt) hot water. Cover tightly, bring to the boil, lower the heat, and simmer for about 10 minutes until the water is absorbed and the rice is cooked.

Soak the dried shrimps (if using) for 5 minutes in hot water.

Sauté the onion and garlic in a wok with 1 tablespoon of oil, until the onion is transparent and slightly browned.

Add the sliced meat and your selection of vegetables, tomato sauce, brown sugar and fish sauce (if using), and sauté for 1 minute. Add the cooked rice and sauté over a high heat for 2 minutes longer.

Push the rice mixture over to one side of the wok, add the remaining oil, and pour in the eggs. Scramble-fry them until cooked, then work them through the body of the dish.

Serve sprinkled, if you wish, with coriander and garnish with the cucumber slices.

Sambals, Sauces, Spice
Mixtures and Chutneys

India

Cardamom is one of those rare, truly exotic spices whose perfume always recalls for me the mysterious essence of the east. A native of southern India and Sri Lanka, it still grows wild in the steaming jungles of those regions. Often it is to be found on the sides of steep ravines, under the shelter of overhanging trees (the same conditions, incidentally, which are favoured by snakes).

The plant is related to ginger, but the flavour of cardamom is vastly different and is better likened to a mixture of lemon and eucalyptus. Curiously, the pods appear not on the main stem of the plant, which can grow to 6 m (20 ft) high, but appear on shoots which sprawl out separately from the root.

Nowadays cardamom is grown in plantations both in India and in central America, often in relatively small jungle clearings with surrounding trees providing cover. Harvesting cardamom is an arduous task. Because the pods must be kept intact, they are carefully hand-cut with scissors. Another problem is that the pods ripen over a long period and must be collected every few weeks. The pods are then either sun dried to a light green colour, or placed over heated sulphur fumes and slowly bleached (supposedly to appeal to the Western market).

Such involved harvesting and preparation explains why cardamom is among the world's most expensive spices. Fortunately, however, a little goes a long way, provided that the seeds are bought still in their pods and crushed just before use (this is easily done as they are fairly soft). Ready ground cardamom should be avoided since it quickly loses its essential oils.

It is sometimes claimed that cardamom was grown in the royal gardens of Babylon before 700BC, but if that were true then the plant would have been well outside its natural habitat. Certainly the Arabs acquired a taste for cardamom very early, as it was brought back from west coast Indian ports on trading dhows. The Bedouin method of making coffee includes dropping a cardamom seed into each cup, or cramming a few bruised pods into the spout of the coffee pot, which adds just the right amount of scent to the coffee as it pours past. In the West, the earliest users of cardamom were the Greeks and Romans, who obtained it from Arab traders and used it mainly as a perfume.

In the Middle Ages the seeds of a closely related plant (*Aframomum melagueta*) from West Africa were mixed with ginger and cinnamon to flavour a wine known as hippocras (from Hippocrates, the father of Western medicine). Was this in fact the drink John Keats had in mind when he referred instead to Hippocrene (a mythical fountain of water) in his 'Ode to a Nightingale'?:

> O for a beaker full of the warm South!
> Full of the true, the blushful Hippocrene,
> With beaded bubbles winking at the brim,
> And purple-stainèd mouth,
> That I might drink, and leave the world unseen.

Certain European peoples make great use of cardamom, the Swedes in particular. It is the main flavouring in the coffee cake aptly named Kardemummakaka, and is found in many Scandinavian pastries. About a quarter of India's output is exported to Sweden. In German cooking, cardamom appears in such classic dishes as sauerbraten and pickled herring, and it also has a small place in French cuisine.

Nowhere, however, has the use of cardamom attained such culinary heights as in India. The Indians distinguish between bari ilaychi, which are big cardamoms with a strong and slightly bitter flavour used only in cooking, and choti ilaychi, a smaller sweeter cardamom which is sometimes sucked and chewed slowly as a breath freshener. The latter variety are also mixed with betel nuts and leaves as a *paan* and sold scented and covered with thin edible silver foil.

Cardamom appears in virtually every recipe for garam masala, those ready-made mixtures of spices (forerunners of that Anglo-Indian concoction, curry powder) used in dal, meat and vegetable dishes. Here is just one combination, particularly rich in cardamom:

Garam Masala

4 tbsp cardamom pods
2 sticks cinnamon, each 8 cm (3 in) long
4 tsp cumin seed
4 tsp black peppercorns
4 tsp whole cloves
1 nutmeg, grated

Spread the cardamom, cinnamon, cumin, peppercorns and cloves in a flat pan and roast in a low (110°C/225°F/Gas Mark 1/4) oven for about 30 minutes, stirring several times. Do not allow the spices to brown.

Break up the cinnamon sticks, open the cardamom pods and place these in a blender with peppercorns, cumin seed and cloves. Grind to a powder at full speed. Add the nutmeg and place the mixture in an airtight jar. This will retain its flavour for about six months.

If you make your own Christmas presents, why not consider giving small jars of home-made garam masala?

This recipe, which I picked up in Kashmir, is a very typical use of cardamom and garam masala in Indian cooking. The potatoes should be very small, little bigger than a walnut. Slice them in half if they are larger.

Alu Dum (new potatoes steamed with yoghurt and spices)

1 kg (2¼ lb) baby new potatoes
1 tbsp oil
seeds of 3 cardamom pods, crushed
2–3 cm (1 in) piece of cinnamon stick, ground (or ½ tsp ready ground)
2 whole cloves, ground (or a pinch of ready ground)
½ tsp cumin, ground
1½ tsp garam masala
¼ tsp cayenne pepper (optional)
½ tsp ground turmeric
1 large onion, roughly chopped
walnut-sized piece of fresh root ginger, roughly chopped
4 cloves garlic, roughly chopped
1 tsp salt
juice of 1 lemon
300 ml (½ pt) plain yoghurt
3 tbsp water

Scrub the potatoes, but do not peel. Boil for 10 minutes in salted water, drain, and then prick each deeply all over with a fork (or use a toothpick for a neater effect).

Heat the oil in a pan and fry the cardamom, cinnamon, cloves, cumin, garam masala and cayenne pepper (if using) for 2 minutes. Add the turmeric and set aside.

Place the onion, ginger and garlic in a blender with the salt and lemon juice and purée to a pulp. (If you have no blender, grate or pound these ingredients.)

Add this pulp to the spices in the pan and fry until they are coated in oil and begin to smell cooked. Stir in the yoghurt and water, then add the potatoes and spoon some of the sauce over them.

Cover the pan with a tightly fitting lid (if it doesn't fit snugly, spread a sheet of aluminium foil over the pot and crimp the edges down the sides before putting on the lid. Cook over a low heat for 20 minutes (this the *dum* or steaming process) then let stand off the heat for a further 5–10 minutes.

Turn the potatoes out on to a heated serving dish and spoon the sauce over the top.
SERVES 6.

After parboiling the potatoes, you could peel them, prick them, and then deep fry for 2 minutes until golden brown. Drain on absorbent paper and then proceed as above.

A distinctive feature of the cooking of Bengal and neighbouring Orissa and Bangladesh is a five-spice mixture known as panch phoron. It combines three well-known spices – cumin, fennel and fenugreek – with mustard seed (replaced in more traditional recipes by a tiny aromatic seed known as radhuni) and kalonji. This is the tiny, black, teardrop-shaped seed of nigella, often mistakenly called onion seed.

Ready-made panch phoron mixtures are sometimes available, but you can of course make up your own, leaving out the kalonji if necessary. Panch phoron can be ground, but more often the seeds are left whole. While most Bengalis mix the spices in equal proportions there are no hard and fast rules. Therefore, if, like me, you are not especially partial to the rather bitter taste of fenugreek, you may like to cut down on the proportion used, as I suggest in this recipe.

Masoor Dal, Bengali Style

300 g (10 oz) red lentils, rinsed if necessary
$\frac{1}{2}$ tsp ground turmeric
1 tsp salt
2 small fresh green chillies, finely chopped
5 tbsp clarified butter
2 medium onions, finely chopped
1 tbsp grated fresh root ginger
3 large tomatoes, finely chopped
4 bay leaves
2 small dried red chillies, chopped
2 cloves garlic, chopped

PANCH PHORON
1 tsp cumin seeds
1 tsp fennel seeds
1 tsp black mustard seeds
$\frac{1}{4}$ tsp fenugreek seeds
1 tsp kalonji (if available)

Put the lentils in a pot with 1.25 litres ($2\frac{1}{4}$ pt) of water, the turmeric, salt and green chillies. Bring to the boil, lower the heat and simmer for 25 minutes, stirring occasionally, until the lentils are reduced to a purée.

Meanwhile, heat 3 tablespoons of the clarified butter over a medium high heat and sauté the onions until golden brown. Add the ginger and tomatoes. Continue to cook, stirring frequently, for about 5 minutes or until the tomatoes have reduced a little, then transfer them to the dal about 10 minutes before the end of cooking.

Just before the dal is ready, heat the rest of the clarified butter and add the panch phoron spices. Cover the pan, and when the black mustard seeds begin spluttering and popping, add the bay leaves dried chillies and garlic. Continue frying for another 30 seconds or so, until the chillies and garlic begin to brown. Stir into the dal and serve.

Since Bengal has produced India's most articulate writers, some of its most stimulating theatre and certainly India's best films, it seems natural that the region should also excel in the culinary arts. A Bengali is likely to be only half joking when he tells you that there are only four great cuisines in the world – French, Chinese, Italian and . . . Bengali!

A great Bengali passion is fish. There is such abundance around the Bay of Bengal that the Bengalis can afford to be choosy. The saltwater varieties, they claim, are tasteless in comparison with the sweet, succulent freshwater varieties caught in the vast Ganges estuary – perch, mullet, prawns, lobsters.

One variety of fish is prized above all. When I was last in Calcutta I was sitting on the veranda of the charming old Raj-era Fairlawn Hotel when the proprietor appeared and announced with obvious pride that hilsa was to be served for lunch.

Hilsa, he explained, was Bengal's finest fish and eagerly sought after. It appears for only a short period toward the end of winter when it begins its migration up the Ganges to spawn.

At lunch the fish duly arrived on a platter. It was served with great ceremony by the Fairlawn's waiters, decked out in turbans, white uniforms, brass buttons, cummerbunds and white gloves. The flavour was delicious – very rich and oily, something of a cross between a salmon and a herring. It had been fried the Bengali way, in mustard oil. This is not as fiery as it sounds, as mustard oil loses its sharpness with heating and actually turns sweet, although it is a completely different story when the fish is fried in a paste of ground mustard seeds, another Bengali favourite.

Considering the number of exotic cultures the British came into contact with in the process of carving out the largest empire in history, it is amazing how little their cooking changed. Not for the British the cultural pastiche which today distinguishes such colourful cuisines as the Creole cooking of New Orleans.

There was, however, one foreign cuisine which managed to wade a path through the mounds of Yorkshire pudding, boiled cabbage and

Watney's best bitter – that of India, the jewel in the imperial crown. The tandoori houses to be found on every High Street in Britain today are just the latest chapter in a love affair with Indian food which began three hundred years ago.

It was kindled by the chutneys and pickles which began to reach England in the late seventeenth century, via the ships of the East India Company. These spicy concoctions, which would keep in jars for months or even years thanks to the preserving qualities of salt, sugar, vinegar and oil, proved the perfect answer to their problem of finding foods that would stand up to long sea voyages and relieve the monotony of diet for both passengers and crew. Introduced back home, they became so popular that in no time at all cooks were busy turning out imitations which substituted apples for mangoes, vinegar for tamarind juice and cane sugar for palm sugar. Some ingredients, such as sultanas, owed nothing to the Indian tradition at all.

Like the chilli pepper, the tomato was introduced to India from its homeland in South America, probably by the Portuguese. Exactly when is unclear, although by 1810 we find the tomato listed in Williamson's *East India Vade Mecum* as being used in India.

The plant grew best in the hills, but was cultivated all over India. Colonel Kenney-Herbert reported in his *Culinary Jottings for Madras* (1878) that they were easily grown in the Madras Presidency and were often available during the hot weather when the stock of garden produce had sunk to its lowest state.

Interestingly, the tomato was initially eaten only by the British. As late as 1889 the botanist George Watt noted that while Indians, particularly Bengalis and Burmese, were beginning to appreciate the fruit, 'the plant is still chiefly cultivated for the European population'. This tends to indicate that the hundreds of tomato-based chutneys, rasams, sambars, dals, bondas, pitlas, bhats, bhurthas, foogaths and vadis of modern Indian cuisine are, at best, only of nineteenth-century origin.

Green Tomato Chutney

The quantities in this recipe are quite large, but then, the whole process is going to take hours anyway, so you may as well make it worth your while. The fact that green tomatoes have little flavour is not important; their function is merely as a bland vehicle for all those pungent spices. Jars of home-made chutney make excellent gifts.

4 kg (9 lb) green tomatoes
1 kg (2¼ lb) onions, sliced
1 kg (2¼ lb) apples, peeled, cored and chopped

1.2 litres (2 pt) white vinegar
1 kg (2¼ lb) sugar
400 g (14 oz) sultanas
4 tsp salt
2 tsp mustard
1 tsp cayenne pepper
3 tsp grated fresh root ginger
2 tsp allspice
8 cloves garlic

Place the tomatoes in one huge or two smaller pots and cover with water. Bring to the boil, then turn the heat down to low and simmer for 10 minutes. Drain off the water and peel the skins off the tomatoes. Slice the tomatoes into quarters.

Return the tomatoes to the pot along with the onions and apples. Add half the vinegar. Bring to the boil and simmer, partly covered, for an hour until the ingredients are soft, stirring from time to time to prevent the mixture catching.

Now add the remaining vinegar along with the rest of the ingredients. Boil uncovered for another 15 minutes or so, until the mixture has reduced but is still runny; remember that the mixture will firm up after it cools.

Wash 12–18 jars of various sizes and then fill each with boiling water, in order to sterilize them. Empty after a few minutes.

Fill the jars with the mixture while it is still hot, and cover with transparent jam covers.

Even today, such Anglo-Indian chutneys remain one of the greatest culinary legacies of the Raj, as the vast number of commercial brands will attest.

These long-life varieties are by no means the complete story, however, for there is also a whole galaxy of Indian chutneys made freshly each day. These are scarcely known outside India but in some ways are even more exciting than the stored chutneys because of their complexity of flavour.

A base of cucumbers, coconuts and other raw fruit and vegetables keeps them cool and refreshing, yet at the same time they have a pungency which can only come from freshly chopped garlic, ginger, coriander leaf or whatever. Even dried seed spices contain volatile oils which evaporate from a chutney within hours of being crushed. In northern India there is a whole tribe based around yoghurt (or rather dahi, or curds, which when fresh have none of the sharp, sour edge of our yoghurt), known collectively as raitas.

Quite apart from gastronomic considerations, these fresh chutneys are better for you as there is no need to use large amounts of salt, sugar and oil to preserve them.

This next recipe I encountered one lunchtime at the Royal Bombay Yacht Club, a genuine relic of the Raj, whose elegant Victorian Gothic headquarters look out over the Gateway to India in Bombay harbour. Until 1948 the club excluded all Indians, even if they were maharajas, but nowadays of course, the membership is almost wholly Indian.

The menu has changed accordingly, even if the food is still served at tables festooned with Edwardian silver candelabras. This delicious mint and coconut chutney accompanied a masala dal and rice, with poppadoms and a dish of mildly spiced bhendi, or ladies' fingers (otherwise known as okra). It does pay to plan mild dishes and plenty of plain rice to accompany these chutneys, as they would clash with a really incendiary south Indian curry, such as nellora mutton curry from Andhra Pradesh, but would also murder the delicacy of fish.

On the same tray as the chutney were quarters of fresh limes and raw Bombay onions, small pink shallots which are sweetly delicious and free of the usual biting acrid sting.

Fresh Coconut and Mint Chutney

I have adapted this and the following recipes to the food processor – in India fresh chutneys are ground in a vast circular mortar with an oversized stone pestle, while coconut is grated with a special implement.

flesh from 1/2 fresh coconut (see pp. 39–40)
walnut-sized piece of fresh root ginger, finely chopped
2 cloves garlic, finely chopped
2 fresh green chillies, finely chopped
3 tbsp lemon juice
large handful of mint leaves
handful of fresh coriander leaves
1 tsp salt

With a sharp kitchen knife, pare the brown inner rind from the coconut and chop the white flesh into smaller pieces (this is to ease the strain on your food processor, particularly if it is under-powered or geriatric). Place in your food processor and grind to a fine paste. Remove and set aside.

Drop the ginger, garlic and chillies into the food processor with the motor going. Turn off the machine and add 4 tbsp water, the lemon juice, mint leaves, coriander leaves and salt. Turn on the machine and grind these to a paste. Now add the ground coconut and blend it in. More water can be added for a creamier consistency.

Fresh Mango Chutney

1 mango, not over-ripe
1 tbsp finely chopped fresh root ginger
1 tbsp fresh coconut, cut into fine slivers
salt
pinch of chilli powder
1 tbsp chopped fresh coriander leaves

Peel the mango with a sharp knife. Now get rid of the stone: lay the mango flat on a board and bring the knife towards you, cutting as close as possible to the broad flat stone in the centre of the fruit. Turn the mango over and repeat the process. Trim off any remaining flesh.

Cut the flesh into cubes and place in a bowl with the ginger and coconut. Sprinkle over a little salt and chilli powder, and stir well. Finally, sprinkle with the coriander leaves.

This chutney comes from the southern state of Andhra Pradesh. The Brahman lady from whom I managed to wheedle the recipe implied I was wasting my time as the main ingredient, a special sour cucumber called dosakai, grows only in that state and would not be available to me when I got home. However, I have since experimented with a regular long cucumber and it works fine.

Dosakai Chutney

1 tbsp oil
1/2 tsp black mustard seeds
1/4 tsp fenugreek seeds
pinch of asafoetida (optional)
1 large dried red chilli, chopped
1/2 cucumber
1 tbsp dried tamarind (cleaned of seed and pith)
1 tbsp finely chopped fresh coriander leaves

Heat the oil in a small frying pan and add the mustard seeds. When they begin to pop and splutter, add the fenugreek seeds, asafoetida (if using) and chilli. Fry briefly.

Transfer to either an electric coffee mill and grind, or grind in a mortar and pestle. Clean the cucumber but do not peel it. Cut it lengthwise, and with a spoon, scrape out the seeds and put them on one side. Chop the flesh roughly and place in a food processor along with the ground spices, tamarind and coriander leaves. Process to a smooth purée and then add the reserved cucumber seeds.

Indonesia

With tearful eyes and numbed mouth, I once watched in awe as the father of a Turkish family casually munched through a whole platter of fresh green chillies, a caustic titbit of which had just blasted me into orbit.

Appetites for chilli are very personal indeed. To anybody cooking for a group of people, this poses quite a problem, but Indonesians have an excellent answer, for while their main dishes are rarely fiery hot, they are invariably accompanied by a small side dish of fresh chilli chutney known as a sambal. The diners then take as much or as little heat with their meal as they wish. To serve an Indonesian meal without sambal would be like serving the roast beef of Old England without a pot of mustard, and Indonesians travelling abroad have been known to take a jar of sambal with them.

Naturally, sambals can be a trap for young players, as can be seen from the following story.

At the close of a successful spice deal, some early Dutch traders in the Indonesian port of Bantam were being entertained in style by the sultan of the region. As dish after dish was being handed around, the Dutch ship's captain noticed that one in particular was being served in a tiny bowl, and furthermore that only minute portions were being taken from it. It must surely, he thought, contain the most exotic and expensive ingredients imaginable.

'Be sure to get a good helping of that one,' he whispered greedily to the first mate, who duly did so. Since the dish was a sambal, the consequences can be imagined.

'Why are you crying?' asked the captain, as the first mate sat spluttering and gasping, with tears streaming down his bearded cheeks. Livid with fury that the captain's gluttony had caused his discomfort, the first mate decided to take his revenge. 'I was just thinking about that seaman we lost overboard near the Cape of Good Hope. He would have loved to be here. But have some of this dish. It is of the most extraordinary sweet taste.'

The captain did so, and when tears appeared in his eyes, the mate enquired: 'May I ask why you are crying too, Captain?'

'Because I'm only damned sorry you didn't fall overboard with that sailor,' came the glowering reply.

While the basic ingredients for sambal are readily available in the West, the instrument for making them unfortunately is not so easy to come by. Known as a ulekan, it is a variation on our Western mortar and pestle, consisting of a flat, solid saucer and a pestle which is bent over at the end. Rather than pound the ingredients, the cook uses a rocking motion with both hands, which I have found to be far more effective for mashing ingredients like chillies and garlic. Of course, an ordinary mortar and pestle can be used instead, and for large batches, a blender or food processor could be brought into action too.

Sambal Ulek

Named after the ulekan, this is the most basic sambal. Here is the recipe I learned in Bali; in Java no shallots are used, nor are the ingredients fried first.

2 cloves garlic
3 shallots or ½ medium onion
2 tbsp coconut oil
4–5 fresh red chillies (each about 2–3 cm or 1 in long)
1 tomato, cut in quarters
1 tsp palm or brown sugar
1 tsp salt

Fry the garlic and shallots or onion in the coconut oil for 10–12 seconds only. Remove and fry the chillies, again for only 10–12 seconds. Now fry the tomato 20–30 seconds, until the skin softens and wrinkles slightly. Pound these ingredients to a paste with the sugar and salt.

This and other sambals are not only served with rice, but are also very nice spread on a prawn cracker. In Indonesia they enliven plain vegetables such as kangkung (a type of spinach), carrots, cabbage, or daun mancok – literally the 'saucer leaf'. Sambals also go wonderfully with Indian food, and indeed were quickly adopted by the Bengalis after British traders introduced them several centuries ago.

The recipe overleaf was taught to me by a young Javanese girl, which is an indication of its simplicity. We were using very mild chillies, each about 10 cm (4 in) in length, from the neighbouring island of Lombok (whose name itself means chilli pepper in Indonesian).

Sambal Terasi

5 large red chillies, sliced
4 shallots, sliced
1 clove garlic, sliced
2 tsp salt
$\frac{3}{4}$ tsp palm or brown sugar
1 tsp terasi (preserved shrimp paste)
juice of $\frac{1}{4}$ lemon

Place the chillies on a ulekan or in a mortar, along with the shallots and gar-lic. Add the salt and sugar and grind to a paste. When it is almost done, add the terasi and lemon juice. There will still be bits of chilli skin in the finished product.

Japan

Soy sauce has been around in the West for so long now that we have ceased to regard it as especially exotic. Even the English, who have never been noted for their adventurousness in food matters, have been using it for over 300 years, and it has always been an ingredient of Worcestershire sauce, surely the most English of all English bottled sauces. I doubt if there are many corner shops nowadays which do not stock it in some form or other.

I say 'one form or other' for, as connoisseurs of the substance will have noticed, the quality of soy sauce can vary very greatly indeed. Some of the so-called soy sauce sold to us today is barely worthy of the name, as it is a synthetic product, made from hydrolysed vegetable protein (defatted soya bean meal) which is treated with acid rather than allowed to ferment naturally, and then bolstered with caramel colouring, corn syrup, salt, monosodium glutamate and preservatives.

At the other end of the scale is shoyu, the Japanese version of soy sauce, which is generally regarded as the finest of them all. The exquisite full-bodied flavour which sets shoyu apart from other soy sauces is a result of it having undergone anything up to three years' natural fermentation.

Soy sauce is thought to have been brought from China to Japan by a Buddhist priest about AD 500, although commercial production in Japan began only in the seventh century, after an edict from a devoutly Buddhist emperor banned the use of meat. The mild, damp Japanese climate was well suited to the growth of bacteria necessary for fermentation, not only of shoyu but also of two other famous Japanese products – sake and miso (a paste made from soya beans and rice or other grains).

By the beginning of the eighth century there were some ten different forerunners of modern shoyu, all of them considerably cruder than today's product but nevertheless used more as a table condiment than in the kitchen. Only about the middle of the fourteenth century, after a long process of trial and error, was an approximation of the modern sauce developed and named shoyu.

The first Portuguese missionaries who arrived in Japan in the mid-sixteenth century ignored shoyu, along with most other Japanese delicacies. St Francis Xavier proclaimed, like the true Jesuit he was: 'God has granted us a grace by leading us to a country where we cannot indulge in luxuries.'

The Dutch traders who followed a century later did notice it, however, and despite the shoguns' ban on international trade, managed to export shoyu from Nagasaki, then a relatively open port for European and Chinese traders. It was shipped to Ceylon and India, and from there to Europe, a rare and precious commodity which began to appear as the 'secret flavour' in opulent dishes of Louis XIV's court.

Only in the nineteenth century did the Japanese perfect the manufacturing process which, apart from a few modern refinements (for example, stainless steel vats, mechanized stirring, and controlled culture of bacteria) has not changed since.

The soya beans are soaked for a few hours and then steamed, to soften them. Wheat is toasted and then cracked, and the two basic ingredients are now subjected to moulds (mainly *Aspergillus*) which break down the protein into amino acids, thus doing part of our stomach's digesting for us.

The wheat and soy beans are then mixed together and a heavy brine solution is added. (The salt content of finished soy sauce is extraordinarily high – about 18 per cent – but it never tastes that salty because of the mollifying effect of the amino acids.)

The resulting syrupy mash is then left to ferment for one to three years, during which amino acids and sugars increase. At the same time, yeast multiplies and turns these sugars into aroma-giving alcohols. Bacteria such as lactobacilli also propagate and produce organic acids, which become the main components of flavour. The aroma of shoyu results from compounds formed by these organic acids and the alcohol.

Finally, the mash is pressed, the oil removed, and the resulting raw shoyu heated, both to kill the now unwanted micro-organisms and to improve colour and flavour.

Just as Zen Buddhism recognizes five spiritual roots (faith, energy, memory, meditation and wisdom), Japanese cuisine emphasizes five methods of food preparation (raw, boiled, grilled, fried and steamed), five colours (green, yellow, red, white and black) and five flavours (salt, sugar, vinegar, hot spices, and – in its own class – shoyu).

Shoyu is used in some form in virtually all Japanese cooking – in grilled or boiled fish dishes, in boiling or pickling vegetables, as a base for soup in which noodles are sometimes dipped, and very importantly, as a base for sauces used for marinating, dipping and grilling various foods. For the latter, a thicker, darker soy sauce known as tamari is often used.

An especially delicious and versatile sauce is teriyaki.

Teriyaki

4 tbsp shoyu or soy sauce
3 tbsp rice wine or dry sherry
1 tsp sugar or honey
walnut-sized piece of fresh root ginger, grated
2 cloves garlic, crushed
1 tbsp sesame or vegetable oil (optional)

Mix all ingredients well.

To make Chicken Teriyaki, cut up a chicken into eight pieces, prick them all over with a fork, and marinate them, turning occasionally. While a Japanese cook would leave it for only 30–40 minutes, my undoubtedly unsubtle Western palate requires that it be left for as long as 24 hours. Barbecue or grill the chicken, and baste with the marinade during the final half of cooking. Reduce the sauce in a pan and brush over the chicken at the end.

Other meat can be treated in the same way. Slice beef thinly or cut into cubes – excellent for shish kebabs. Simmer pork spare ribs in water for about 20 minutes, drain, and marinate them in the teriyaki sauce for 3 hours. Grill for 5 minutes per side. It also goes with lamb (which is not traditionally eaten by the Japanese).

For fish teriyaki, use steaks or fillets from an oily fish such as mackerel. Marinate for about 20 minutes, then grill for about 5 minutes per side, basting with the marinade near the end of cooking. Glaze the cooked fish with reduced marinade.

I have also used teriyaki sauce for tofu, and have concocted a rather nice dish by marinating cubes of aubergine in the sauce, and then simmering them in it until almost cooked. Finally, I finish off the dish under the grill to crisp up the aubergine cubes a little.

Middle East

Almost every Eastern country seems to have its favourite spice mixture. In China it is the anise-dominated Five Spices, in Japan it is the chilli and sesame scented sishimi-togarashi, in Malaysia the fabled Seven Seas Spice, in Yemen zhug, while in India, the entire cuisine is centred on masalas which we in the West grind up and package as curry powder.

Right across North Africa, from Libya and Tunisia through Algeria to Morocco, the clear favourite is harissa, a fiery mixture based on chilli, with the addition of caraway, cumin, coriander and garlic. Apart from the chilli, which is an import from South America, it is easy to see why this particular mixture should have come into being: coriander grows wild throughout North Africa, cumin is grown there commercially, and caraway is native to the Middle East.

I first encountered harissa in the Grand Socco of Tangier, a confusion of market stalls and shops lining the steep streets of that port city. There it was being sold ready-made in jars and tins, but it is a relatively simple matter to make it up yourself at home:

Harissa

5 tbsp chilli powder (or, even better, dried chillies which have been soaked
    for an hour in water and then pounded)
1 clove garlic, crushed
2 tsp ground caraway
1 tsp ground cumin
1 tsp coriander
salt to taste

Mix together thoroughly to a paste. Store, covered with a layer of olive oil, in a clean jar.

If making harissa in large quantities, work on the principle of 15 parts ground chilli to two parts caraway, and one each of coriander, cumin and garlic.

There are innumerable uses for this mixture. It can be added to soups for extra zest, or thinned down with oil and water for a sauce to accompany couscous, the famous Moroccan dish of crushed and reconstituted wheat cooked with stock and meat or vegetables. Mixed with tomato purée and olive oil, it becomes a spread for bread. It is also very good with fish.

Cauliflower with Anchovies

This is excellent as a starter and can be served either hot or cold.

1 small cauliflower, broken into florets
3 medium potatoes, quartered
3 tbsp oil
3 cloves garlic, crushed
1 tsp harissa
½ tsp salt
1 tsp ground caraway
juice of 1 lemon
1 tin anchovy fillets

Steam the caulfliflower and potatoes until cooked.

Meanwhile, heat the oil in a pan, add the garlic, harissa, salt, caraway and lemon juice. Chop the anchovies finely and add to the pan. Stir the mixture for several minutes longer.

Pour this mixture over the cooked vegetables in a serving dish and toss well.

The harissa in this side salad adds a interesting bite. Although very popular in Morocco, the Greeks claim this as a national dish too.

Orange and Olive Salad

4 large oranges
1 small onion, sliced very thinly into rings
20 black olives
pinch of salt
½ tsp ground cumin
½ tsp harissa
1 tbsp lemon juice
1 tbsp olive oil

Break the oranges into segments and cut each segment into three pieces. Place in a bowl with the onion rings, olives, salt, cumin and harissa, diluted with the lemon juice and olive oil. Toss thoroughly and, if time permits, refrigerate before serving.

Even more arcane than harissa is another North African spice mixture known as ras-el-hanout (literally 'head of the shop'). There are well over twenty-five ingredients for this mixture, including all the better-known spices and not a few bizarre items as well. These include belladonna berries, almond husks, the roots of the lesser galangal and wall brome-grass from Sudan, reputedly an aphrodisiac.

Since sesame seeds are so cheap I am tempted to use them by the hand-ful, particularly as there is scarcely a vegetable or a crust or a topping which is not improved by a generous sprinkling.

It almost goes without saying that sesame seeds need to be toasted in order to bring out their nutty flavour. Do not make the common mis-take of frying them, however, as the oil causes them to stick together in lumps and makes it impossible to turn all sides of the seeds an even brown. Rather, toast them over a medium high heat in a heavy frying pan without any oil, shaking the pan away from you and then quickly tilting it back towards you to circulate the seeds. It is all too easy to over-toast sesame seeds, since they can taste burnt even before they actually look it. This applies specially when you are grinding the seeds to make tahina.

There is really no mystery at all to tahina, or sesame seed butter, which is used so often in Middle Eastern cooking. It is merely ground sesame seeds with nothing added or subtracted and can be made in a minute in a food processor, although the result will not be as oily as some commercial preparations made from fresh, undried seeds.

The best known use for tahina is in hummus, but another equally delicious but lesser known Middle Eastern tahina dish is baba ghanoush, in which a large aubergine is placed under the grill (having first been punctured in the side with a knife to prevent it exploding) and turned on all sides until the skin is blackened. The flesh is then scraped out, and tahina, garlic, lemon juice (and perhaps a little cumin) added to taste. The mixture is then puréed in a food processor or blender.

Those who enjoy the undiluted flavour of tahina can try this sauce, intended either for aubergine or for fish:

Tahina Sauce

250 ml (9 fl oz) home-made or shop-bought tahina
3 cloves of garlic, peeled
2 tbsp lemon juice
1 tbsp vinegar
$\frac{1}{2}$ tsp cumin
250 ml (9 fl oz) stock or water

Into a running food processor place the cloves of garlic (or crush by hand), then add to the rest of the ingredients. If you are serving this sauce with fish, it should be fish stock, or vegetable stock if you are serving it with aubergine. Purée this mixture in the food processor or stir by hand. As you can see, it is dead simple.

To serve with aubergine, slice the aubergine fairly thickly. Heat olive oil in a pan (whichever way you fry aubergine it will soak up the oil, though less so if it is hot) and fry the slices on both sides until browned patches appear, then place in an oven dish and pour over the sauce. Cover and bake in the oven at 180°C/350°F/Gas Mark 4 for 15 minutes.

If using with fish, simply pour the sauce over the raw fillets, cover the dish and bake in a moderate oven for 15 minutes or until the fish flakes easily when tested with a fork.

The sesame plant probably originated in Africa and was being turned into flour 3000 years ago by the Egyptians. It reached India in ancient times and China by about the first century AD. The Chinese burnt the oil to make soot for their inks. Slavers took the plant to America and it is now cultivated in all temperate regions of the world. The plant thrives wherever there is no frost.

It is also popular in Japan, despite the opinion of one Isabella L. Bird, who wrote in 1881 that it produces 'one of the most horrific smells in Japan'. The Japanese grind toasted sesame seeds and mix them in the proportion of five to one with salt to make gomasio, which is recommended as a table condiment to those who are trying to reduce their salt intake.

The Romans, who brought sesame seeds from Egypt, used to make a kind of hummus with sesame and cumin, and sprinkled the seeds over cakes and breads, as bakers still do today. Throughout the Middle East the seeds are ground and bound with honey and flavourings to produce halva, one of a number of confections which share this name (*see* pp. 249–50).

One recipe for a sesame seed confection listed in the Kama Sutra promised that the man eating it would 'enjoy innumerable women'. Perhaps this aphrodisiac reputation is derived from the fact that sesame seeds are very high in vitamin E, the 'vitamin of sexuality', so named following the isolation of *Dalpha tocopherol*, the chemical name for vitamin E, by Doctors Katherine Bishop and Herbert Evans in 1922. Their experiments on rats led to the theory that vitamin E makes men better lovers and gives women a stronger sex drive.

Desserts and Confectionery

Egypt

Boulevards pockmarked with unfinished roadworks, the tide of humanity forced to spill from the pavements out on to the roads, the horns of impatient taxi drivers trying to cut a swathe through this, and the piles of rubbish everywhere, are all the result of decades of uncontrolled urban drift which have erased all sense of Cairo's ancient roots.

To any tourist expecting a scene from A *Thousand and One Nights*, the reality of modern Cairo would prove somewhat shocking; my visit to Old Cairo lasted approximately five minutes.

A stench of dung and excrement assailed my nostrils as I viewed a scene of utter desolation: streets of crumbling mud buildings, not a leaf or a twig in sight, and an ankle-deep layer of rubbish everywhere – frayed remains of plastic bags, scraps of cardboard packaging, bits of yellowed newspaper. A group of dirty children played and wallowed in the midst of this, obviously knowing nothing else.

Stepping back aboard the grimy ferry, I was accosted by a commission agent who invited me to view his 'father's' perfume shop. Father, my foot, I thought, but I followed him in any case. I was not sorry, for The Thousand and One Nights Perfume Shop proved to be everything that Old Cairo should have been.

Pushing aside the beaded glass curtain over the doorway, I entered a dimly lit room which was the embodiment of a nineteenth-century Orientalist painter's fantasy: a silk canopy hung from the ceiling, finely woven kilims covered the floor with a riot of colourful patterns, and around the walls were richly carved cabinets containing jars of perfume, the scent of which pervaded the whole shop.

I was ushered to a chair inlaid with mother-of-pearl while the tout's 'father' launched into a well-polished spiel: what is sold in the West as French perfume, he claimed, is made at Grasse from a much diluted base of Egyptian perfume oil, distilled from flowers grown in commercial crops in the Nile valley. Once home in New Zealand, I could dilute his Chanel No. 9 or Opium base nine times with ethyl alcohol, and end up with French perfume.

Our deal haggled over and successfully concluded, the merchant lit up his hookah and sent his shop boy out on an errand. Several minutes later he arrived back with glasses of heavily sweetened tea and a plate of scented semolina and coconut cakes, the simple but very delicious basboosa.

Basboosa

350 g (12 oz) sugar
juice of ½ lemon
½ tsp rose essence
125 g (4½ oz) butter
300 g (10 oz) semolina
100 g (4 oz) plain white flour
200 g (7 oz) caster sugar
50 g (2 oz) desiccated coconut
1 tsp baking powder
1 tsp cinnamon
150 ml (¼ pt) milk

Put the sugar in a pan with 125 ml (4 fl oz) of water and boil together for 8 minutes, until the syrup is thick enough to coat the back of a spoon. Stir in the lemon juice and rose essence. Allow to cool.

Melt the butter in a saucepan and add the semolina, flour, sugar, coconut, baking powder and cinnamon. Pour in the milk and stir until you have a smooth batter.

Spread it about 1 cm (½ in) thick over a greased baking dish. Bake in the oven at 180°C/350°F/Gas Mark 4 for 30–40 minutes, until golden brown and crisp on top.

Remove from the oven and immediately cut into diamonds. Pour over the reserved syrup and serve hot or cold.

India

While desserts in the Western sense are not often eaten in India, the range of exotic sweets to be found in Indian cooking is truly amazing.

The Bengalis are India's master confectioners. There are more varieties of sweets from Bengal than any other state in India, and many a Bengali has a passion for sweets which borders on an obsession. It is not unknown for a Bengali to make a whole meal of sweets. Bengal is one of the main producers of gur, or sugar made from the sap of various palms. Besides being used in sweetmaking, Bengali cooks often add it in small amounts to savoury dishes. It may even be offered in the form of small lumps to nibble as a condiment at the table.

References to sweet foods are woven right through Hindu mythology. Spiritual enlightenment is often likened to the taste of nectar or honey, and the gods and goddesses, we are told, are child-like in their love of sweet offerings. Lakshmi, in particular, has a penchant for offerings of sweetmeats.

There is the story of Rama, who gave each of his queens a magic rice ball to produce offspring. One of the queens discarded her ball, which was swooped up by a bird and then accidentally dropped over a forest. A monkey found it and ate it, and gave birth to Hanuman, the monkey-general who helped Rama win his battle with Ravana. These rice balls are still made today from a mixture of milk, rice, sugar and cinnamon, rolled in coconut.

Most Indian sweets are high in cholesterol, carbohydrates and other horrors, but the *Bhagavad Gita* provides a marvellous rationalization for eating them. It tells the budding yogi to avoid foods which contain the quality of passion (*rajas*) – food that is too acid, too sour, too pungent, too dry or too hot. Rather he or she should eat food which contains the quality of harmony (*sattva*). Conveniently, Indian sweets are said to contain just such a quality.

When a Hindu priest bathes a holy statue in a temple, it will most likely be with panchamrita, a mixture of milk, ghee, honey, sugar and water. These five ingredients form the basis of nearly all Indian sweetmaking. Milk, in particular, appears in perhaps half of all Indian sweet recipes, usually in a much condensed form. This is a result of having been kept at boiling point for an hour and a half or more.

Sweets are integral to many Indian festivals, such as Divali, the Hindu New Year, but their making and eating is by no means confined to special occasions and they can be usually seen on sale in almost any chai (tea) shop. In Indian bazaars I saw stalls piled high with sweets of all shapes and colours, many of them covered with thin, supposedly edible, silver leaf. Often these are the specialized products of the Halvai, a caste of confectioners in northern India whose art is passed down from father to son.

Halva seems to mean different things to different peoples, but in India the base is often fruits or vegetables rather than semolina (*see* pp. 249–50).

Gajar ka Halwa (carrot halva)

1.2 litres (2 pt) milk
500 g (1 lb) carrots, grated
175 g (6 oz) jaggery or soft brown sugar
125 g (4½ oz) white sugar
3 tbsp ghee or clarified butter (*see below*)
225 g (8 oz) blanched almonds, ground
3 tbsp sultanas (optional)
¼ tsp cardamom seeds, ground
30 toasted almonds, in slivers

Place the milk and carrots together in a heavy-bottomed pan, bring to the boil, lower heat and simmer over a moderate heat, just bubbling, for about an hour, stirring occasionally. The milk should reduce to about half its original volume.

Add the sugars, stir to dissolve, and cook for 10 minutes longer.

Stir in the ghee, almonds and sultanas, and cook the halva for a further 10 minutes, by which time the mixture should be leaving the side of the pan. Add the cardamom seeds and then turn the mixture on to a flat plate, piling it up towards the centre. Decorate by studding it all over with slivered almonds. Ignore facetious comparisons to a hedgehog.

In India, ghee can refer to almost any frying medium, including vegetable oils, but in sweetmaking it usually means a substance resembling clarified butter. This is made by melting unsalted butter, stirring in the froth and leaving over a very low heat for 45 minutes or so, until the protein solids settle at the bottom and the clear fat rises to the top. This is strained through several thicknesses of fine cloth and stored in a screw top jar in the fridge, where it will solidify. If you are pressed for time ordinary clarified butter can be substituted. Simply melt some butter and skim off the foam which rises to the top. Scoop out the clear butter, avoiding the solids at the bottom of the pan. Packets of ghee and clarified butter are also becoming increasingly available.

Gulab Jamon

Anybody who has travelled through India should be familiar with these deep-fried milk balls in syrup, which are standard fare in chai shops everywhere.

SYRUP
1 kg (2 lb) sugar
1/2 tsp rose essence
1/2 tsp ground cardamom
few drops cochineal

BALLS
150 g (5 oz) milk powder, preferably full cream
50 g (2 oz) self-raising flour
2 tsp baking powder
1/4 tsp ground cardamom
225 g (8 oz) ghee
oil for deep frying

First make the syrup by placing the sugar, rose essence, cardamom and cochineal in 600 ml (1 pt) water. Boil quite vigorously for about 10 minutes, stirring until the sugar is thoroughly dissolved (it will crystallize back if it isn't).

Mix together the milk powder, flour, baking powder and cardamom in a bowl. Make a well in the centre and mix in the ghee and about 150 ml (1/4 pt) water. Mix to a pliable dough, adding more water if necessary, then form walnut-sized balls.

Heat the oil in a wok or a heavy pan to a temperature of about 180°C (350°F). Deep fry the balls. If the temperature is correct they should take about 4 minutes to turn a fairly deep brown. They will also puff up in size.

As each one is done, drain on absorbent paper, then transfer to syrup. They can be served either hot, at room temperature, or cold.

MAKES ABOUT 18 BALLS.

Consider how incongruous is the singing of 'Jingle Bells' by a roving choir of Indian children on the palm-fringed beaches of Goa, in the sweltering equatorial heat of southern India:

Oh, what fun it is to ride,
Riding all the way.

Such fudging of the lyrics is understandable. After all, what relevance has a one-horse open sleigh to an eight-year-old who cannot even properly conceive of snow?

Dressed in their school uniform, holding candles, and headed by a boy bearing a pole from which is suspended a huge, brightly painted cardboard star illuminated from within by a candle, the groups proceed from café to café, collecting tips from tourists.

Not that this is any reason to doubt their sincerity, for Christianity in India is as old as the religion itself. Hindu scholars will tell you that Christ travelled through India and the East during the so-called lost years between AD12 and 30, visiting Hindu temples and Buddhist monasteries, and they point to a 2000-year-old manuscript in the Himis monastery in Tibet which records this.

Even more widely accepted by historians is that Thomas the Apostle ('doubting Thomas') travelled to India soon after Christ's crucifixion, settling in what is now the state of Kerala and founding the sect known as the Syrian Malabar Christians, who can thus trace their history back as far as any Church in the West.

In the case of the Christians of neighbouring Goa, their faith is a legacy of 400 years of Portuguese colonial domination, which has left Goa dotted with hundreds of whitewashed Catholic churches in the striking and graceful Portuguese colonial architectural style.

Like most Goan Christians, my landlords at Colva Beach were of mixed Portuguese and Goan descent. In the days leading up to Christmas a succession of delicious aromas emanated from their rather primitive darkened kitchen, and the daughter was set to work in the backyard, grating the flesh from a small heap of coconuts.

Finally, on Christmas Day, the landlord appeared on our doorstep and, with his saintly, toothless smile, presented us with a platter of traditional Goan sweets, some rather gaudily coloured, but all delicious. The pick of them was this halva-like confection:

Dholdhol

600 g (1¼ lb) sugar
400 ml (¾ pt) coconut cream
225 g (8 oz) ground rice
pinch of salt
¾ tsp ground cardamom
75 g (3 oz) cashew nuts, roasted and ground to a powder
¾ cup clarified or ordinary butter
3 tbsp sliced almonds (or any mixture of nuts), toasted

Place the sugar with 250 ml (9 fl oz) of water in a saucepan, bring to the boil and keep at a steady rolling boil for 5–8 minutes. Add the coconut cream then stir in the ground rice, salt and cardamom.

Stir the ground cashew nuts into the mixture and then, little by little, stir in the butter. Continue to cook, uncovered and stirring frequently, until the mixture thickens and the butter begins to separate out.

Pour into a shallow dish and sprinkle with the toasted nuts. Refrigerate and slice when cold.

Early one summer's morning (before the heat of the day set in), I took a stroll through the south Indian town of Mysore, home of incense, sandalwood carvings and coffee. An unseasonal rain shower the previous night accompanied by dramatic flashes of forked lightning had washed the city clean. Scattered under the hedgerow were carpets of fallen flowers – pink, white and yellow, and especially the purple of jacaranda.

Obviously an early morning constitutional is the thing to do in Mysore, for the streets were full of people, including a couple of elderly gents dressed in the traditional Mysore garb – laced turban, high-collared coat, and dhoti. From the houses drifted the delicious smells of breakfast cooking, and through one open doorway I could see a woman packing steamer moulds with uncooked iddlies. These are without a doubt south India's most popular breakfast dish, consisting of a mixture of ground rice and dal, which is partially fermented and then steamed into dumplings and served with fresh coconut chutney and a spicy vegetable broth.

Soon the cooking aromas became too much for me, and I headed for a restaurant on Ramanuja Road which had been recommended to me. For over twenty years the proprietor had resisted giving his establishment a name, a cunning marketing ploy since it now enjoys local fame as the 'nameless' restaurant.

Seeing that everybody else seemed to be ordering a 'set', I followed suit. The 'set' was served on a banana leaf, and consisted of four dosas – south Indian pancakes crisp and brown on the bottom and spongy in the middle – topped with coconut chutney, potato, and two dabs of butter which tasted more like cream. All this was washed down with a couple of cups of Mysore coffee.

Later that day I visited the Devaraja Market in the centre of the city and marvelled at the piles of fruit and vegetables, meticulously arranged in cones. Among the more familiar cabbages, cauliflowers and beetroot, I detected the long tubular drumstick, which is a tasty vegetable provided you remove its leathery skin. Mysore is especially noted for its many varieties of banana, each with its own particular flavour. Almost every corner shop has a bunch of little bright yellow hands hanging from the ceiling.

The most famous food product of Mysore, however, is a sweet

known as Mysore Pak. This can be bought everywhere in the city from confectionery shops, each with piles of hand-made Indian sweets under the counter. *Pak* means pure.

Mysore Pak

500 g (1 lb) sugar
500 g (1 lb) besan (chickpea flour)
750 g (1½ lb) clarified butter
1 tsp powdered cardamom
1 tsp saffron (optional)

Boil the sugar in 250 ml (9 fl oz) of water for 5 minutes to make a syrup. Set aside. Sift the flour and also set aside.

Melt the butter in a small saucepan and transfer a third of this to a large pot. Add the sifted flour to the pot and stir well, then pour in the syrup and stir again. Add the cardamom and, if you have it, the saffron (ground in a mortar and pestle with a little hot water).

Continue to fry, stirring continuously, for 10 minutes, dribbling in the remaining butter with your other hand. This process is essential to obtain the porous drawn-thread consistency of a perfect Mysore pak. Keep the heat low, as the mixture easily catches on the bottom of the pan.

When all the butter has been absorbed, transfer the mixture to a greased biscuit tray. Allow to cool a little, and cut into large squares before the pak sets completely. It hardens very quickly and will break in the wrong places if you try to cut it once it has set.

If you wish, you may press some slivered almonds, cashews or pistachios into the surface before the pak sets. This, however, is a modern innovation, frowned upon by the orthodox, who insist that no solid bits should interfere with the fine consistency of the sweet.

Indonesia

Somewhere in everybody's vision of a tropical paradise is fruit, and with good reason, for on an island like Bali, coconuts and bananas bulge from self-sown trees everywhere. The combination of sun, rich soil and heavy rainfall results in lush growing conditions and allows the Balinese a great deal of leisure, for after the rice crop has been sown and the fruit trees planted, there is little to do other than sit back and let it all grow. This largely explains why the Balinese have been able to develop such extraordinarily rich dance, music, art and cuisine.

Fruits sold in Balinese markets are rarely the perfect specimens seen on our greengrocers' shelves. Usually they are the products of scattered smallholdings, or even a single tree grown in a family's compound, and lack the careful rootstock selection, pruning, spraying and all the other pampering which takes place in Western orchards. But compare the sheer variety. Besides our familiar apples, pears and bananas is a whole assortment never seen outside the tropics, perhaps because they do not travel well, or simply because they are not widely known outside Bali.

A good example is the salak, a small tear-shaped fruit with a beautiful reddish-brown scaly skin which looks like it belongs on a snake, and crisp, mildly astringent white flesh with the flavour of a pineapple. Then there is the exquisitely perfumed mangosteen, for which Queen Victoria offered a prize to the first person who could get it to England in an edible condition, or the curious jackfruit, with its sweet stringy flesh, sticky with sap and simultaneously rubbery and crunchy.

Any of these fruits and more can be combined to make a delicious sweet-sour fruit salad known as rujak. Although the recipe originated in neighbouring Java, rujak is enormously popular in Bali, and is sold everywhere from carts by street vendors.

To some, the idea of adding chilli and shrimp paste to a syrup for fruit salad may seem bizarre, but that is only because we are accustomed to eating fruit salad as a dessert. In Indonesia, rujak is eaten more as a snack, although certainly it is served as dessert in hotels catering to Westerners. It is ideal as an appetizer. The list of fruits is flexible – the oranges here are substitutes for the juruk Bali or pomelo, the apples for the sour, egg-shaped kedondong.

Rujak

1 orange, peeled
2 slightly unripe pears or mangoes
1 slightly unripe apple
1/2 fresh pineapple, peeled
1 cucumber
1 tbsp dried tamarind pulp
1 fresh red chilli or 1/2 tsp dried chilli
1/2 tsp terasi (preserved shrimp paste)
3 tbsp brown sugar or palm sugar
large pinch of salt

Divide the orange into segments. Cut all the remaining fruit and the cucumber into equal-sized pieces. If preparing the rujak in advance, place the fruit in slightly salted water.

For the sauce, break the tamarind pulp into pieces and place in a bowl. Pour over 4 tbsp boiling water and allow to stand for 5 minutes. Meanwhile, pound the chilli, shrimp paste, sugar and salt. Strain the tamarind pulp to get rid of pith and stones, and mix in. Pour over the fruit and mix well. Alternatively, pour into a separate small bowl and allow guests to help themselves.

Turkey

With a place in every national cuisine from Greece through the whole of the Middle East to India, halva is the best-loved of all Oriental sweetmeats.

Although the same word is used for some quite different confections, a halva is usually based on a flour such as semolina, ground rice or cornflour, which is enriched with butter or ghee, sweetened with a syrup, and flavoured with nuts, raisins, spices and perhaps rosewater or orange flower water. The imported Lebanese halva which you see in wrapped blocks in shops is based on sesame seed paste.

Here is a Turkish recipe (where it is spelled helva) but, with minor variations (*see* below), it would be equally at home in any of the halva-making countries.

Helva

225 g (8 oz) sugar
225 g (8 oz) semolina
125 g (4½ oz) butter
12 almonds, toasted and sliced lengthways
¼ tsp vanilla essence or rosewater

Place the sugar and 500 ml (scant 1 pt) of water in a saucepan and boil for a few minutes.

Meanwhile, place the semolina in another, larger saucepan over a low heat and stir for 5 minutes or until it begins to give off an appetizing smell. Add the butter and continue to stir for a few minutes longer.

Now, add the syrup and stir for another 5–10 minutes until the mixture leaves the sides of the pan. This may not seem much cooking but is sufficient to remove the raw taste of the semolina. The texture is supposed to be grainy.

Finally, add the toasted sliced almonds and the vanilla essence or rosewater. If serving cold, press into a greased tin and, when cold, unmould and cut into diamond shapes.

This halva can be eaten as a pudding rather than a sweetmeat, in which case it would be advisable to reduce the amount of sugar. Try using honey instead of sugar.

For a Syrian version, increase the amount of water to 1.2 l (2½ pt) and add to it 2 tbsp lemon juice. Omit the nuts and substitute 1½ tsp cinnamon for the vanilla essence. This is known as mamounia and is said to have been created for the Caliph Al-Manum (AD813–833). Originally rice rather then semolina was used. In Syria, this is a common breakfast dish and is usually eaten warm, with cream. Great claims are made as to its health-giving properties and it is also fed to women in labour, or convalescing after a pregnancy.

An Indian cook would use ghee rather than butter, and might add the crushed seeds of a cardamom pod and some raisins. Some or all of the almonds might be replaced with pistachios. Indian halvas also utilize some unlikely ingredients such as pumpkin or potatoes (*see* p. 242 for carrot halva).

A Greek halva would be made using half milk and half water and substituting pine nuts for the almonds.

In the week preceding Easter, devout Greek Christians observe a fast which precludes all meat and even food prepared with olive oil. The austerity of this time is broken, however, with dishes of halva.

Originally Greek halva was made with honey and olive oil, and the recipe is said to go back to the travels of Alexander the Great (356–323BC). The earliest documentary reference to halva, however, is in a cookery book written in 1226, describing the recipes prepared in the kitchens of the caliphs of Baghdad. This 'halwa' bears little resemblance to modern recipes, being more like pulled toffee spiked with almonds.

Glossary of Ingredients

ALLSPICE
The dark, pea-shaped, partly dried berry of a tropical tree of the myrtle family. The world's largest supplier is Jamaica and the berry owes its name to the belief that it combines the flavours of cinnamon, nutmeg and cloves. While is is popular in Turkey, allspice is used more in Western than Eastern cooking.

ANISEED
Most common in Bengali and Kashmiri cooking, the pale grey-green elongated seeds of the aniseed have a distinct liquorice-like aroma, and are usually roasted before use. Aniseed does not last beyond two years, and turns brown as it goes stale and loses its flavour. It is easily crushed, so avoid the relatively tasteless powdered form.

ASAFOETIDA
The dried gum resin of a plant akin to fennel, with a potent flavour. It is also known as hing. It is popular all over India but forgotten in the West since Roman times. Powdered asafoetida is often sold ready mixed with flour, not just to increase the manufacturer's profits but also to reduce the strong sulphuric, garlic-like odour (which is greatly mellowed with cooking). Indeed, the spice is used as a garlic substitute by Brahman cooks, and is also greatly valued as a digestive.

BAMBOO SHOOTS
Every bamboo plant produces thick, pointed shoots from below ground level which, if left unharvested, would grow into new stems. However, only 10–15 per cent of the hundred or so species of bamboo produce edible shoots. Of these, the most prized, and expensive, are the winter shoots, which have a meat-like chewiness; spring shoots are more tender. Unless otherwise specified on the label, tinned bamboo shoots are likely to be the summer variety, succulent but inclined to bitterness. Fresh bamboo shoots are very rarely seen in the West outside Chinatowns, which is no great loss, as the raw shoot contains a bitter poison, hydrocyanic acid, which must be eliminated by cooking.

Tinned bamboo shoots may be used straight from the can, although they may need blanching to reduce a 'tinny' taint. Once opened, they will keep for a month provided the water is changed every few days.

BANANA LEAVES
Used extensively as a wrapping in South-East Asian cooking, the leaves, when steamed, impart a faint banana flavour to some foods. They are sometimes available in the West, either fresh, dried or frozen, but are not essential. Aluminium foil or greaseproof paper may be substituted.

BASIL
Although native to India and grown in the courtyards of the pious, basil is worshipped rather than eaten by Hindus. In Thailand, however, three varieties are

consumed with gusto: the conventional European basil (horapa), a slightly paler, hairier version known as lemon basil (mangluk) and the holy basil (grapao), which has narrow, slightly purplish leaves. Other South-East Asian basil varieties have flavours closer to mint, anise and eau de cologne.

BEANSPROUTS
While many types of bean can be sprouted and eaten, Chinese and South-East Asian cooks use almost solely mung beans, and occasionally the longer, coarser soya beansprouts. The latter are seen in Hong Kong markets, tied, unlike mung beansprouts, into neat bundles. A common sight in Hong Kong markets is of the stallholder laboriously picking the heads and tails from beansprouts, later to be sold at a premium to gourmets and the restaurant trade as 'silver sprouts'. Soya beansprouts are slightly poisonous raw; correct cooking (over a fierce heat, to minimize the accumulation of moisture) benefits the flavour greatly.

BELACHAN OR BLACHAN
The Malay name for the pungent paste made from shrimps and spices: *see* Preserved shrimp paste.

BESAN
A heavy, musky flour made from skinned and roasted chickpeas, much used in Indian cuisine, either as a thickening agent or as a batter for pakoras, pancakes, dumplings and sweetmeats. It is best kept in the refrigerator, as it has a tendency to go rancid when stored at room temperature, and may have to be sieved before use.

Ordinary pea-flour may be substituted.

BITTER MELON
A member of the gourd family, called karela in India (*see* pp. 159–60).

BLACK BEANS
Soya beans which have been steamed, spiced, fermented and preserved in salt. They are found in the cuisines of south China (dow see), Thailand (tao jiew kawo or tao jiew leung) and Malaysia/Indonesia (tauco).

Two types of bean are used, black and yellow. Sold in the East in tins or jars labelled 'salted black beans' or 'salted yellow beans' or sometimes as black, yellow or white 'bean sauce', even though the beans are still partially intact. The whole beans should be lightly crushed to release their flavour. They can be kept almost indefinitely in an airtight container.

Soy sauce substitutes for the flavour but not the texture.

CANDLE NUT
This staple of Indonesian cooking is so named because the indigenous Orang Asli used to thread the nuts on the midrib of a palm leaf and burn them like candles. This gives an idea of the extreme richness of this waxy, cream-coloured, heart-shaped nut. In cooking it is ground and used to thicken curries.

The closely related macadamia nut is an admirable substitute, preferred even by many Indonesians.

CARAWAY
More of a European than an Oriental spice, caraway is nevertheless occasionally found in the curries of northern India. The seeds should be bruised with a mortar and pestle prior to using them, to bring out their flavour.

CARDAMOM
A highly aromatic spice used to flavour dishes and drinks right across North Africa, western Asia and India. In the West, cardamoms are most commonly sold as greenish white pods containing half a dozen or so rather soft dark seeds, although larger black varieties are also sometimes available. *See* pp. 217–18.

CASHEW NUT
see pp. 128–9.

CHILLI
Unsurprisingly, Eastern cuisines call upon a far greater range of chillies than we have in the West, but the type and the amount can usually be adjusted, anyway, to suit individual tastes. *See* p. 109.

CHILLI BEAN SAUCE
Otherwise known as hot bean sauce, this is not to be confused with ordinary chilli sauce, as it is made with yellow soya beans and other seasonings in addition to chilli, and provides a key flavouring in Sichuan cooking. Several brands are quite widely available, although the best tend to come from China itself rather than Taiwan. Once opened, store in a jar kept in the refrigerator, where it should last indefinitely.

CHINESE CHIVES
see Garlic chives

CHINESE GREENS
The Chinese grow a number of members of the cabbage family which are quite different from our familiar tight-headed or crinkly Savoy cabbages. Many are becoming increasingly available here.

Most widely known is the pale, crinkly leaved, barrel shape of what the Cantonese call wong nga bok but is usually labelled, rather vaguely, as 'Chinese cabbage'. It keeps well, and indeed the Chinese insist it sweetens as it wilts. While Westerners now eat Chinese cabbage raw in salads, a Chinese chef would typically braise it with garlic and ginger, or use it to absorb strong flavours.

Also commonly known by its Cantonese name, pak choi or Chinese white cabbage is easily identifiable by its ivory white stalks topped by a cluster of two-toned green leaves. The plant is used in its entirety, although the stems are traditionally added only at the end of cooking. A greatly favoured green of modern fusion cooking.

Mild-flavoured, long-stemmed Chinese flowering cabbage (choi sum) is often hailed as the best of the Chinese cabbages. It resembles its close cousin, Chinese kale, but its flowers are yellow rather than white.

Chinese kale (gai laan) is less common than its relations and its robust, slightly bitter flavour is not to everybody's taste. It is stouter than Chinese flowering cabbage and distinguished by its white flowers. Ideally, these should be in bud rather than full flower, and the stems either very thin (no need to peel) or very thick (when the pith is sweet).

See also Preserved cabbage.

CHOI SUM
see Chinese greens

CINNAMON
Cinnamon quills, which have more flavour than ground cinnamon, are the innermost bark of branches from the true cinnamon tree (*Cinnamomum zeylanicum*), harvested mainly in Sri Lanka, the Seychelles and Madagascar. What is sold as ground cinnamon is often a mixture of true cinnamon and the coarser, stronger-flavoured cassia, the bark of a tree belonging to the laurel family found in Vietnam, China and the eastern Himalayas. A 'warm' spice, cinnamon is an essential ingredient of Indian garam masala (*see* p. 218).

CLOVES
The dried, unopened flower buds of a tree native to the Moluccas and grown in Indonesia, Malaysia and southern India. Today, the world's largest suppliers are Zanzibar and its neighbouring island of Pemba. The slightly citrusy pungency of cloves is an essential element both of Indian garam masala (*see* p. 218) and Chinese five spice powder (*see* pp. 255–6); look for plump, oily specimens.

COCONUT CREAM
see pp. 39–40.

CORIANDER
An emblem of fusion cuisine, fresh coriander is steadily creeping into even quite conservative Western kitchens. Americans generally use the Italian name, cilantro, and older cookery books sometimes refer to it as 'Chinese parsley'. The leaves resemble flat-leaved parsley, but this is not a suitable substitute, as is sometimes suggested.

Like all acquired tastes, acceptance swiftly becomes passion, and Western cooks are now discovering that the pungency of fresh coriander enhances a remarkable range of dishes. In the East, it is used in all cuisines in the arc from Asia Minor through India, South-East Asia, southern China and up to Korea.

Fresh coriander is (or should be) sold with the roots still intact, for all parts of the plant yield flavour. In Thailand, the stems and roots are pounded before being added to curries. The plant withers easily, and once limp cannot be revived; it is best stored in the refrigerator, arranged like a bunch of flowers in a jar of water, with a plastic bag loosely over it.

Coriander can be grown successfully as an annual in the garden. Sow only small amounts at a time, to give a succession of young leaves for picking; if left for long the plants will soon develop flower heads and set seed, and the flavour in the leaves will be lost.

Coriander seeds are especially important in Indian cuisine, and should be bruised or ground before being lightly roasted in order to bring out their orange-like flavour.

CUMIN
A basic spice of Indian cuisine, in which it frequently accompanies coriander. Although cumin seeds may look like caraway or fennel, they smell and taste distinctly curry-like (*see* pp. 151–2).

CURRY LEAF
Aptly named, since it does taste vaguely like commercially produced curry powder. The small, thin, shiny, dark green curry leaf comes from an ornamental shrub of the orange family. Especially popular in south Indian cookery (where it is known as metha neem or, in Tamil, karuvapillai), it is also used in Indonesia and Malaysia – it is called daun kari in Malay. It is sometimes confused with the Malay/Indonesian daun salam (*see* below), for which it can be substituted.

Ideally, they should be used when fresh, but curry leaves can nevertheless be wrapped in plastic and frozen or, at a pinch, used dry, although the flavour is much reduced.

DAIKON
A large white winter radish, extremely popular in Japan (*see* p. 176).

DAL
The collective name for pulses and lentils in Indian cookery. *See* pp. 130–4.

DAUN KESOM
see Mint

DAUN SALAM
This large, shiny, pointed leaf, used fresh in Indonesian cooking, vaguely resembles a bay leaf, which is often used as a substitute. Closest in flavour, however, is the curry leaf (*see* above). Dried salam leaf is available in the West, but has minimal flavour.

FENNEL SEEDS
Similar in appearance to aniseed, only longer and plumper, fennel also has a mild anise flavour. Used in Indian and Malay/Indonesian cooking, it has digestive properties and thus is an important component of the aromatic spice mix known as mukwas, chewed on completion of an Indian meal.

FENUGREEK
Both leaves and the gritty seed of the fenugreek are used in Indian cookery, with great discretion, to lend a faintly bitter edge to a dish. The leaves should only be used young, and the seeds not over-roasted, in order to keep the bitter, celery-like flavour to an acceptable level. Some Indian cooks, however, literally char the seed into a state of docility before use.

FISH SAUCE
A condiment widely used in Thailand (*see* pp. 95–6).

FIVE SPICE POWDER
A pungent, slightly sweet brownish powder, concocted from star anise, Sichuan

peppercorns, fennel, cloves and cinnamon. It is commonly used in southern Chinese cooking as a marinade for pork and poultry.

A quite different five spice mix (known as panch phoron) is used in Bengali cooking: *see* pp. 220–1.

GAI LAAN
see Chinese greens

GALANGAL
Also known as galanga, lengkuas, laos or ka, galangal is a relative of ginger, to which it bears a close resemblance (except for its pink shoots). It fell out of favour in Europe after the Middle Ages, but remains central to the cuisines of Thailand, Malaysia and Indonesia.

It has a uniquely medicinal flavour, quite different from fresh ginger, which is not a suitable substitute. Ideally use it fresh, frozen or bottled. it is very much less satisfactory as dried slices, which need to be infused in boiling water or stock before use. It is better to leave it out of the recipe than to buy the little jars of powdered galangal, which are more expensive than plain white flour and about as tasty.

A related plant, lesser galangal or kencur, is mostly used in Asia as a medicine.

GARAM MASALA
Literally 'hot spices', this mixture of warm sweet spices such as cardamom, cloves, cinnamon, cumin and nutmeg, originated in the colder climates of northern India and is designed to heat up the body. Since these spices turn bitter when overcooked, they are usually added at the very end of cooking, after the heat has been turned off. *See also* p. 218.

GARLIC
Happiness begins where garlic is used in cooking, and one of the great advances of the twentieth century has been its adoption by English-speaking peoples. Chinese cooks peel garlic by giving it a good whack with the flat side of a cleaver, but a more delicate technique is to hold top and bottom of each clove between thumb and forefinger, and gently squeeze until the skin pops open at the seam. Pickled garlic, processed commercially and sold in jars, is an important ingredient in Thai cuisine.

GARLIC CHIVES
The leaves of garlic chives (also known as Chinese chives or, in Cantonese, gau choi) are longer and tougher than Western chives, and flat rather than tubular, giving them a grassy appearance. They have a stronger garlic-onion flavour and need to be chopped finely. Occasionally Chinese growers blanch the plants (i.e. grow them in the dark) for a more tender texture. Eventually the plant forms flower heads at the end of tubular stalks, which are then sold as flowering garlic chives (gau choi fa).

GELUGUR
This large species of tamarind is generally sold dried in markets throughout Malaysia, but is difficult to obtain even there, let alone in the West. A common use for gelugur is in Malaysia's national dish, rendang (*see* p. 46). Ordinary tamarind (*see* p. 262) is an acceptable substitute.

GHEE

Today the term ghee is used loosely in Indian cookery to mean any frying medium, oil or butter. Traditionally, however, it refers to expensive clarified butter, which has the advantage, from the cook's point of view, of not burning when heated for deep frying. You can make your own (*see* p. 242) but packets of ghee are becoming more widely available not only in Indian shops, but delicatessens and supermarkets too.

GINGER

One of the universals of Asian cuisine, the root of the ginger plant is at its freshest and juiciest when the skin has a slight sheen, and is stretched tight by the plumpness within. A wrinkled skin and shrivelled form are sure indications of the nasty dry, fibrous interior which develops in old age. Store in the refrigerator and freeze what you won't be using in the next month or so, or peel and store covered in a screwtop jar of sherry. Peel with a potato peeler and either grate or chop by hand, or drop slice by slice into a running food processor, followed by a small quantity of water.

The tight buds of wild ginger flowers, seen in Malaysian markets but generally unavailable in the West, are sometimes shredded as a garnish over a bowl of Penang laksa soup (*see* p. 180).

Dried ground ginger imparts a completely different taste to food and is no substitute for the fresh root.

HEIKO

see Preserved shrimp paste

HING

see Asafoetida

HOISIN SAUCE

A thick, syrupy, reddish brown sauce manufactured from soya beans and flavoured with sugar, vinegar, garlic and spices. It is especially popular in southern Chinese cooking and is used both as a dipping sauce for the table and as an all-purpose barbecue marinade for pork, poultry and seafood.

JAGGERY AND PALM SUGARS

Jaggery is used loosely to cover all types of unrefined sugar in South-East Asia and India, but strictly the term refers only to the sugar cane juice processed in India's villages (accounting for over half the sub-continent's sugar consumption). Gur, in India, refers to the sugar made from the sap of various palms, such as the celebrated tal palm of Bengal, or of the date, coconut, sugar or palmyra palms. In Malaysia palm sugar is known as gula melaka and the best quality comes from Melaka (Malacca).

Jaggery and palm sugar are usually sold in solid brown blocks; the best is fudge-like and breakable, rather than rock-hard in texture. Ordinary soft brown, raw, muscovado or even demerara sugars make acceptable substitutes.

KAFFIR LIME

The glossy round leaves and rind of this knobbly fruit are much used in Asian cookery, especially Thai (*see* pp. 170–1). The fruits are little known outside South-East Asia, but the leaves are obtainable here, occasionally fresh, but more often frozen or dried. Both forms can be added directly to soups. In Asian shops the leaves may be sold as bai makrut. For a similar flavour, substitute lemon verbena, lemon grass or finely pared lime peel.

KALONJI
Beloved in India but obscure in the West (where it sometimes dubbed nigella, after its botanical name, *Nigella sativa*), this small, black, teardrop-shaped seed tastes rather like a peppery form of oregano. It is especally popular in the Muglai cooking of the north, sprinkled over naan bread and is used in lamb korma, dals, vegetable dishes and pickles. It is also an ingredient in the Bengali spice mixture, panch phoron (*see* p. 220).

KAPEE
see Preserved shrimp paste

KARELA
A long, pale gourd which needs careful preparation to lose the unpalatable bitterness in the flesh (*see* pp. 159–60).

KATSUO BUSHI
Dried flakes of bonito, a fish related to tuna. Katsuo bushi is used to flavour Japanese stock and soups.

KECAP MANIS
Indonesia's celebrated sweet soy sauce, made from fermented soya beans and palm sugar, is also used to a lesser extent in neighbouring Malaysia. An acceptable substitute is ordinary Chinese dark soy sauce, to which brown sugar, molasses or honey has been added.

KERUPUK OR KRUPUK (UDANG)
The Malay name for prawn crackers (*see* p. 170).

KOMBU
A type of seaweed commonly used in Japanese cooking, especially for making stock (*see* p. 145). It is sold in sheets.

LAOS
see Galangal

LEMON GRASS
The gorgeous citric perfume of lemon grass so thoroughly pervades the kitchens of South-East Asia that Thai cooking, in particular, seems impossible to contemplate without it. Fortunately, the proliferation of Thai restaurants has resulted in commercial cultivation in many other parts of the world. However, lemon grass, which resembles a fibrous spring onion, needs hot growing conditions to bring out its full flavour, and imported Thai stalks are often a better alternative to those grown closer to home.

To use, either grind to a powder in a food processor or with mortar and pestle, or simply whack and thoroughly bruise the stalks with the side of a cleaver, and the use in the dish whole, discarding before serving.

Stalks bottled in acidulated water are an acceptable but less aromatic alternative to the fresh stems, but powdered lemon grass is virtually useless, and dried lemon grass is effective only when infused into stocks by the handful; I sometimes wonder whether the authors of recipes which tell you to substitute a miserable teaspoon or two of powdered lemon grass for the fresh stems have actually tried following their own advice. If you can't find fresh or bottled lemon grass, boil 75 g (3 oz) dried lemon grass in some coconut cream or cooking liquid to obtain an infusion.

There is no substitute, although lemon peel has often been suggested.

LENGKUAS
see Galangal

LIMES
The Asian lime is smaller and darker than that of the West, but our limes are a perfectly good stand-in. The small, knobbly kaffir lime is prized primarily for its leaves (*see* pp. 170–1), and Malays and Indonesians also use the limau, a strongly aromatic little relation of the kaffir lime. Lime pickle is an important table condiment in Indian cuisine.

Lemon rind and juice is not the same but can be substituted should limes be unobtainable.

MACE
see Nutmeg

MANGE-TOUT
Another icon of fusion cuisine, mange-tout have been enthusiastically adopted in the West. Although all young pea pods are edible, mange-tout lack the parchment-like layer that usually toughens the pod. Mange-tout keep well – up to a week in the refreigerator. Whether you first snap the stem off and peel off the string along the length, or leave them intact depends on whether you are cooking for ease of eating or for presentation.

MINT
Many varieties of mint, including peppermint and spearmint, are used in Asia, primarily in India (for fresh chutneys and raitas) and in Vietnam and Thailand (in stir fries, salads and as a garnish). Vietnamese mint (otherwise known as daun kesom or laksa leaf – a reference to its use in Penang Nonya-style laksa soup) is now grown commercially in Australia, New Zealand and California, but is difficult to find elsewhere in the East. Its cloying, highly perfumed, minty flavour is an acquired taste.

MOOLI
A long white winter radish (*see* Daikon).

MUSHROOMS

While there are an estimated 500 varieties of mushrooms used in Chinese cooking along, the most popular cultivated variety by far is *Lentinula edodes*, known to the Chinese as dong-gu and to the Japanese – and in the West – as shiitake (*see* pp. 172–3).

A close second in popularity is the straw mushroom, grown from early times, as the name suggests, on beds of rice straw. When fresh they are very tasty, but they are only available tinned or dried in the West.

European button mushrooms are a recent introduction to China, where they are now grown for export and internal consumption. They can be used a substitute in most recipes, but will add neither the flavour nor texture of most Chinese varieties. Better are dried mushrooms, European if not Chinese.

Some mushrooms are added for flavour, but others, such as cloud ear (also called wood ear) don't taste of much but contribute a unique gelatinous texture difficult to reproduce with anything else.

When using dried mushrooms, soak for up to half an hour in tepid water and rinse thoroughly to dislodge particles of sandy earth and grit. The stalks will often remain tough and will need to be sliced very thinly or used to flavour a stock.

MUSTARD SEEDS

The large European whitish yellow mustard seed scarcely features in Asian cooking at all, except as a Chinese dipping sauce for meat. The two native Indian mustard seeds – one black and the other a dark reddish brown – are much smaller and have a distinctly different flavour. They are quite widely sold. The leaves, seeds and even the oil of the mustard plant are much used in Bengal. Usually the seeds are popped in very hot oil before being added to an Indian dish.

NAM PLA

Thai fish sauce (*see* pp. 95–6).

NUTMEG AND MACE

When the fruit of the nutmeg tree ripens, it splits like a chestnut to reveal the mace, a red cage-like covering for the inner kernel, the nutmeg itself. Native to the Moluccas and grown throughout the Malay archipelago as well as in Sri Lanka, nutmeg exudes a far better flavour when freshly grated. Mace has a similar flavour, but is milder.

ONIONS

The onions most widely used throughout the East are not our white or yellow variety, but the much smaller (and usually cheaper) shallots. Recipes in the book usually give either as alternatives.

Bombay onions are a deliciously sweet type of shallot, for which red onions are an acceptable substitute.

OYSTER SAUCE

Originating in southern China but now adopted by all cuisines of South-East Asia, oyster sauce is the strained, thickened essence of oysters boiled down to a rich concentrated broth in a mixture of soy sauce and brine. Surprisingly free of any 'fishy' odour, it will keep indefinitely if refrigerated. Quality varies greatly, and the more expensive brands are usually worth the extra cost – beware of bottles marked 'oyster-flavoured sauce'. In cooking, it is Asia's answer to the stock cube.

PAK CHOI
see Chinese greens

PALM SUGAR
see Jaggery

PANDANUS OR SCREWPINE
The beloved daun pandan of Malay and Indonesian cooking grows easily in their gardens, and a young spear-shaped leaf is often tied into a loose knot and added to give a fresh-mown hay scent to savoury food, or more commonly to colour desserts and sweets green.

There is no substitute, although the rose-like essence of the flowers is available in the West in Indian shops, usually under its Indian name of kewra or, less commonly, kevda.

PANIR
Indian white curd cheese (*see* p. 136). Of the same derivation is Turkish beyaz peynir (*see* p. 21).

PINE NUTS
The nutty, tear-shaped seeds of certain pine trees (*see* pp. 86–8).

POPPY SEED
The Indian poppy seed is white and smaller than the blue-grey variety common in Europe, yet despite protestations of Indian cooks, I find the two fairly interchangeable in the kitchen. The nutty flavour of the roasted seed may seem deliciously addictive, but rest assured that morphine alkaloids are only found in the latex of the poppy bud.

PRESERVED CABBAGE
An ingredient in some Chinese dishes, tinned preserved cabbage is sold in Chinese supermarkets as tse choi or 'preserved vegetable'. It may need to be soaked in water if it is too salty.

PRESERVED SHRIMP PASTE
The Malaysians call their version belachan, the Indonesians terasi, the Thais kapee, but the three are interchangeable. All are made from salted, fermented shrimps which are dried in the sun before packaging. The final paste is dark reddish brown, has the consistency of raw pastry and an unforgettable smell.

Fishy, even slightly rotten-flavoured it may be, but preserved shrimp paste is essential to South-East Asian cooking. Without a tiny, barely distinguishable amount of shrimp paste, the food would not have the same depth of flavour.

Shrimp paste is never added to a dish raw – opening the packet is likely to set you recoiling in an ammoniacal daze. To mellow the flavour, it has to be zapped briefly in the microwave or wrapped in a little aluminium foil and grilled before use. This creates a horrendous stench at the time, but its contribution to the finished dish should be unidentifiably subtle.

Much rarer is the black heiko, somewhat milder in flavour and used only for a few specialist dishes of Penang.

RICE VINEGAR

The vinegar used in Japanese cuisine is usually distilled from rice wine. It is stocked in Asian shops and some supermarkets, but cider vinegar can be used instead.

SAFFRON

The price may be prohibitive, but since each saffron crocus must be picked individually and the stamens plucked out by hand, it is also justified. *Crocus sativa* is today cultivated around the Mediterranean and in Asia Minor, Iran, Pakistan and China, but the consensus is still that the finest saffon comes from the traditional producers – Spain and Kashmir. Buy only the whole dried stamens; powdered saffron makes adulteration all too easy.

Extraction of both flavour and colour is greatly improved by lightly toasting the saffron in a non-stick frying pan until the colour darkens, then crumbling it into a very little amount of hot milk and allowing it to infuse. The liquid is then poured over the food as it cooks. Even then the colour of most foods will become light primrose rather than a violent yellow.

Alternatives to saffron are dried marigold, which adds colour but no flavour, and turmeric, which adds more colour than saffron, but greatly alters the nature of a dish.

SCREWPINE

see Pandanus

SESAME

Both seed and oil are used in Asian cuisines, but in different ways from country to country (*see* pp. 149–50, 157).

SHALLOTS

see Onions

SHOYU

Japanese soy sauce (*see* pp. 229–30).

SHRIMPS, DRIED

Integral to Asian cooking, dried shrimps should be soaked in only a little water before using, and the water incorporated into the dish if possible.

STAR ANISE

Star-shaped, as the name suggests, this pretty liquorice-flavoured spice marries well with fatty meats such as duck and pork, and is often associated in both Chinese and Malaysian cooking with cinnamon and soy sauce. Stored whole in an airtight jar, it keeps almost indefinitely.

TAMARIND

A block of the semi-dried flesh of the tamarind pod might easily be confused with mangled dates, a thought which may have occurred to the Arabs, who coined the name 'tamr-hindi', or Hindu date.

It is used as is a delicious souring agent in South-East Asian as well as Indian cooking, and there is no real substitute, although lemon juice can be used at a pinch.

Tamarind is not too difficult to find, both in the dried form and, more recently and conveniently, as an extract. To use the dried form, soak in hot water for 20 minutes (or, preferably, overnight), then squeeze the pulp with your fingers, strain out the liquid and discard the remaining pith. If using extract, which can be quite concentrated, just follow the directions on the jar.

TARO
A relation of the yam (*see* p. 27).

TAUCO
see Black beans

TERASI
The Indonesian name for the pungent paste made from shrimps and spices: *see* Preserved shrimp paste.

THAI FISH SAUCE
A translucent amber liquid which seems to be squirted into just about every cooked dish in Thailand, where it is called nam pla (*see* pp. 95–6).

TOFU
Beancurd (*see* p. 125).

TURMERIC
While powdered turmeric is both convenient and readily available, it is worth trying to seek out fresh tubers of turmeric at Indian greengrocers. Used fresh, turmeric has a delightfully pungent scent which is lacking in the powder. Added sparingly to curries, it contributes both a bright yellow colour and a unique flavour, but when overdone a bitter element is introduced.

Turmeric leaves are occasionally used as a herb in Indian cooking, but as they do not add a great deal of flavour and there is no adequate substitute, they are best left out if unavailable.

WATER CHESTNUT
A crisp addition to Chinese stir fries, unpeeled water chestnuts do look a little like chestnuts, though we are more familiar with them as peeled white balls in tins.

WONG NGA BOK
see Chinese greens

YARD-LONG BEANS
Yard-long is perhaps a slight exaggeration, though these green beans, also sometimes called asparagus beans, do regularly reach 30 cm (1 ft) or more in length. While they are stronger in flavour than conventional green beans and remain crunchier when cooked, the latter can always be substituted.

Equipment and Techniques

Equipment

Regardless of where you visit a kitchen in the East, whether in an Indian village, on the veranda of a Thai hut or in a cramped high-rise apartment in Singapore, you are likely to find an austerely furnished room containing only the simplest equipment.

No great problems accompany the conversion of a Western kitchen to Asian cooking, since it is more a matter of ignoring equipment than adding to it. The Western oven, for example, is largely redundant, since virtually all domestic cooking in the East is done on a stove top which may be nothing more than a kerosene burner or a bucket of live coals. Most Oriental utensils such as ladles, strainers, graters, pots and pans have similar counterparts in the West. A metal pot or casserole dish is admirable substitute for the Indian *dekchi*, while a cast-iron or non-stick frying pan stands in well enough for the slightly concave Indian griddle known as a *tava*.

There are, however, three pieces of equipment which, while not absolutely necessary, will greatly add to the ease of cooking Oriental style: they are a wok, a Chinese cleaver and an electric blender and/or food processor (to replace the traditional pestle and mortar or stone rolling pins and slabs of India and South-East Asia).

WOK

So entrenched is the wok in the contemporary European kitchen that some smart (and expensive) hobs include a wok burner. As Western cooks have discovered, the uses of a wok extend far beyond stir-frying. I always use mine for cooking risotto and for boiling ravioli and gnocchi (they have more room to spread out), while for deep frying, there is no better implement, since its convex shape means less oil has to be used.

Known as a *kuali* in Malaysia and a *wajan* in Java, the wok also has a close relation in the Indian *karai*, which has a deeper bowl, and is often thicker and heavier, being made of iron, silvered brass or aluminium.

While woks vary in size, for domestic purposes the best is probably one about 35 cm (14 in) in diameter. They are now manufactured in aluminium and even copper, but the traditional cast iron or steel wok remains the best because these surfaces are slightly porous, absorbing oil and thus making the surface non-stick. The modern non-stick wok should be avoided, since the coating interferes with the evaporation process, causing food to stew in its own juices.

If you are going to use your wok solely for stir-frying, buy a wok with a Western-style long handle. However, since this causes the wok to tip over when left free standing, a better all-purpose wok is the traditional design, with a little handle either side, like ears. These handles do get hot during stir frying, but it is a simple matter to remember to hold them with an oven mitt or folded towel.

The traditional wok works best over a gas ring, where the flames can lick up around the sides of the bowl, heating everything evenly. Electric hot plates are not ideal, as heat tends to concentrate at the bottom of the wok. To sit a wok over a flat electric or solid fuel hot plate, you will need to buy a metal collar with perforated holes to allow the convection of heat. You can buy flat-bottomed woks especially for non-gas hot plates and, although not as easy to use as the traditional bowl shape, they are probably better than the free-standing electric wok. Most electric woks do not respond well to sudden changes of temperature which a cook so often requires. Perhaps a better investment, for those without gas hobs, would be a portable gas stove or separate mini-hob hooked up to bottled gas.

The wok should have a lid for steaming, preferably fitting a little below the lip of the wok, so extra water can be poured in during steaming. To use a wok for steaming a trivet or metal steaming basket is useful, although purists prefer the traditional Chinese bamboo steaming baskets, insisting that the bamboo absorbs extra water, not allowing the steam to condense on the underside of the lid and drip back into the food. However, bamboo steamers are more difficult to keep clean.

Another cheap and very useful wok accessory is a shovel-shaped spatula, whose gently curved edge follows the curve of the wok. Add to this a long-handled Chinese wire straining basket and your Oriental batterie de cuisine is virtually complete.

A new wok may have to be seasoned, to remove the coating of machine oil applied at the factory to prevent the wok from rusting in transit.

First, scrub the wok with a scouring pad. Unless your wok should later develop rust, this is the first and only time you will be doing this; a nicely seasoned wok needs only to be gently scrubbed with a nylon dishwashing brush (or traditional bamboo wok-cleaning brush). Next, rub the entire wok, inside and out, with a paper towel soaked in cooking oil. Then place the wok on a hot ring and allow the oil to burn. Leave to cool, then wipe off with another paper towel. Repeat this process two or three times, until nothing comes off on the towel once it has been wiped across the wok.

With constant use over time, the wok will turn black as a result of the build-up of a thin layer of charcoal and unused oil. This is to be encouraged, as it provides the wok's natural, rust-proof 'non-stick' surface. Fastidious Western housekeepers must temporarily set aside their prejudices. Arriving back from holiday, I once discovered a well-intentioned house guest had scoured every trace of black from the inside of my wok, thus undoing ten years of careful seasoning! To the Oriental eye, a blackened wok is an object of beauty, symbolic of all the delicious food which has been prepared in it over the years.

CLEAVERS

If you have quality European chef's knives, they will do an excellent job of slicing meat and vegetables Oriental-style, despite being held somewhat in disdain by Chinese chefs. Their weapon of choice is the Chinese cleaver, which comes in several grades: heavy for bone chopping, medium for all-purpose slicing and chopping, and a lightweight version with a narrower blade for more delicate work.

Unless your existing kitchen knives are razor sharp, I strongly recommend buying a cleaver from a Chinese supermarket or other Asian shop. Its sharpness will richly reward the modest financial outlay. Cleavers are made either from carbon steel, which rusts easily but is easier to sharpen, or stainless steel, which is easier to maintain. For an initial purchase, a medium weight stainless steel cleaver is probably best.

On buying a stainless steel cleaver, it is absolutely essential to take it along to a professional knife sharpener, who will put the requisite edge on it. From then on it is simply a matter of giving it frequent licks with a steel.

Westerners seem to find the Chinese cleaver vaguely disquieting, perhaps due to its very sharpness and its maniacal connotations, which are undeniable. So routine is the use of cleavers in gang fights between rival Triads, that 'chopping' is now an accepted abbreviation in Hong Kong media reports.

Properly handled, the heaviness of a cleaver is a boon to chopping dense vegetables, and you can become every bit as dextrous as with a Western-style knife, provided it is correctly held. Chinese chefs say they can instantly tell the worth of a new boy in the kitchen by the way he holds the cleaver. Rest the index finger down the top of the blade, in order to give better control. It seems an unnatural grip at first; only with perseverance does its wisdom become apparent. As with Western knife handling, use your other hand to feed the food into the path of the blade, with a tight row of protective fingernails pointing towards the lethal metal.

The broad, flat side of a Chinese cleaver is very handy: use it like a shovel to transfer food from the chopping board to the wok, and to smash cloves of garlic before chopping.

BLENDERS AND FOOD PROCESSORS

For the modern home cook with a demanding daytime job, blenders and food processors are what make preparing Asian food accessible and feasible, It may be, as the die hards insist, that these machines do not pulverize spices as finely as the old-fashioned pestle and mortar, but I challenge anybody to detect a significant difference in the flavour of the finished dish.

Food processors are best for grinding coconut and the aromatic fresh bulbs, roots and stems (garlic, ginger, galangal, turmeric and lemon grass), which should be dropped in through the feeder tube while the metal blade is turning.

Blenders and electric coffee grinders, on the other hand, are best for pulverizing dry whole spices (which generally should be heated first). If there are insufficient spices to get the blades working properly, add a small amount of the liquid appropriate to the eventual cooking method (i.e. oil if the spices are to be fried, coconut cream or water if they are to be simmered). Little or no extra oil will be needed in the pan when you then fry the spice mixture, as heating will coax out the existing oil.

In affluent middle-class kitchens of South-East Asia, blenders, coffee mills and food processors are today a common sight. There may also be an electric rice cooker, an appliance still relatively rare in the West. While the rice cooker does not necessarily produce better results than a conventional saucepan, there is no denying its convenience, or the consistent excellence of the rice it produces. Being a stand-alone appliance, the electric rice cooker also frees up space on the stove, an important consideration in the cramped domestic kitchens of Tokyo, Hong Kong and Singapore.

Techniques

CUTTING

The basic methods of shredding and dicing are common to Oriental and classical French cuisine: first cut the food into slices, then stack several layers on top of each other and cut into matchstick lengths, or into thicker lengths if they are then to be cut crossways into cubes.

An Oriental cook, however, will also commonly slice carrots, courgettes and other long, round vegetables at an angle, in order to expose more surface area to the wok, speeding up the cooking process and thus better preserving the texture and nutrients of the vegetables. These cylindrical vegetables are also subjected to the peculiarly Chinese technique of roll-cutting. Beginning from one end, the chef makes a diagonal cut, then rolls the knife or cleaver around 180 degrees and makes another cut, the final effect being a series of aesthetically pleasing triangles.

BONING A CHICKEN LEG

To bone a chicken leg, slit it down its length, cut around the bone both top and bottom, then cut with almost a scraping motion down the length of the bone.

DEVEINING A PRAWN

Shrimps and small prawns do not need deveining, but the technique will improve the appearance of king prawns. To devein, peel off the shell (the tail may be removed or retained for more elegant presentation, as you wish), then slit down the back and remove the dark, thread-like digestive cord.

STIR FRYING

Only a wok allows for satisfactory stir frying – the rapid turning over of a small amount of food over a high heat. Usually the right time to add the food is when the heated oil is rolling freely around the wok but is not smoking hot. Garlic and ginger are often tossed about first, before adding the meat and finally the vegetables.

A common mistake is to overfill the wok, slowing down the heating process and causing the vegetables and meat to stew rather than remain sizzling hot and reasonably dry. It is better to stir fry a large amount of food in several batches.

STEAMING

If you don't already steam your vegetables, start doing so today. Quite apart from their considerable health benefits, steamed vegetables taste better than boiled vegetables because they remain crisper and retain more of their natural flavour.

Although steam is no hotter than boiling water, it absorbs extra heat as it vaporizes. This extra heat is transferred to the vegetables as the steam condenses on their surfaces. However, unlike boiled vegetables, steamed vegetables do not reach boiling point. As the condensed steam trickles back into the water, it does leach out some soluble salts, vitamins and natural flavours, but far less than had the vegetables been boiled.

For best results, steaming requires some sort of gadget to separate the food from the boiling water underneath. You can, of course, steam food simply by cooking with a minimum of water at the bottom of the pot, but the longer cooking time required for steaming means the vegetables on the bottom tend to be rather over-done and waterlogged before those on top are cooked.

The cheapest and most adaptable of all steamers is a handy little gadget with collapsible sides, enabling it to fit inside any size of pot (although it works best in a large saucepan). Then there are steaming attachments which fit over the top of an ordinary saucepan. These work satisfactorily, but often are on the small side – a steamer works best where there is a large confined space in which the steam can circulate.

The most ancient of all steamers is a Chinese invention still in common use today. These bamboo baskets with woven bottoms are traditionally filled with vegetables or steamed bread (man-tou) and placed over boiling rice in a wok. In rural communes of China these steamers are so large they require two people to handle them, and seven or eight stacked on top of each other contain sufficient food for a whole canteen of workers. South of the Yang-tse river, fish is also steamed in this way (the northern Chinese do not care for it) and the Cantonese use tiny versions of these steamers for their equally tiny, delicate dim sum dishes. They are widely available here and come in a variety of sizes; baskets the same size stack neatly on top of each other so that different foods can be kept separate but steamed over the same pot.

BHOONA
The Indian bhoona technique is a combination of braising and reducing. A dish (usually meat) is stirred over a medium to high heat so that any accompanying liquid evaporates into a spice paste covering the cubes of meat, resulting in a so-called 'dry curry'. This is done not only to make food more manageable to Indian diners who eat with their fingers, but also to force the spices inside the meat.

DUM
An Indian method of cooking, whereby a dish is fried, then tightly covered and allowed to steam in its own natural juices. The idea is to capture the 'breath' (dum) of the food.

BAGHAR
Otherwise known as chonk, this is another uniquely Indian technique. Spices are fried in oil or ghee in a separate frying pan, then added to a dish only in the last stages of cooking. Alternatively, spices can be dry roasted by stirring about in a heavy cast iron pan until they just begin to brown.

Index